Accounting

second edition

Michael Fardon
David Cox

**OSBORNE
BUSINESS**

© Michael Fardon, David Cox, Second edition 1998

Published by Osborne Books Limited
Unit 1B Everoak Estate
Bromyard Road
Worcester WR2 5HN

Printed by The Bath Press, Bath

A CIP catalogue record for this book is available from the British Library

ISBN 1 872962 28 9

foreword

Accounting is a foundation text in financial, cost and management accounting. In its first edition it has been widely used on a variety of vocational, Higher National, and first year degree courses. It is written in a straightforward style, and can be easily understood by the reader who has had no previous accounting training. This second edition contains substantially revised chapters on Cash Flow Statements and the published accounts of public limited companies.

Accounting is divided into four self-contained sections:

The first section, *Accounting Records*, contains a clear and comprehensive introduction to the basic principles of double entry book-keeping, and a detailed description of the books of the business, the emphasis being on the wide variety of book-keeping systems currently in use.

The second section, *Accounting Statements*, sets out the various forms of accounting statements prepared for sole traders, partnerships and limited companies. There is a separate Chapter on the published accounts of public limited companies.

The third section, *Cost and Management Accounting,* aims to give a thorough grounding in the subject, and provide a clear view of how businesses operate.

The fourth section, *Presentation and Analysis of Accounting Information,* explains the statistical techniques of presenting figures such as sales and profits, and examines the use of statistics in forecasting future trends.

This second edition is published as the millenium rapidly approaches. The authors have therefore looked forward to this event: dates in the text and activities have in most cases been set in the twenty-first century and quoted, for example, as '20-1'.

Michael Fardon
David Cox
Worcester, 1998

93815

acknowledgements

The authors wish to thank the following for their assistance in the production of this book: Jean Cox, Michael Gilbert, Hedgehog Design, Jon Moore, Caroline Morgan, Peggy Rossiter, Jed Stone, Tony Warburton, and P J Wellspring. They would also like to thank The Body Shop International PLC for granting permission to quote published material.

the authors

David Cox has more than twenty years' experience teaching management and accountancy students over a wide range of levels. Formerly with the Management and Professional Studies Department at Worcester College of Technology, he now lectures on a freelance basis and carries out educational consultancy work in accountancy studies. He is author and joint author of a number of textbooks in the areas of accounting, finance and banking.

Michael Fardon has extensive teaching experience of a wide range of business and accountancy students at Worcester College of Technology. He is now a writer and educational consultant in the area of business and finance.

contents

section one
accounting records

	Introduction: Accounts and Accountants	6
1	Double Entry Book-keeping	10
2	Balancing the Books; the Trial Balance	19
3	The Books of the Business	28
4	Computer Accounting Systems	33

section two
accounting statements

5	Sole Trader Final Accounts	42
6	Adjustments to the Final Accounts	52
7	Incomplete Records	62
8	Partnership Accounts	73
9	Limited Company Accounts	80
10	Cash Flow Statements	91
11	Published Accounts of Limited Companies	105

section three
cost and management accounting

12	Cost Accounting and Manufacturing Accounts	118
13	Accounting for Materials and Labour	130
14	Overhead Costs	142
15	Break-Even; Marginal and Absorption Costing	152
16	Job Costing and Process Costing	163
17	Standard Costing and Variance Analysis	175
18	Budgets and Budgetary Control	185
19	Cash Budgets and Forecast Final Accounts	195
20	Working Capital Management	208
21	Further Aspects of Working Capital	215

section four
presentation and analysis of accounting information

22	Accounting Ratios	226
23	Statistical Techniques and Accounting Data	238
24	Statistical Forecasting Techniques	246

index 253

assignments

1   Bolton Sports: Writing up the Books   26

2   Compusoft Limited: Computer Accounting   38

3   Joan Pearce: Incomplete Records   71

4   Published Accounts of Public Limited Companies   115

5   Manufacturing Accounts   128

6   Newtown Printers: Overhead Absorption and Job Costing   172

7   Health 'n Burger Park: Feasibility Study for a New Shop   204

8   Interpreting the Accounts   235

Assignment work forms a important part of accounting studies. In order to assist tutors and students, eight fully developed assignments have been included in the text to consolidate the learning of each subject area.

It is hoped that the Assignments should not be seen by students as staged 'exercises', but as part of the whole learning process, complementary to the other subjects that they are studying. Assignment 7, *Health'n Burger Park,* was written with the concept of integration specifically in mind. The authors hope that the Assignments will prove stimulating, and they welcome any feedback.

accounting
records

introduction ACCOUNTS AND ACCOUNTANTS

Does a business have to keep books?

Who keeps the books; the owner, a book-keeper, or an accountant?

What is the difference between book-keeping and accounting?

What is the difference between an auditor and an accountant?

These questions are asked as frequently by people starting up in business as by students taking a course in Accounting. In this introduction to accounting we have two aims: first, to distinguish between book-keeping and accounting, and secondly to describe the various types of accountant that an organisation is likely to encounter or to employ. We will conclude with a revision of some important accounting terms which you should already have encountered in your studies.

the need for the 'books' of a business

If anyone asks you how much you are worth at any particular time, or how much you have spent within a particular period, you will probably be unable to give an accurate figure, and will probably consider it an invasion of your privacy. You could add up the total of your assets and produce a basic personal balance sheet showing how your belongings are financed, whether out of your own capital or from borrowed money. Valuation may be difficult, and you may have little in the way of written records to guide you. You may be able to give a general estimate of what you have spent since pay day, but it is unlikely that you will have precise written details of money spent on smaller items such as travel or food. You are, as you will readily point out, accountable only to yourself.

A business, on the other hand, must keep *books* to record its financial transactions. It will carry out the process of book-keeping to provide information for a number of interested parties:

*   the owner(s)
*   the Inland Revenue (for taxation of profits)
*   H M Customs & Excise (the VAT authorities) if the business is registered for VAT
*   the bank manager (if the business is borrowing from the bank)

It is essential then that the financial transactions of the business are recorded in a way that is both *precise* and *standardised*, as these transactions are likely to be examined and monitored by a number of interested parties, not least the owner himself. Whereas the *book-keeping* is essentially a mechanical procedure, the process of *accounting* will use the recorded information to provide analytical statements which are either *retrospective:*

- trading account, profit and loss account and the balance sheet

or *forward looking:*

- costing statements and budgeted accounts

In each case these statements are invaluable aids for monitoring the business, and provide a basis for making financial decisions.

forms of accounting record

The two main types of accounting records are those in *handwritten* form (the traditional method), or records maintained on a *computer*.

Written Accounting Records
The traditional, and still by far the most common method of keeping accounting records is by keeping *books of account.* The term "ledger", which is still used in referring to some of the accounting records owes its origin to stiff-covered leather bound volumes, neatly ruled into columns, in which the book-keeper would enter each financial transaction in immaculate copperplate handwriting into individual *accounts.* In modern times the format of the books has changed surprisingly little, and many commercial stationers stock 'paperback' ledgers for the smaller business. We will look at the mechanism of manual book-keeping fully in Chapters 1, 2 and 3.

Computer Accounting Records
The introduction of low-priced computers has meant that many businesses can record all financial transactions by inputting all the details onto computer disc. This can be a very accurate and convenient method of keeping records, but it can also be cumbersome and time-consuming to set up, particularly for the smaller business. We will examine the use of computer accounting systems fully in Chapter 4.

book-keepers and accountants

Who keeps the books of a business? The answer is simple: *anyone* can maintain the accounts. The important point is that they *must* be maintained: either by the owner, or by a full or part-time book-keeper brought in for the purpose. A book-keeper does not have to be professionally qualified, but the owner of a business will be looking to employ a proficient and reputable book-keeper.

The role of the accountant - who does have to be professionally qualified - is to check, summarise, present, analyse and interpret the accounts for the benefit of the owner and other interested parties. It is possible, if the owner has been lax in compiling the accounting records, that the accountant will be brought in to do the job of the book-keeper and prepare the accounts from incomplete records. This situation is dealt with in full in Chapter 7.

accounting personnel

Financial Accountant
The function of the *financial accountant* is very much concerned with business transactions, and with taking further the information produced by the book-keeper. The financial accountant extracts information from the accounting records in order to provide a method of control, for instance over debtors, creditors, cash and bank balances. The role also requires the preparation of year-end accounts from a trial balance (a summary of all the accounts in the books - see Chapter 2) and may also include negotiation with the Inland Revenue on tax matters for the business. Limited companies, in particular, must comply with the accounting requirements of

the Companies Acts 1985 and 1989 (see Chapter 11). This Act requires the directors of a company to report annually to shareholders, with certain minimum financial accounting information being disclosed.

Cost and Management Accountants

It is the *cost accountant* who obtains costing information, for example costs of raw materials, labour and overheads. This information is then interpreted by the *management accountant* who prepares a report for the decision-makers of the business. In many organizations, the different roles of the cost accountant and management accountant have been merged; however, larger businesses usually still make the distinction between the two.

The cost accountant is particularly concerned with recent costs incurred by the organization, and in estimating costs for the future. One task often undertaken is that of setting *standard costs*; this subject is covered in full in Chapter 17.

Auditors

Auditors are accountants whose role it is to check that accounting procedures have been followed correctly. A distinction should be made between:
- external auditors
- internal auditors

External auditors are independent of the firm whose accounts are being audited. The most common type of audit conducted by external auditors is the *statutory audit* of a limited company. In this, the auditors are reporting to the shareholders of a company, stating that the legal requirements laid down in the Companies Acts 1985 and 1989 have been complied with, and that the accounts represent a "true and fair view" of the state of the business. External auditors are usually appointed by the shareholders at the Annual General Meeting of the company.

Internal Auditors are employees of the business which they audit. Their duties are concerned with the internal check and control procedures of the business, for example setting down the procedures for the control of cash, authorisation of purchases, and disposal of property. The nature of their work requires that they should have a degree of independence within the company; they often report directly to the financial director.

Organization of Accounting Personnel

The chart below shows the inter-relationship of the accounting personnel described. The business in this instance is a medium-sized limited company.

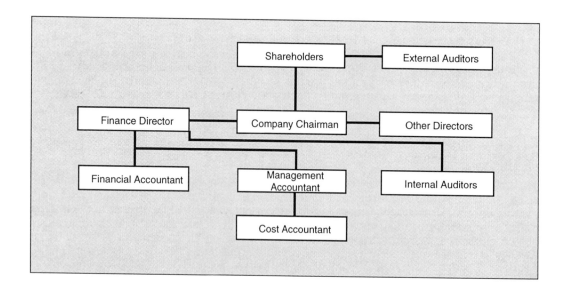

accounting terms

Before studying the next four Chapters, which deal with double entry book-keeping, the trial balance, the layout of the accounts in the ledger, and computerised accounting systems, you are advised to read and study carefully the list of accounting terms set out below. You may be familiar with some of the terms already.

Cash Sales are sales which are paid for immediately, by cash or by cheque.

Credit Sales are sales which should be paid for by customers within a stated time period stated on the invoice (30 days or 60 days are common credit periods)

Debtors are customers to whom sales have been made on a credit basis.

Cash Purchases are purchases of goods which are paid for immediately.

Credit Purchases are purchases of goods which may be paid for within an agreed time limit.

Creditors are suppliers to whom the business owes money.

Assets are items *owned* by the business, either *Fixed Assets* (items such as premises and equipment, retained for the long term), or *Current Assets* (items such as stock, debtors and cash, retained for the short term).

Liabilities are items *owed* by the business, either *Long Term Liabilities* (such as a bank medium-term loan) or *Current Liabilities*, to be repaid within 12 months (such as creditors).

Capital is money contributed to the business by the owner, and hence owed by the business to the owner.

Drawings are amounts (money or goods) taken out of the business by the owner for his or her own use.

CHAPTER SUMMARY

❏ A business must maintain hand-written or computerised books of account.

❏ A business may employ a book-keeper to maintain the accounts.

❏ An accountant is normally employed to prepare financial statements from the accounts.

❏ The term "accountant" may be used to describe a wide variety of accounting functions, including
  - financial accountant
  - management accountant
  - cost accountant
  - auditor (external or internal)

1 DOUBLE-ENTRY BOOK-KEEPING

Before studying accounting in any detail it is important to understand and practise the basic principles of *double entry book-keeping*; without doing so is like studying a language and ignoring the grammar, or on a more simple level, trying to run before one can walk. In this Chapter we will study the principles of double entry book-keeping; in Chapter 3 we will examine the layout of the books of the business and see exactly where the transactions are recorded.

the principles of double entry book-keeping

The Dual Aspect of Double Entry

Double entry book-keeping involves the making of two entries for every transaction in the books of account of the business. It therefore follows that these two entries represent a two-fold or dual aspect of each transaction, and it is the appreciation of this dual aspect which is crucial to an understanding of double entry. Take, for example, three common business transactions: the purchase of goods for cash, the sale of goods with a cheque received in payment, and the payment of wages by cheque. When you examine them they involve a *dual* aspect in which the situation of the business has changed, and must be recorded:

- *Purchase of goods for cash :* *1.* goods have been received; *2.* cash has decreased.
- *Sale of goods for cheque:* *1.* goods have gone out of the business; *2.* the bank balance has increased.
- *Payment of wages by cheque:* *1.* wages have been paid for work done; *2.* the bank balance has decreased.

Ledger Accounts

It is essential that, for each transaction, two entries are made in the books of the business. These entries are recorded in *ledger accounts*. A separate ledger account is kept for each different type of transaction. In practice each ledger account will be on a separate page in the books of the business, but in this book, and we suggest in your exercises, a number of different ledger accounts can be set out on an individual page. Set out below is a typical ledger account; this example is a wages account, used for recording the wages paid out by a business.

Debit   **Wages Account**   Credit

Date	Details	Folio	£		Date	Details	Folio	£	
20-1 5 Sept	Bank	CB12	1,200	00					

You should note the following points about the layout of this account:

- the name of the account is written at the top
- the account is divided into two identical sides (separated by a central ruled line)
- the left hand side is labelled "debit", often abbreviated to "Dr."
- the right hand side is labelled "credit", often abbreviated to "Cr."
- the date and details of the transaction are entered on *one* side only of the account
- the "Folio" is the page reference of the other entry of the double entry transaction
- the description of each entry is the name of the other account involved

The wages account illustrated above is a typical layout of a double entry ledger account. For the purposes of clarity of illustration in this book, the account format will be simplified as follows:

Dr.				Wages Account			Cr.
20-1			£	20-1			£
5 Sep	Bank		1,200				

debits and credits in double entry book-keeping

We have just seen that for every transaction in double entry book-keeping there will be two entries in the ledger accounts. In the case of wages paid there will be an entry in the wages account (set out above) and another entry in the bank account. The two basic rules of double entry book-keeping are therefore:

1. *Every transaction involves one debit entry and one credit entry.*

2. *Debit entries are on the left of the appropriate account, and credit entries are on the right.*

You may find the second rule more easy to remember by thinking of "<u>c</u>orrect = <u>r</u>ight" (credit = right hand side), or for UK drivers, "<u>dr</u>ive on the left."

The most difficult aspect of double entry book-keeping, however, is working out *which entry is the debit and which entry is the credit.*   There are two ways of approaching the problem, the first is a *conceptual* approach, and the second is a *practical* approach involving the cash and bank accounts of the business. The second approach is useful in reinforcing the first.

The Conceptual Approach to Debits and Credits

As we have seen, for every transaction an entry is made in one ledger account, and a corresponding entry is made on the opposite side of the other ledger account concerned. One method of working out which entry is the debit and which the credit is as follows:

Debit Entry: the account which gains value or derives a benefit
Credit Entry: the account which gives value or records some obligation

Once you have decided whether any *one* entry is a debit or a credit, the other entry will follow on the *opposite* side of the other account.

Double Entry and the Cash and Bank Accounts: a Practical Approach

In order to examine double entry book-keeping in practical terms, consider the following five transactions carried out by a long-established stationery wholesaler, Sidbury Traders:

1 Sep 20-1   Sale of goods for £120 cheque received
5 Sep 20-1   Payment of wages of £1,200 by cheque
6 Sep 20-1   Purchase of goods for £3,000, paid for by cheque
7 Sep 20-1   Received loan of £5,000 from Ian Watson, and paid cheque into bank
9 Sep 20-1   Purchase of computer costing £4,000, paid for by cheque

If you look at these five transactions for Sidbury Traders, you will see that they all involve the bank account. One invariable rule for both bank account (bank transactions) and cash account (notes and coin transactions) is that money *received* is recorded on the *left* hand side, and money *paid out* is recorded on the *right* hand side. By applying this rule to debits and credits you can say:

Money in *is a debit (on the left);* **money out** *is a credit (on the right)*

Using this rule, the bank account for Sidbury Traders, after entering the five transactions, appears as set out below (ignoring any other transactions or opening balance on the account):

Dr.		Bank Account			Cr.

20-1			£	20-1			£
1 Sep	Sales		120	5 Sep	Wages		1,200
7 Sep	Ian Watson Loan		5,000	6 Sep	Purchases		3,000
				9 Sep	Computer		4,000
	Money in				**Money out**		

It is now a simple step to work out onto which side, debit or credit, the entries are recorded in the other accounts involved. If you bear in mind that money received is a debit (left hand side) and money paid out is a credit (right hand side), by looking at any double entry transaction which involves the bank account (or equally the cash account) you should

- identify on which side of the bank account, debit (money in) or credit (money out), the item is recorded
- record the other double entry item on the *other* side of the appropriate account

We are now in a position to set out the other accounts involved in the five transactions entered in the bank account. Note that in each case the description in the account is "Bank."

1 September 20-1: sale of goods for £120 cheque received
Debit bank account (money in); *Credit* sales account

Dr.		Sales Account			Cr.
20-1		£	20-1		£
			1 Sep	Bank	120

5 September 20-1: payment of wages £1,200 by cheque
Debit wages account; *Credit* bank account (money out)

Dr.		Wages Account		Cr.
20-1		£	20-1	£
5 Sep	Bank	1,200		

6 September 20-1: purchase of goods for £3,000, paid for by cheque
Debit purchases account; *Credit* bank account (money out)

Dr.		Purchases Account		Cr.
20-1		£	20-1	£
6 Sep	Bank	3,000		

7 September 20-1: received loan from Ian Watson, £5,000, and paid cheque into bank
Debit bank account (money in); *Credit* Ian Watson loan account

Dr.				**Ian Watson Loan Account**			Cr.
20-1			£	20-1			£
				7 Sep	Bank		5,000

9 September 20-1: purchase of computer costing £4,000, paid for by cheque
Debit computer account; *Credit* bank account (money out)

Dr.				**Computer Account**		Cr
20-1			£	20-1		£
9 Sep	Bank		4,000			

Note that the acquisition of a computer is a purchase of an item which will be retained in the business. It is therefore a *fixed asset* and will be recorded in a separate account, and *not* in purchases account, which is used solely for recording the purchase of goods for resale.

double entry for credit sales and credit purchases

So far in this Chapter we have examined the treatment of double entry transactions involving the bank account, and have used the bank account as a guide to working out which entry is a debit and which is a credit. In business many entries will involve the cash account or bank account, because cash and cheques are a very common medium of exchange; there will, however, be certain transactions which do not involve the bank account. Purchases and sales on credit are the most common, and the double entry rules for these follow the same logic: the book-keeper on entering a credit purchase or credit sale, records the item in the sales account or purchases account as normal, but then records the second entry in the relevant account in the name of the debtor or creditor, instead of in the bank account, because no money has yet changed hands. The entries are therefore:

Credit Sale: Debit debtor's account, Credit sales account

Credit Purchase: Credit creditor's (supplier's) account, Debit purchases account

Let us now take an example of a credit sale made by Sidbury Traders, and payment received after thirty days. On 10 September 20-1 Sidbury Traders sells goods invoiced at £5,000 on credit to Arco Engineering. The ledger entries are: Credit sales account; Debit Arco Engineering's account.

Dr.				**Sales Account**			Cr.
20-1			£	20-1			£
				10 Sep	Arco Engineering		5,000

Dr.				**Arco Engineering**		Cr.
20-1			£	20-1		£
10 Sep	Sales		5,000			

On 10 October, thirty days after this sale has been made, Sidbury Traders receives a cheque for £5,000 from Arco Engineeering in settlement of the amount due; the cheque is paid into the bank. Sidbury Traders' book-keeper will

- *debit* the bank account £5,,000 (money received)
- *credit* the account of Arco Engineering

The accounts will appear as set out below. Note the existing entry from 10 September on the account of Arco Engineering.

Dr.	Bank Account				Cr.
20-1		£	20-1		£
10 Oct	Arco Engineering	5,000			

Dr.	Arco Engineering				Cr.
20-1		£	20-1		£
10 Sep	Sales	5,000	10 Oct	Bank	5,000

Credit purchases made by a business are recorded in a similar way. If Sidbury Traders purchases £2,500 of goods from Newland Supplies on 12 September, and is given 30 days in which to pay, the entries in the books will be:

- *debit* purchases account
- *credit* Newland Supplies' account

Dr.	Purchases Account				Cr.
20-1		£	20-1		£
12 Sep	Newland Supplies	2,500			

Dr.	Newland Supplies				Cr.
20-1		£	20-1		£
			12 Sep	Purchases	2,500

Settlement of the invoice by cheque by Sidbury Traders in thirty days' time will be recorded by their book-keeper *debiting* the supplier's account and *crediting* the bank account:

Dr.	Newland Supplies				Cr.
20-1		£	20-1		£
12 Oct	Bank	2,500	12 Sep	Purchases	2,500

Dr.	Bank Account				Cr.
20-1		£	20-1		£
			12 Oct	Newland Supplies	2,500

Balancing Off Accounts

You will probably have noticed that in the above examples, the accounts of the debtor (Arco Engineering) and the creditor (Newland Supplies) have finished up with identical amounts on each side; in these cases, nothing is owing to Sidbury Traders, or is owed by it. In practice, as the business trades, there will be many entries on both sides of debtor and creditor accounts. As we will see in the next Chapter, it is a useful exercise to *balance off* each account periodically, to see how much in total each debtor owes, and how much is owed to each creditor of the business. This balancing off procedure will also be applied to other accounts in the books of the business.

Returns In and Returns Out

There are, of course, other double entry transactions which may not involve the bank and cash accounts. For example Returns In (goods sold and then returned to the business) and Returns Out (goods returned by the business to a supplier).

Returns In are unwanted or faulty goods returned to the business, normally with a document known as a *debit note*. The returned goods are an expense or loss and therefore a debit. The entries for returned goods sold on credit are:

- *Debit* returns in account
- *Credit* the debtor's account

The transaction is completed by the business sending the debtor a *credit note*, advising the debtor that his or her account has been credited with the amount of the returned goods.

Returns Out are goods returned by the business, normally with a *debit note*. They are therefore a gain and a credit; the entries will be:

- *Debit* creditor's (supplier's) account
- *Credit* returns out account

Capital

Capital is the money invested in the business by the owner, and is *owed* by the business to the owner. A capital account will be set up to record the amount(s) paid into the business, normally by cheque. The entries will be:

- *Debit* bank account
- *Credit* capital account

general principles of debits and credits

If you now examine the nature of the five transactions of Sidbury Traders we looked at earlier in the Chapter and the notes set out above, you may deduce some further rules which help with deciding which item is a debit and which is a credit. Some further items have also been added to the following list:

Debits include:
- *purchases* of goods for trading purposes
- *expenses* incurred by the business (wages in the case of Sidbury Traders)
- *purchase of assets* for retention in the business (a computer, a fixed asset, in this case)
- *money received* (as in Sidbury Traders' bank account)
- *drawings* made by the owner of the business

Credits include:
- *sales* made by the business
- *income* received by the business
- *incurring a liability* (Ian Watson's loan, or alternatively, capital contributed by the owner)
- *money paid out* (as in Sidbury Traders' bank account)

These rules might be illustrated as follows:

Debits	Credits
Money received (cash and bank)	Money paid out (cash and bank)
Purchases	Sales
Fixed assets acquired	Liabilities incurred
Expenses	Income
Drawings	Capital

CHAPTER SUMMARY

❏ Double entry book-keeping transactions involve two entries, a credit and a debit.

❏ Debits are recorded on the left hand side of an account, credits on the right hand side.

❏ Entries in the bank account or cash account are:
- Debit (left hand side) money in
- Credit (right hand side) money out.

❏ Many transactions involve the bank account, in which case the corresponding entries are easily worked out. These entries, and those not involving the bank account, comply with the following rules:

Debit entries include
- an acquisition or an increase in an asset
- expenses or losses incurred
- purchases made for trading purposes
- money owing by customers (debtors)

Credit entries include
- a liability incurred (a loan from an outsider or capital from the owner)
- income or benefit received
- sales income received from trading activities
- money owed to suppliers (creditors).

✍ STUDENT ACTIVITIES

You are a trainee accountant in the firm of Arthur Andrews & Co.. You are at present assisting with the accounts of start-up businesses, a number of which have no double entry records. You are to carry out the following tasks.

1.1 Will Watney has kept his bank account up to date, but hasn't got around to the other double entry items. Rule out the other accounts for him, and make the appropriate entries.

Dr.			Bank Account			Cr.
20-1		£	20-1			£
1 Feb	Sales	5,000	1 Feb	Purchases		3,500
2 Feb	Sales	7,500	2 Feb	Wages		2,510
3 Feb	Bank Loan	12,500	3 Feb	Van purchase		12,500
5 Feb	Sales	9,300	3 Feb	Purchases		5,000
			4 Feb	Rent paid		780

1.2 Sarah Banks has opened up a health food shop "Just Nuts", but hasn't started to write up the books. As she is inexperienced she asks you to set up an accounting system for her. She provides you with the following list of transactions for the first week's trading, starting on Monday 8 June 20-1. You are to enter up the accounts for her.

Monday:
paid £ 5,000 cheque as capital into the bank; purchases of £4,000, paid by cheque
paid £750 sales into the bank; paid week's rent £75 by cheque.
Tuesday:
paid £500 sales into the bank; made purchases of £425 by cheque.
Wednesday:
paid £420 sales into the bank; bought computer £890 by cheque.
Thursday:
paid £550 sales into the bank; made purchases £510 by cheque.
Friday:
paid £925 sales into the bank; paid assistant's wages £75 by cheque.

1.3 Jim Ruddles has made a mess of recording entries in his bank account . You are to set out the bank account as it should appear, rule up the other double entry accounts and make the appropriate entries.

Dr.			Bank Account			Cr.
20-1		£	20-1			£
1 Jan	Purchases	1,000	2 Jan	Sales		5,000
5 Jan	Wages	2,700	3 Jan	Sales		7,000
5 Jan	Rent paid	150	4 Jan	Bank Loan		5,500
8 Jan	Rates paid	6,210	9 Jan	Machine purchased		4,000
9 Jan	Sales	5,205	10 Jan	Sales		9,520
10 Jan	Purchases	6,750	12 Jan	Wages		2,850
11 Jan	Car purchase	5,500	12 Jan	Rent paid		150

1.4 Sam Smith is a lazy individual and has not entered up his double entry accounts. He has listed all his transactions, and mentions that all cheques are paid into the bank account on the day of receipt. You are to draw up the accounts for Sam Smith and make the necessary entries.

1 March	Received £5,000 cheque as loan from brother
2 March	Bought goods £200; paid by cheque
3 March	Bought goods £1,200 on credit from H Lomax
4 March	Sold goods £800; cheque received
5 March	Sold goods £1,200 on credit to V Firth
6 March	Paid rent £955 by cheque
9 March	Bought cash register £1,200 on credit from Broadheath Business Supplies
10 March	Paid wages £780 by cheque
11 March	Bought goods on credit £5,920 from W Gould
12 March	V Firth pays for goods £1,200 by cheque
15 March	Bought goods £1,650 on credit from H Lomax
16 March	Made payment £750 by cheque to H Lomax

1.5 James Davenport has recently started in business as a wine importer, and being inexperienced in the trade, he has occasionally sent out incorrect items and also ordered the wrong wines. As a result he has an unusually large number of returned items. He hands you a list of transactions for the week and asks you to set out his double entry accounts for him.

1 August	Sold champagne £7,500 on credit to Excelsior Hotel
2 August	Sold 2 cases fino sherry £100 on credit to Bishops Palace
3 August	Bought 10 cases claret £600 on credit from Pinot Ltd.
3 August	Bought 12 cases Muscadet £480 on credit from Boissons Bros.
4 August	£500 champagne returned by Excelsior Hotel (1 August consignment)
4 August	£50 sherry returned by Bishops Palace (2 August consignment)
5 August	Returned £100 claret bought on credit from Pinot Ltd.
5 August	Returned £40 Muscadet bought on credit from Boissons Bros.
5 August	Pay pharmacist £10.40 by cheque for tranquilisers

1.6 When undertaking an audit you discuss book-keeping with a client. He says that he finds double entry very confusing because different people tell him different things about how to decide whether an item is a debit or a credit. He complains that the whole system seems very illogical. You are to set out in writing for his use guideline rules, with examples, to help him decide whether an item is a debit or a credit. You should mention all types of transaction - cash and credit transactions - in your *aide memoire*.

2 BALANCING THE BOOKS – THE TRIAL BALANCE

Double entry book-keeping involves the making of a debit entry and a credit entry for every transaction. It therefore follows that if the book-keeper has done his or her job accurately, the total of all the debit entries will equal the total of the credit entries for any given period. To test this accuracy the book-keeper will regularly, often on a monthly basis, check that the total of the debit entries equals the total of the credit entries by extracting a *trial balance,* which will hopefully show that these totals do in fact agree.

A trial balance is a summary in two columns of the balances of all the accounts, listing debit balances on the left and credit balances on the right, and showing the total of each column.

You should note that this definition refers to *balances* rather than *entries* in the accounts. The reason for this is that the book-keeper *balances off*, and calculates the running total of each account before setting out the trial balance. It would clearly be cumbersome and time-consuming for the book-keeper to enter *every* transaction in the trial balance. Balancing off is therefore regularly carried out both to speed up the preparation of the trial balance and also to provide the owner(s) of the business with valuable information about items such as sales, purchases, expenses and income.

balancing off

The mechanics of balancing off are straightforward, and have already been seen in their initial stages in our examination of the transactions of Sidbury Traders in the last Chapter. When Sidbury Traders issues an invoice for goods sold on credit, it enters the amount on the debit (left hand) side of the debtor's account in the Sales Ledger (with a corresponding credit to sales account). In the example of Arco Engineering set out below the debit balance of the account is £5,000.

Dr.			**Arco Engineering**			Cr.
20-1			£	20-1		£
10 Sep	Sales		5,000			

When Arco Engineering settle up by sending a cheque, the amount is entered into Sidbury Traders' bank account (a debit entry), and a corresponding credit entry is made to Arco Engineering's account:

Dr.			**Arco Enginering**			Cr.
20-1			£	20-1		£
10 Sep	Sales		5,000	10 Oct	Bank	5,000

Arco Engineering, according to the account, now owes *nothing;* the arithmetic difference between the debit side and the credit side is *nil.* If Arco Engineering on 25th October buys further goods from Sidbury Traders for £10,000, simple arithmetic states that as the invoice for £5,000 has been paid, they now owe £10,000, and the debit balance of their account will be £10,000. You will see from the account below that this £10,000 owing is the difference between the total of the debit side and the total of the credit side (£15,000 less £5,000 = £10,000).

Dr.				Arco Engineering			Cr.
20-1			£	20-1			£
10 Sep	Sales		5,000	10 Oct	Bank		5,000
25 Oct	Sales		10,000				

On 31 October, the month-end, the book-keeper will balance off the double entry accounts, in preparation for the trial balance. Study the account below very carefully.

Dr.					Arco Engineering					Cr.
20-1				£	20-1					£
10 Sep	Sales			5,000	10 Oct	Bank				5,000
25 Oct	Sales			10,000	31 Oct	Balance c/d		2		10,000
		3		15,000				3		15,000
1 Nov	Balance b/d	4		10,000						

The book-keeper, when balancing off, takes the following steps, indicated (except for the first step) by the numbers in the shaded boxes in the account above.

Step 1
The debit and the credit columns are separately added up and the totals noted in pencil. It is important to appreciate that *nothing* is entered in the account at this stage.

Step 2
The difference between the two totals (the balance of the account) is entered in the account
- on the side of the *smaller* total
- on the next available line
- with the date of the balancing off
- with the description "Balance c/d", an abbreviation of "Balance carried down"

Thus the balance of the above account is £10,000. This is the amount owed by Arco Engineering to Sidbury Traders on 31 October 20-1.

Step 3
Both sides of the account are now added up and the totals (which should be identical) are entered on the same line in the appropriate column and double underlined. The double underlining indicates that the account is *ruled off* and the figures above them should not be added to the figures below them.

Step 4
As we are dealing with double entry book-keeping, the book-keeper must, in order to complete the transaction of entering the difference (see Step 2), now enter the same amount *on the other side of the account,* below the totals entered in Step 3. In doing this, the book-keeper will have completed both a debit and a credit entry. The entry in this example reads "1 Nov Balance b/d £10,000." The date here is not the month-end date (October 31) but the first day of the following month; the abbreviation "b/d" stands for "brought down".

Here are two more examples of accounts which have been balanced off:

Dr.			Wages Account				Cr.
20-1			£	20-1			£
1 Jan	Bank		1,000	31 Jan	Balance c/d		5,150
8 Jan	Bank		1,200				
15 Jan	Bank		800				
22 Jan	Bank		1,000				
29 Jan	Bank		1,150				
			5,150				5,150
1 Feb	Balance b/d		5,150				

Dr.			Bank Account				Cr.
20-1			£	20-1			£
1 Jun	Sales		1,000	1 Jun	Wages		800
3 Jun	Sales		3,500	4 Jun	Rent paid		560
6 Jun	VAT refund		450	5 Jun	Purchases		2,500
				30 Jun	Balance c/d		1,090
			4,950				4,950
1 Jul	Balance b/d		1,090				

Note on the Wages Account

You will note from the wages account set out above that the balancing off process is carried out even if there are entries on only one side of the account. It should be added that balancing off should normally be carried out *even if there are no entries at all for the period in question:* it is important that the book-keeper carries out the process to all accounts to prevent possible errors occurring through omitting to balance off an active account.

Note on the Bank Account

In this account there are entries on both sides and the balance brought down is the difference between them; if the balance is on the debit side, this represents money in the bank. You should note that the bank itself will be keeping a similar account on its books and will regularly balance off and send the business a *bank statement.* It will then be the job of the book-keeper to reconcile the two balances in a *bank reconciliation statement:* this is a further check on the book-keeper's accuracy.

extracting the trial balance

When the book-keeper has balanced off the accounts, he or she can then proceed to the *trial balance.* As we saw at the beginning of the Chapter, the *trial balance* lists and totals in *two* columns the *balances* of the double entry accounts, debit balances on the left and credit balances on the right. If the book-keeper has been accurate in the day-to-day recording of transactions, the total of the two columns should agree. You should note that before proceeding to the trial balance, the book-keeper will add up the balances of the debtors' accounts to produce a single *debtors* figure, and total the balances of the creditors' accounts to produce a single *creditors* figure.

To understand the process of constructing the trial balance you should examine the list of account totals of Sidbury Traders on the next page, and decide which items are debits and which are credits. You should then set them out in a trial balance, listing the titles of the accounts in a further column to the left of the figures. Total the money amount columns and see if they agree.

If you are not sure which are debits and which are credits, refer to these guidelines:

Debits: assets (including debtors), purchases, expenses (including returns in), drawings

Credits: liabilities (including creditors), capital, sales, income (including returns out)

Account balances of Sidbury Traders as at 31 December 20-1

	£
Capital	50,000
Bank	1,500
Purchases	110,000
Sales	200,000
Returns out	5,000
Returns in	4,000
Wages	22,000
Equipment	25,000
Sundry expenses	59,000
Debtors	58,500
Creditors	25,000

The Trial Balance you have created should appear as follows:

Trial Balance of Sidbury Traders as at 31 December 20-1

	£ *Debit*	£ *Credit*
Capital		50,000
Bank	1,500	
Purchases	110,000	
Sales		200,000
Returns out		5,000
Returns in	4,000	
Wages	22,000	
Equipment	25,000	
Sundry expenses	59,000	
Debtors	58,500	
Creditors		25,000
	280,000	280,000

You will see from this exercise that the account balances making up the trial balance can easily be identified as debits or credits by following the guidelines set out at the top of the page. The only frequently occurring item which can appear on either side of the trial balance is the *bank account:*

• money in the bank = an asset = a debit balance = an entry on the left of the trial balance

• a bank overdraft = a liability = a credit balance = an entry on the right of the trial balance

As we will see later in the Chapter, the trial balance is an important step in the preparation of the *final accounts* of the business: the trading and profit and loss accounts and balance sheet. First, however, it is useful to see how a business using a computer accounting package arrives at the trial balance.

computer produced trial balances

If the business runs its accounts on a computer system, the ledger accounts on computer file will automatically balance off, and the balances can easily be accessed by inputting the appropriate enquiry on the keyboard. Similarly a trial balance can be produced on the computer by inputting an enquiry. This saves the book-keeper a great deal of time and trouble, and ensures complete accuracy. As the entry of each transaction into the computer file is a single entry with the corresponding entry generated by a code, there can be no imbalance in the trial balance: the total of the debits must equal the total of the credits. Unless an incorrect code has been input, the trial balance should be reliable. This may not be the case with a manual accounting system, which, depending on the calibre of the book-keeper, may be prone to error.

trial balances that fail to balance

It is possible that the extracted trial balance does not balance. In this case the book-keeper must locate the error as soon as possible, because the error may affect other people with whom the business trades, for example debtors and creditors. The procedure that should be adopted on finding a trial balance that does not balance is as follows:

- check the addition of the trial balance
- check that the balances have been entered correctly from the accounts
- check that all the balances have been entered
- find the difference between the differing totals
- look for the amount of the difference as an item in the accounts
- divide the difference by two: a transaction could have been entered as two debits or two credits

Certain errors made by the book-keeper in entering the accounts will *not* be picked up by the trial balance. These include:

- transactions not entered at all
- transactions entered for the wrong amount in both accounts
- transactions entered on the wrong side of both accounts
- transactions entered in the wrong accounts
- compensating errors where two errors cancel each other out

Such erors may, and hopefully will, emerge in due course when either a customer points out a mistake (charged too much, too little, or not at all), or when an auditor inspecting the accounts locates a discrepancy.

production of final accounts from the trial balance

A business will extract a trial balance on a regular basis to confirm the arithmetical accuracy of the book-keeping. It will also use the account balances as a basis for the production of its *final accounts*, normally once a year, but sometimes more frequently. The final accounts comprise:

- trading account
- profit and loss account
- balance sheet

These final accounts show the owner how profitable the business is, what it owns, and how it is financed. We will deal with the preparation of final accounts in detail in Chapter 5. The trial balance therefore is an important exercise in any business' accounting process: it proves the book-keeper's accuracy and also extracts the account balances which form the basis for the final accounts of the business.

CHAPTER SUMMARY

❏   In order to balance the books the book-keeper must adhere strictly to the double entry rules.

❏   The book-keeper's accuracy can and should be proved regularly by the extraction of a trial balance.

❏   The book-keeper must balance off each account before proceeding to the trial balance.

❏   The trial balance balances the total of all debit accounts with the total of all credit accounts.

❏   The trial balance is used periodically as a starting point for the preparation of the business' final accounts.

STUDENT ACTIVITIES

You are a trainee accountant with Porterhouse & Co. and have been called in to assist Robert Jefferson, a bookshop owner, who needs help with his double entry book-keeping. You visit his premises and he hands you the following lists of items for the first two months of trading. He asks you to deal with them for him.

Task 1
You are to enter up the January transactions in double entry accounts and balance off each account as at 31 January.

Task 2
You are then to draw up a trial balance as at 31 January to prove your accuracy.

Task 3
You are to enter up the February transactions in the same accounts and balance off at the end of the month.

Task 4
You are to draw up a trial balance as at 28 February to prove your accuracy.

Transactions for January 20-1

1 Jan	Introduced £5,000 capital, paid into bank account
2 Jan	Paid rent on premises £200 by cheque
4 Jan	Bought shop fittings £2,000 by cheque
5 Jan	Bought stock of books £2,500 on credit from Northam Publishers
8 Jan	Book sales £1,200 paid into bank
9 Jan	Book Sales £1,000 paid into bank
12 Jan	Bought books £5,000 on credit from Broadheath Books
15 Jan	Book sales £1,500 paid into bank
17 Jan	Book sales £1,250 paid into bank
19 Jan	Bought books from Financial Publications £2,500 by cheque
23 Jan	School returned books £580, unsuitable, cheque refund sent
30 Jan	Sold books on credit Wyvern College, £1,095

Transactions For February

3 Feb	Book sales £2,510 paid into bank
5 Feb	Paid rent on premises £200 by cheque
7 Feb	Bought shop fittings £1,385 by cheque
10 Feb	Book sales £3,875 paid into bank
11 Feb	Sent cheque £2,500 to Northam Publishers
13 Feb	Bought books £1,290 on credit Northam Publishers
14 Feb	Sent cheque £5,000 to Broadheath Books
17 Feb	Book sales £1,745 paid into bank
18 Feb	Wyvern College returned books £250
21 Feb	Book sales £1,435 paid into bank
24 Feb	Bought books £1,250 Associated Publishers on credit
28 Feb	Book sales £3,900 paid into bank

You are presented with two further lists of balances :

Task 5
Produce the trial balance of Brian Montagu as at 28 February 20-1

	£
Cash	130
Sales	3,970
Bank	720
Car	2,500
Machinery	1,500
Capital	5,000
Purchases	4,220
Debtors	192
Returns out	168
Creditors	254
Returns in	130

Task 6
Produce the trial balance of Jane Greenwell as at 28 February 20-1. She has omitted to open a capital account.

	£
Bank overdraft	1,250
Purchases	850
Cash	48
Sales	730
Returns out	144
Creditors	1,442
Equipment	2,704
Van	3,200
Returns in	90
Debtors	1,174
Wages	1,500
Capital	?

ASSIGNMENT

Bolton Sports:
Writing up the books

---

covering
books of account, the double entry book-keeping system.

SITUATION

You are a trainee accountant in the firm of Porterhouse & Co., 78 High Road, Greenham, GR1 2AZ. Your present job involves assisting small businesses in setting up accounting systems. Dave Parks, proprietor of Bolton Sports, a local sports shop (110, The Broadway, Greenham, GR2 3RF), has approached your firm after attending a lecture "Book-keeping for the Smaller Business" at the local College. He is not a methodical person, and has kept little in the way of financial records. His only documentation is:

- a cheque book with completed counterfoils
- a paying-in book with details on carbon copies of items paid in
- a box file containing sales invoices, sub-divided into paid and unpaid items
- a box file containing purchase invoices, sub-divided into paid and unpaid items

When you visit him at his shop he states that he has been trading for exactly three months (1 January to 31 March). He is a worried man. He has three concerns:

1.   He seems to be losing track of who owes him what; no-one seems to be paying him (apart from his shop cash customers), despite the fact that he gives only 30 days' credit to the clubs, schools and colleges that he supplies.

2.   Early in March he received a sharp note from Superior Sports, one of his creditors, for non-payment of a 30 days' invoice for £5,000. He had no idea at the time that the money was owing.

3.   He knows he has money in the bank because he regularly pays in at the branch and asks for the balance of his account over the counter; but he does not know the exact amount. His bank statement for the first quarter has not yet arrived.

When you examine his accounting documents, such as they are, you find that they are generally in rather a mess, but you are able to extract the following details:

Cheque book counterfoils		
20-1		
2 Jan	Fixtures & fittings	£3,000
3 Jan	Purchases	£3,500
5 Jan	Rent	£500
7 Jan	Cash	£450
30 Jan	Wages	£350
4 Feb	Purchases	£3,560
5 Feb	Rent	£500
15 Feb	Cash	£590
28 Feb	Wages	£295
3 Mar	Superior Sports	£5,000
5 Mar	Rent	£600
9 Mar	Cash	£695
10 Mar	Purchases	£3,410
12 Mar	Van purchase	£15,000
31 Mar	Wages	£375

Paying-in Book Details		
20-1		
1 Jan	Capital	£10,000
5 Jan	Sales	£4,500
15 Jan	Sales	£3,900
30 Jan	Sales	£7,200
5 Feb	Sales	£4,000
15 Feb	Sales	£2,500
23 Feb	Sales	£6,920
5 Mar	Sales	£3,170
15 Mar	Sales	£2,240
15 Mar	Greenham College	£2,542
31 Mar	Sales	£8,395

Note:
Items marked "Sales" are takings from the shop, paid straight into the bank account.

File for Sales Invoices
Invoice dated 23 March to Greenham College £1,907 (not yet paid)
Invoice dated 8 Feb to Greenham College £2,542 marked "paid in full 15 March 20-1"

File for Purchase Invoices
Invoice received 10 Feb from Superior Sports £5,000 (not yet paid)
Invoice received 12 March from Superior Sports £3,000 (not yet paid)
Invoice received 22 March Willow Supplies £2,000 (not yet paid)
Invoice received 10 Jan Superior Sports £5,000 annotated by Dave Parks "paid in full 3 March"

Dave Parks also brings two other points to your attention:

- He shows you a letter from Greenham College stating that they are returning ten defective cricket bats under separate cover and requesting credit for £100. Mr Parks has prepared a credit note for £100, dated 31 March.

- He mentions in passing that the three cheques for "cash" were in fact drawings for his own living expenses rather than for use in the business.

TASKS

1. You are to rule up double entry accounts for Bolton Sports and enter all the transactions for the three months.

2. You are to balance off all the accounts at 31 March 20-1 and prepare a trial balance as at that date.

3. You are to write Mr Parks a letter explaining succinctly and in jargon-free language what you have done. The letter should include:

   - an explanation of why you have made two entries for each transaction
   - the purpose of balancing off the accounts
   - the purpose of the trial balance

   The letter should take into account the fact that Mr Parks has an elementary knowledge of book-keeping (he has after all been to a lecture on the subject), but, more importantly, the pressing need for him to be able to work out his debtor and creditor positions and his bank balance.

3 THE BOOKS OF THE BUSINESS

Double entry book-keeping involves, as we have seen, the making of two entries in the ledger accounts for each transaction. The traditional meaning of a *ledger* is a weighty leather bound volume into which each account is entered on a separate page. The term "The Ledger" is also used in a technical sense to refer collectively to the four main divisions of the books of the business:

- *Sales Ledger*, containing the accounts of debtors
- *Purchases Ledger*, containing the accounts of creditors
- *Cash Book*, containing cash account and bank account in separate columns
- *General (or Nominal) Ledger*, containing the remaining accounts

These four divisions comprise *The Ledger* and are illustrated in full on the next page. Before studying the diagram in detail, examine the nature of the four very common transactions set out below, the accounts into which they are entered, and the ledgers in which they are recorded.

Purchase of goods on credit	*Debit* General Ledger: the amount is entered in the purchases account *Credit* Purchases Ledger: the amount is entered in the creditor's (supplier's) account
Purchase of goods by cheque	*Debit* General Ledger: the amount is entered in the purchases account *Credit* Cash Book: the amount is entered in the bank account column with the cheque details
Sale of goods on credit	*Debit* Sales Ledger: the amount is entered in the personal account of the debtor who has made the purchase *Credit* General Ledger: the amount is entered in the sales account
Sale of goods for cash	*Debit* Cash Book: the amount is entered in the cash account column *Credit* General Ledger: the amount is entered in the sales account

the divisions of the ledger

CASH BOOK

The Cash Book records all entries for

- *Bank* Account transactions (e.g cheques, standing orders)
- *Cash* Transactions (notes and coins)

Entries are made in ruled columns, there being one each for
- debit side: cash in, bank transactions in
- credit side: cash out, bank transactions out

The Cash Book can also be used for *listing* cash discounts.

SALES LEDGER

The Sales Ledger contains debtors' accounts and records:
- Sales made on credit to customers of the business
- Payments received from debtors
The Sales Ledger does *not* record Cash Sales

The Sales Ledger contains an *account* for each customer. Each account, normally on a separate page, shows the transactions for that particular customer. Each customer is a *debtor* of the business. The total of the Sales Ledger account balances is the *debtors* figure which appears in the balance sheet.

PURCHASES LEDGER

The Purchases Ledger contains creditors' accounts and records
- Purchases made on credit from suppliers of the business
- Payment of amounts owing to creditors
The Purchases Ledger does *not* record Cash Purchases

The Purchases Ledger is divided into accounts for each supplier *(creditor)*, each account recording the transactions for that particular creditor.
The sum of the Purchases Ledger accounts is the *creditors* figure which is shown in the balance sheet of the business.

GENERAL OR NOMINAL LEDGER

This Ledger is termed the *General Ledger* or *Nominal Ledger* because it contains a wide variety of accounts which record:
- Fixed assets
- Long term liabilities
- Running expenses incurred, income received
- Sales account (total of cash and credit sales)
- Purchases account (total of cash and credit purchases for *trading* purposes, not fixed asset purchase)
- Capital account, drawings, trading and profit and loss accounts
- VAT account (where the business is registered for VAT)
- Stock account

other books of the business

The four ledgers set out on the previous page form the basis of the standard double entry book-keeping system. There are also a number of other books which may be used by a business, if the volume of transactions is sufficiently high. These include the *Petty Cash Book* and the *Journals.*

Petty Cash Book

If a business has a large volume of small cash (notes and coin) payments, it will keep in the office a float of cash, known as *petty cash,* so that staff can make purchases of necessary items such as stationery, instant coffee and postage stamps. A separate *Petty Cash Book* will be maintained to record and analyse these transactions to prevent the columns of the main cash book becoming congested with 'petty' items. The petty cash float will be 'topped up' from time to time from the main cash book, the two book-keeping entries being a withdrawal from the main cash book and a corresponding entry in the petty cash book.

The Journals

The four principal books illustrated on the previous page are known collectively as 'The Ledger'. As you might imagine, if a business has a heavy volume of, say, sales transactions, it would be very inconvenient every time an invoice was produced to have to record it in the General Ledger (sales account) and in either the Sales Ledger (credit sale) or the Cash Book (cash sale). Many businesses therefore use a *Journal* or *Day Book,* as it is termed, to list all the transactions as they occur. These journals include:

* *Sales Journal,* for listing credit sales (from the invoices produced by the business)
* *Purchases Journal,* for listing credit purchases (from invoices received from suppliers)
* *Sales Returns Journal,* for listing items returned to the business (from credit notes prepared)
* *Purchases Returns Journal,* for listing items returned out (from debit notes prepared)
* *General Journal,* for recording other transactions for later reference

It must be stressed that the Journals are merely a means of listing transactions which are totalled up periodically - daily, weekly, or monthly, depending on the volume. For example, the Sales Journal may list ten sales invoices prepared during the course of a day. At the end of the day the book-keeper will enter the transactions as follows:

* each invoice entry is posted *individually* to the appropriate debtor's account in the Sales Ledger
* the *total* of all the invoice entries for the day is posted to the sales account in the General Ledger

The Journals or Day Books are often referred to as *Books of Original Entry* for the simple reason that it is in these books that transactions are first recorded. It is important to bear in mind that Journals are *not* Ledgers, they are merely listing devices used for convenience.

variations from the standard ledger accounting system

It cannot be stressed too often that the full double entry ledger accounting system as we have seen it so far is a standard system. Many businesses, however, do not need a full set of ledgers, either because they are too small, or because they deal on a cash (immediate payment) basis, or both. Variations from the standard system include the single entry system (the 'shoe box' system), packaged 'Write it Once' systems, and computer based systems.

Single Entry Systems

For the small business, which needs little more than a cash book and records of amounts owing and owed, the single entry or shoe box system will suffice. It is called 'single entry' because all that is recorded are income and expenditure in the cash book (sometimes ruled with analysis columns for individual items), and 'shoe box' because all it requires additionally is four shoe boxes (or box or other files): a set of two for *unpaid* sales invoices and purchases invoices, and another set of two for *paid* sales and purchases. Each 'unpaid' box or file of invoices represents either debtors or creditors. This is a basic system, but for many businesses it is quite adequate.

The 'Write it Once' System of Book-keeping Records

For businesses which are not sure *how* to keep the books there are a number of commercially available systems of record-keeping files, together with full instructions of how to keep the 'books' using loose leaf record sheets. The advantage of this type of system is that it saves time through being a 'write it once' system, which uses 'no carbon required' paper to produce copies: when entering each transaction the book-keeper can enter up to three record sheets simultaneously.

Computer Based Systems

Most computer based systems, which involve the book-keeper entering transactions into a computer rather than into a handwritten book, are to all appearances single entry because each transaction is entered once only. On computer file however the system is double entry based because each transaction is coded by the computer operator: as each transaction is entered it is given a code which automatically posts it to the relevant book of account maintained in the computer file. The use of computer based accounts will be dealt with in full in Chapter 4.

information available from the ledgers

Whatever book-keeping system a business adopts, it is the role of the accountant to advise in the making of the choice. It will also be up to the accountant to judge how much information the owner of a business will need to extract from the accounts. A full set of double entry accounts will tell the owner a number of useful facts about his or her business:

- the total of the business assets (General Ledger)
- the cash and bank balances (Cash Book)
- the total of debtors (Sales Ledger)
- the total of creditors (Purchases Ledger)
- the total of sales and purchases (General Ledger)
- the VAT position, if the business is VAT registered (General Ledger)

As we will see in later Chapters, the information can be used in a variety of ways for the production of accounting statements, such as the trading account and profit and loss accounts, the balance sheet and costing and budget statements. These statements will be of value not only to the owner, but also to other interested parties, such as the bank manager and the Inland Revenue. It is therefore vital that the books of the business are maintained efficiently, as they are the only reliable basis for measuring and comparing business performance.

CHAPTER SUMMARY

❏ The basic ledgers of a business are the Cash Book, Sales Ledger, Purchases Ledger and General Ledger, collectively known as *The Ledger*.

❏ These four books form the basis of the standard double entry book-keeping system.

❏ Additionally, businesses may use other books, which include the Petty Cash Book and various types of Journal.

❏ Not all businesses need to adopt the double entry system; many use a single entry system.

❏ It is important that the books are maintained accurately; most accounting statements will be prepared from them.

✍ STUDENT ACTIVITIES

As a trainee accountant in the firm of Price Waterston, 26 Hunt Street, Lime Hill, LM7 9DW, you are faced with a number of enquiries from businesses seeking help in setting up book-keeping systems. You are to answer the enquiries as indicated in activities 1 to 3. Activity 4 is a a task set you by your Senior Partner.

3.1   Mrs Hetty James, who has recently taken over the local Post Office at Wellbrook, is not trained in book-keeping, and is having difficulty in interpreting the accounting system used by the previous owner. She telephones and asks you what the following mean:
* *Sales Ledger* (she says that not all her sales are listed here)
* *Sales Day Book* (she does not understand how this works)
* *Cash Sales* (she is confused because these seem to include cheques received)
* *Cash Discount* (she asks if this is the same as trade discount)

You are to write out headed explanations of these items to assist Mrs James.

3.2   Jim Hitchen, a self-employed plumber, is finding difficulty in dealing with his double entry ledgers - Sales, Purchases, General and Cash Book - which he has bought from a commercial stationers. He asks in which ledgers the following transactions should be entered:

(a)   bought £3,000 materials on credit from Dynopipe Limited
(b)   bought £1,250 materials by cheque from Dynopipe Limited
(c)   withdrew £300 cash from the bank for use in the business
(d)   paid his assistant wages of £250 in cash
(e)   paid rates bill of £120 by cheque
(f)   received £1,275 by cheque for work done three weeks ago for Miller Fashions Ltd.
(g)   replaced hot water tank for S Taylor for £147, payment to be in 30 days
(h)   repaired burst pipe for Frank Watts and is paid £75 cash 'on the nail'
(i)   completed VAT return and wrote out cheque for £1,239.75 for VAT payable

Write out a schedule containing columns setting out:
* a list of the transactions
* the *two* books into which, in the *majority* of cases, the entries will be made

Note: there is one transaction which is entered twice in the same book.

3.3   You receive a letter from Mr Andrew Bone who keeps a meat stall in the local market. He asks what books he should use to record his business transactions, as at present he only uses his bank statement, cheque book, and paying-in book as accounting records. He mentions that his receipts are all in cash and cheques, but adds that he does obtain some of his supplies on credit from a single supplier, Welland Meats Limited, who issue him with invoices and monthly statements.

You are to write him a suitable reply, suggesting a book-keeping system appropriate to his needs. Mr Bone's address is 25 Malvern View, Welland, Worcester.

3.4   You are approached by your senior partner, who is going to give a lecture at the local Further Education College to owners of small businesses on the subject of "The Books of the Business: Help or Hindrance?" He asks you to set out for him a draft text for the talk, which will deal with the importance of choosing the right book-keeping system for the individual business. He mentions that he wants to cover the double entry book-keeping system, the single entry system, and computerised accounts.

4 COMPUTER ACCOUNTING SYSTEMS

As we have already seen, a computer accounting system can replace the manual handwritten accounting records, the Ledgers and Daybooks, examined in Chapter 3, with information input over a computer terminal and stored on computer disc. Many businesses now use computerised accounts because they find them beneficial in terms of cost and the information they provide. For many businesses, and particularly smaller businesses, computerising the accounts can be a marginal proposition.

There are two opposing points of view about the computerisation of accounts:

> *"Owners of businesses sometimes think that if they computerise their accounts, they will automatically save time, money and effort. Tempted by advertising hype they rush out and buy the latest and cheapest system, which they probably don't understand and will seldom use. They believe that technology equates with progress."*

> *"A computerised accounting system can be of great benefit to a business; it will enable the owner to control the business better by streamlining procedures and providing more management information."*

In fact both points of view are correct. Large businesses invariably use computers and reap the benefits of efficiency and accessibility of information. It is for the smaller business that the decision whether to instal a computer accounting system becomes more difficult. A computer accounting system, if it is to be introduced, must be chosen with great care and with proper professional advice.

These are the questions a business owner should consider before investing in a computer accounting system:

- Can my present manual system cope? If not, why not?
- Will a computer system improve the situation?
- What benefits will a computer system bring to my business?
- What professional advice should I seek? Do I involve an accountant?
- Should I computerise all of my accounting system?
- What type of system should I instal?
- What happens to double entry in a computer accounting system?
- How important is training and a backup service?

In this Chapter we will answer these questions and examine in the following Assignment the way in which a typical small business computerises its accounting system.

examination of the manual accounting system

As we have seen in Chapter 3, there are four main divisions within the organisation of business accounts using the double entry system:

- Sales Ledger
- Purchases Ledger
- General or Nominal Ledger
- Cash Book

In addition, a business may keep Stock Control and Payroll records. But, as must be obvious when one considers the different forms of business and the differing expertise of business owners, a full set of accounting records is not always maintained. A small jobbing builder is likely to keep only a basic analysed cashbook and two piles of invoices as a "Sales Ledger" and a "Purchases Ledger" on a single entry basis. A builders' merchant, on the other hand, who has many transactions to record, will probably keep a full set of double entry accounts. If either of these two businesses cannot cope with the manual system and is considering using a computer, it should look very carefully at the reasons for not being able to cope.

These could be some of the reasons:

- lack of skill in entering up the accounts (unfortunately all too common)
- shortage of time/shortage of staff for entering the accounts
- an increasingly large volume of transactions
- too much time spent on VAT returns
- too little information available for management decisions
- not knowing which customers are late in paying

The first two reasons - lack of skill and staff shortage - may well point to the need for an improvement in the management of the manual accounting system and not necessarily to the need for a computerised accounting system. The solution would be either to consult an accountant, or in the case of lack of expertise, enrolment on a book-keeping class at a local College of Further Education. The remainder of the reasons suggest that a computerised system would be beneficial to the business.

what type of computer accounting software?

Before appreciating the benefits that a computer accounting system can bring, it is important to examine exactly what prorammes (software) are available. There are basically two types of system: the simple *cash trader* programme and the *complete ledger* programme. The latter can either be *integrated* 'all in one' packages or *modular* systems.

Cash Trader Programmes
These simple systems assume that the business keeps only a Cash Book and needs to keep track of money received and money spent, and to analyse the expenditure. Such programmes are inexpensive and are clearly suitable for small businesses which deal on a cash only basis.

Complete Ledger Systems
These programmes are suitable for businesses that keep a full set of double entry accounts. The following facilities are normally available:

- Sales Ledger
- Invoicing (sometimes integrated with Sales Ledger)
- Purchases Ledger
- General Ledger (incorporating the Cash Book)
- Stock Control
- Payroll

Complete Ledger systems are available in two formats: *the integrated format* and the *modular format:*

Integrated packages will normally contain all of the functions listed above. An integrated pachage may be expensive and intially more complex to operate, but eventually it will prove very useful because it also automatically produces reports such as the trial balance, the trading and profit and loss accounts and the balance sheet.

Modular Systems are suitable if the business considers that it does not need the full range of facilities offered by the integrated package. It may select individual functions, for example the Sales Ledger and Invoicing, which may be purchased separately as *modules*. This approach is useful because a business can purchase extra modules, for example Purchases Ledger and General Ledger, as the need arises. Each module added is completely compatible with other modules from the same software house.

what computer hardware is required?

Most of the computer accounting systems are produced to the IBM PC standard. Accounting software is also available for other types of computer, but the variety is more limited. A recommended system might therefore include:

- an IBM or IBM compatible computer with built in floppy or hard disc storage system
- a compatible dot matrix printer, with tractor feed to take continuous stationery (e.g. invoices)

A larger business which employs many accounts staff may consider *networking* a number of computer terminals in different parts of the office, linking them to a central storage system, or printer. This can be a cost-effective solution, but professional advice must be taken for its implementation.

the benefits of a computer accounting system

The main benefits of a computer accounting system include its ability to handle a high volume of transactions, its simplification of double entry, its improved credit control, instant VAT reports, and rapid access to management information.

Volume Transactions
Although a computer accounting system may take time to set up, and may have teething troubles, one of its principal benefits is its ability to handle large volumes of transactions and to enable the owner of the business to access that information immediately, or "real time" in computer jargon. If a customer telephones to query an invoice amount or discount allowed, the owner does not need to search through paper files (with the invoice possibly missing or misplaced), he can instead call the transaction up on his screen to give an immediate answer. Also, as the business expands, the ability of the computer to deal with a high volume of transactions will lead to a saving in staff costs, as fewer accounts staff will be needed. To some, this is a mixed blessing.

Avoidance of Double Entry
One major advantage and time saving element of a computer accounting system is the fact that double entry is automatic. Each transaction is recorded as a *single* entry into the system with an appropriate code input for the automatic entering of the corresponding double entry transaction. For example, the receipt of a cheque from a debtor is a *single* entry for the amount of the cheque in the customer's account in the Sales Ledger with the appropriate code entered for the bank account; two entries are posted in the accounts, but only one entry made on the computer keyboard.

Credit Control
The use of computerised Sales Ledger and Invoicing functions can help the owner of a business in keeping track of overdue payments from his customers and will reduce the time-consuming paperwork generated by credit control. The best packages will produce:

- invoices
- statements with remittance advices attached
- aged debtor summaries (lists of debtors showing the amount of time invoices have been outstanding)

VAT Reports

Many businesses are registered for Value Added Tax (VAT), and are required to make regular returns of the amounts of VAT paid on purchases and charged on sales. Manual calculations of the VAT position can be time consuming and tedious. Computer records which contain Sales and Purchase Ledger functions will automatically produce VAT reports and save many troublesome hours.

Management Information

Accounts packages containing a General Ledger should be able to produce trading and profit and loss accounts and balance sheets automatically. This will be of benefit to the owner, as not only will he or she be able to obtain up-to-date information on profitability, but computer produced financial statements will impress the bank manager and save the accountant's time and fees.

the necessity for professional advice

There are, as we have seen, considerable benefits derived from introducing computer accounting systems. There are also, inevitably, problems and drawbacks:

- the difficulty of deciding on the appropriate computer software and hardware
- the necessity for keeping a parallel manual accounting system for a suggested twelve months
- the danger of mechanical breakdown, and software problems or "bugs"
- the need to train staff who may not like computers
- the problem of security (the wrong person obtaining access to the system to "cook the books")

It is clear that anyone considering the purchase of a computer accounting system must obtain reliable professional advice. This can be provided by accountants and computer consultancy firms.

The accountant should be consulted at an early stage so that the manual system can be assessed and the appropriate type of computer package (cash trader or complete ledger system) be recommended. It is quite possible at this stage that the accountant will advise against buying a computer system, and will instead suggest ways of improving the manual system, thus saving the owner considerable expense.

The computer consultancy firm should be contacted, if a purchase is recommended, and discussions entered into, possibly with the accountant present, about suitable hardware and software. Although this approach is more expensive than buying 'off the shelf', there are a number of advantages:

- expert advice on the necessary hardware and software
- assistance with setting up the system in the office
- after sales service for hardware and software
- often a telephone 'hotline' for operational problems
- staff training arranged

It must be remembered that computers, to date at least, are essentially unintelligent; they will only do precisely as instructed and cannot anticipate or correct. Unless a business obtains appropriate professional advice from an accountant and/or a computer consultancy, the cost benefits of a computer accounting system may be totally lost.

other uses for the business computer

So far we have looked solely at the accounting uses of a computer system. It must be remembered that the purchase of a computer will also enable the business to improve its performance by introducing other programmes such as word-processors, databases, and spreadsheets.

Word processing packages are now the standard for any efficient office. *Databases* are computer filing systems which enable a large amount of information, such as client names and addresses to be held on file and accessed immediately, and more importantly, analysed for management reports. *Spreadsheets* enable a large amount of numeric data to be tabulated and processed into formats such as budgets, financial statements (trading and profit and loss accounts, for example) and cash flow forecasts.

CHAPTER SUMMARY

❏ Computer accounting systems can greatly improve business efficiency.

❏ Computer accounting systems can either be simple cash trader programmes or a full ledger system in an integrated or modular form.

❏ Computer accounting systems, by providing management information, can assist the business owner in making decisions.

❏ Computer accounting systems cannot work miracles; they should only be introduced after a thorough feasibility study, and full staff training.

❏ Professional advice should be sought when introducing a computer accounting system.

STUDENT ACTIVITIES

4.1 You have been asked to recommend to a small business (Sidbury Traders) a suitable computer and software for accounting, word-processing and spreadsheet functions. Obtain from your library or local newsagent copies of professional computing magazines. Investigate hardware and software from reviews and advertisements; send away for details if necessary. Draw up a shortlist of 3 suitable machines together with compatible software, bearing in mind the considerations of value for money and reliability. Present your findings in the form of a report addressed to Tom Elliott, Accounts Manager, Sidbury Traders, Deansway, Worcester.

4.2 Answer the following letter from Mrs. Rose Turner, Arco Engineering, Unit 7, Westbury Trading Estate, Greenham, GR6 9TY:

```
J Rudd
White Peterhouse, Chartered Accountants,
Castle View, Greenham.                              7 July 2000

Dear Mr Rudd,

I have been considering the possibility of computerising our accounts. As you
know, we run a double entry system here at Arco Engineering, and  I want to
convince the higher management that computerisation will bring great benefits.
They are an old-fashioned lot, and are bound to bring up any number of
objections. I shall be very grateful if could set out for me the advantages of
computerisation, particularly for management, and also the disadvantages, so
that I can answer their criticisms. I know that you are expert in the field, so
I hope you will be able to help me.

Yours sincerely,

Rose Turner
Rose Turner
Accounts Manager
```

ASSIGNMENT

2 *Compusoft Limited: Computer Accounting*

> *covering*
> books of account, manual and computerised accounting systems, credit control

Equipment required
This Assignment requires the use of microcomputer equipped with an accounts package which has at least a sales ledger and purchase ledger function.

SITUATION

Compusoft Limited is a small shop situated at 108 Friar Street, Worcester WR1 6TG. It is run by its systems analyst owner, Ron White. Most of the sales, which are of both hardware and software, are cash sales in the shop, but it does sell to a small number of customers on credit, many of them educational establishments. Compusoft Ltd. gives on average a 30 day payment period.

Ron White bought a business microcomputer six months ago. Although he is a computer expert, he is slow to practise what he preaches, and he has only recently realised that his manual system of recording credit purchases and sales has been rather "hit and miss": it takes him a long time to work out the balance of his debtors' accounts, and his credit control is consequently lax. He has therefore purchased an integrated accounts package and wishes to use it to record his credit sales and purchases.

You are the assistant in the shop and have been deputed to keep the accounting records. Mr White hands over to you his manual accounting records, which include:

• a list of ten customers to whom he sells on credit, together with the outstanding invoices
• a list of five suppliers, together with outstanding invoices

These are set out below.

Debtors and Outstanding Invoices
Note: the limit stated is the credit limit; the invoice details include the invoice date and the details of the goods sold. Note that the year on each invoice is the current year.

```
Electra Ltd., 123 High Street, Hamble, SS1 2TH.  Limit £1,000.
Invoice 2453, 23 May, £750, (10 x Wordplay wordprocessing programmes)

Systemsgo, Orchard House, The Green, Helford, TR9 6FD.  Limit £1,500
Invoice 1989, 20 April, £1,350.65 (20 x games packages)
```

Bigbyte, 43 Summer Street, Sunborough, SN8 6VC. Limit £1,000.
Invoice 1675, 4 March, £650 (600 floppy discs)
Invoice 2091, 5 May, £450 (400 floppy discs)

Compustore, Wilson House, Waterston Lane, Waverley, OL8 5AS. Limit £3,000
Invoice 2654, 13 June, £2,500 (2 x databases)

Bufton College, Deans Yard, Witterbury, WR6 9IN. Limit £10,000.
Invoice 2001, 1 May, £5,675.95 (5 x Armstrong PC107 microcomputers)

Norton Sixth Form College, Stratford Road, Wimbury, WM9 7LK. Limit £5,000.
Invoice 1945, 30 March, £4,385 (2 x Compact 2 microcomputers)

Llanfair College, Berwen Road, Derwenlas, LL8 2CV. Limit £2,000
Invoice 2703, 23 June, £1,567.35 (1 x Armstrong PC107 microcomputer)

Sunbury College, Worthing Road, Twickenham, HA9 8BG. Limit £1,000
Invoice 2507, 15 June, £239.89 (200 floppy discs)

Eliot Supplies, 43 The Crest, Palmers Green, London N13 7MA. Limit £500
Invoice 2508, 16 June, £340.35 (1 x spreadsheet)

Telesystems, Holloway House, High Road, London NW3 2EM. Limit £5,000
Invoice 1812, 12 March, £3,500 (2 x Electroputer F14 microcomputer)
Invoice 2603, 23 June, £2,509.65 (1 x Compact 2 microcomputer)

Creditors and Outstanding Invoices

Note: no addresses are quoted here, as the accounting packages do not require them.

Hyposoft, Limit £15,000
Invoice 20987, 15 May, £12,095.25 (assorted software)

Clifford Systems, Limit £2,500
Invoice 3981, 29 April, £1,987.46 (1250 x floppy discs)

Electroputer UK, Limit £35,000
Invoice 16543, 21 May, £14,325.75 (10 x F14 microcomputers)

Compact Systems plc, Limit £20,000
Invoice 19867, 21 March, £15,562.50 (10 x Compact 2 microcomputers)

Armstrong plc, Limit £15,000
Invoice 2546, 20 May, £14,575.87 (10 x Armstrong PC107 microcomputers)

TASKS

1.   You are to enter all the above details on the Sales and Purchase Ledgers of your accounting package. *Important Note: the date is 30 June of the current year.* It is quite likely that you will first have to open the accounts and then post the invoices in a separate routine. If in doubt, consult the computer manual. The amounts quoted are net of VAT. You are to assume that the items involved are *zero rated*. (You will probably have to input a VAT code into the computer).

2.   Mr White hands you some items from the day's post which have not yet been entered into the accounts. You are to deal with them as appropriate. *Remember, the date is 30 June .* The items are as follows:

- A cheque No. 298647 from Systemsgo for £1,350.65, quoting invoice No.1989.

- A cheque No.245637 for £340.35 from Eliot Supplies quoting invoice No.2508.

- A cheque No.456735 for £2,500 from Compustore quoting invoice No.2654.

- A cheque No.198563 from Sunbury College for £239.89 quoting invoice No.2507.

- A package from Bigbyte containing 50 floppy discs which the company claims to be faulty. The discs relate to your invoice No 2091, and you have issued a credit note for £58.50.

- A letter of complaint from Telesystems stating that your recent invoice No. 2603 was incorrect. You check your records and find that you have not given them their customary discount. You issue them with a credit note for £510.00.

3. You are to write a letter of apology to Telesystems enclosing the credit note for £510 issued in respect of your incorrect invoice No.2603 . The letter should be for Mr White's signature.

4. On 6 July your boss has at last found time to examine the credit sales and purchases position. He asks you to extract the following information:

- A printout of the Sales Ledger and Purchases Ledger balances.

- An account history (if available) of Bigbyte, whom he suspects to be bad payers.

- Aged debtor and creditor summaries to enable him to see what action needs to be taken.

After examining this information he asks you to

(a) Write an appropriate letter to Bigbyte pointing out the present position (you are to assume that statements have been sent out at each month-end), and requesting payment. The letter is to be signed by Mr White.

(b) Write him a memorandum stating which invoices he needs to pay.

(c) Write him a memorandum giving your recommendations for action to be taken regarding Telesystems, bearing in mind your recent error on invoice 2603. He asks you to look carefully at the credit limit and the time Telesystems takes to pay.

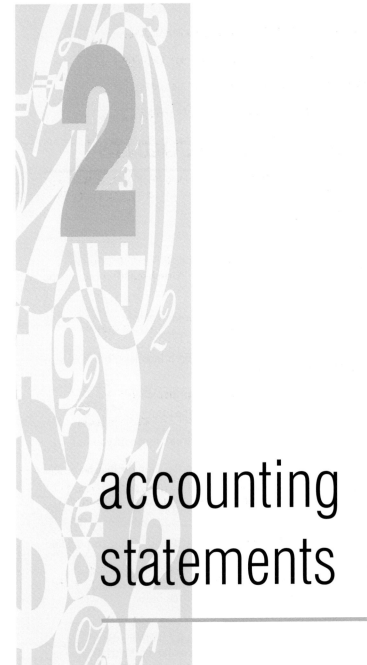

accounting
statements

5 SOLE TRADER FINAL ACCOUNTS

A person setting up in business on his or her own, not involving partners and avoiding the expense of forming a limited company does so as a *sole trader.*

A sole trader is an individual trading alone in his or her name, or under a recognised trading name.

Becoming a sole trader is the simplest and cheapest way of setting up a business, but it is also the most risky:

* the responsibility for managing the business is entirely your own
* it will involve long hours and short holidays and will require good health
* you may have to provide and risk all of the start-up capital
* you are solely liable for all *business* debts and risk losing your *personal* assets if you fail

Having accepted all these risks, the sole trader can take comfort from the thought that he or she is the 'boss', and is entitled to all the profits earned.

accounting records of a sole trader

It will be clear from what we have seen of the status of a sole trader that he or she is responsible for the maintenance of the accounting records. This may be achieved by

* the sole trader keeping hand-written accounts personally (the most common situation)
* the sole trader employing a book-keeper on a full-time or on a part-time basis
* the sole trader using a computer (an increasingly popular option)

If there is a manual book-keeping system maintained by the sole trader and/or a book-keeper, the records, in the case of a double entry ledger system, will be taken as far as the trial balance. The trial balance and the balanced off double entry books will then be handed to the accountant, usually on an annual basis, for the production of the *final accounts* of the business. These are termed "final accounts" because they are produced at the end of the financial year of the business. The end of the *financial* year can be any date in the calendar, but is often 31 December. Nevertheless, many businesses produce trading and profit and loss accounts more frequently - monthly or quarterly - as a means of management control.

If the business has only a single entry system, the accountant will have more of a job on his hands, as we will see in Chapter 7 *Incomplete Records,* but will still be able to calculate and construct a set of final accounts. If the business runs a computer accounting package, the owner will be able to extract these final accounts automatically. This will be of great benefit to the owner, and will also save the accountant's time and fees. The accountant will still, of course, be needed to advise on tax and other matters.

The final accounts comprise:

* trading account
* profit and loss account
* balance sheet

final accounts of Express Pasta from the trial balance

Express Pasta is a food importing business which supplies hotels, restuarants and retail stores with a wide range of Italian pasta and other delicacies. The following trial balance was extracted by the owner, Toni Ricci, at 31 December 20-1, the end of the first financial year.

Trial Balance of Express Pasta as at 31 December 20-1

	£	£
Sales		250,000
Purchases	156,000	
Returns in	5,400	
Returns out		7,200
Discount received		2,500
Discount allowed	3,700	
Stock 1 Jan 19-1	nil	
Salaries	46,000	
Electricity and gas	3,000	
Rent and rates	2,000	
Sundry expenses	4,700	
Premises	78,000	
Equipment	30,000	
Vehicles	21,500	
Debtors	23,850	
Bank	1,239	
Cash	125	
Creditors		28,756
Capital		62,500
Drawings	10,442	
Long term loan		35,000
	385,956	385,956

As it was the first year of trading there was no stock at the beginning of the year. Stock at the end of the year was valued at £25,300. From these figures the accountant will prepare the trading and profit and loss accounts and balance sheet. In the following examples we will present the accounting statements

* *before adjustments* for items such as accruals, prepayments, bad debts and depreciation, which we will deal with in the next Chapter
* in *vertical format*, ie in *columnar* form rather than in *horizontal* format

trading account: gross profit

The Italian food importing trade involves the purchase from abroad of a variety of foodstuffs, such as pasta, cheeses and speciality sausages. In accounting terms these are known as the *purchases* of the business. These are then sold to retail stores and caterers in the UK. The items which are sold are known as *sales*. Purchases and sales are recorded in purchases account and sales account respectively. The arithmetic difference between sales and purchases, after making certain adjustments explained below, represents the *gross profit* of the business. The trading account is set out in full on the next page.

TRADING ACCOUNT OF EXPRESS PASTA
FOR THE YEAR ENDED 31 DECEMBER 20-1

	£	£	£
Sales			250,000
Less Returns in			5,400
			244,600
Opening stock		-	
Purchases	156,000		
Less Returns out	7,200		
		148,800	
Less Closing stock		25,300	
Cost of Goods sold			123,500
Gross Profit			121,100

Note the following points about the trading account:

- Sales and Purchases only include items bought and sold in the normal trading pattern of the business. They do not include items like machinery, which will be kept for use in the business and are classed as fixed assets.

- Adjustment must be made to the Purchases figure for stock in the store or warehouse at the beginning of the year; this would be *added* to Purchases because it will be sold during the year. In the case of Express Pasta, opening stock is nil because 20-1 is the first year of trading.

- Adjustment must be made for stock in the store or warehouse at the end of the year; this figure is *deducted* from Purchases because it has not been sold. It will form the opening stock for the next financial year.

- Purchases, adjusted for the change in level of stock is known as *cost of sales* or *cost of goods sold*. It is this figure which is deducted from Sales to give *gross profit*.

profit and loss account: net profit

The profit and loss account deducts from gross profit the day-to-day running expenses of the business, known as revenue expenses, to give *net profit*. Net profit is an important figure: it shows what has been earned by the business for the owner, and it is on this profit, after certain adjustments, that the owner's tax liability will be based. The profit and loss account is set out as follows:

PROFIT AND LOSS ACCOUNT OF EXPRESS PASTA
FOR THE YEAR ENDED 31 DECEMBER 20-1

	£	£	£
Gross Profit			121,100
Add Discounts received			2,500
			123,600
Less			
Salaries		46,000	
Electricity and gas		3,000	
Rent and rates		2,000	
Sundry expenses		4,700	
Discounts allowed		3,700	
			59,400
Net Profit			64,200

It is normal practice to combine the trading account and the profit and loss accounts into a single format showing both net profit and gross profit:

TRADING AND PROFIT AND LOSS ACCOUNT OF EXPRESS PASTA
FOR THE YEAR ENDED 31 DECEMBER 20-1

	£	£	£
Sales			250,000
Less Returns in			5,400
			244,600
Opening stock		-	
Purchases	156,000		
Less Returns out	7,200		
		148,800	
Less Closing stock		25,300	
Cost of Goods sold			123,500
Gross Profit			121,100
Add Discount received			2,500
			123,600
Less			
Salaries		46,000	
Electricity and gas		3,000	
Rent and rates		2,000	
Sundry expenses		4,700	
Discounts allowed		3,700	
			59,400
Net Profit			64,200

You should note the following points about the combined trading and profit and loss accounts:

Net Profit
The net profit for the year of £64,200 is the amount the business earned for the owner. It would be wrong, however, to state that this is cash which is available on 31 December 20-1, because the owner will already have drawn on it during the year as *drawings* (£10,442 according to the trial balance), and possibly spent it some of it on fixed assets for use in the business. The trial balance in fact shows the final bank balance to be £1,239.

Returns in and Returns out
You will note from the trading account that returns in and returns out are shown as *deductions* from sales and purchases respectively. This is logical when one considers that returned goods are in fact amending the figures for goods sold and goods purchased.

Discounts received and Discounts allowed
The discounts referred to here are *cash discounts*, i.e. discounts for early settlement of invoices, and not *trade discounts* which would already be included in any invoice total, and for which no adjustment would therefore be necessary. *Discounts received* are added to gross profit (as would any incidental income) and *discounts allowed* (i.e. by Express Pasta) shown among the running expenses of the business.

double entry book-keeping and the trading and profit and loss accounts

Each item entered in the trading and profit and loss accounts represents the balance of the appropriate double entry account in the books of the business. We are in effect 'emptying' each account that has been storing up a record of the transactions of the business during the course of the financial year, and transferring it to either the trading account or to the profit and loss account.

Trading Account

In the trading account of Express Pasta the balance of the purchases account will be transferred as follows:

Dr.		Purchases Account			Cr.
20-1		£	20-1		£
31 Dec	Balance b/d	156,000	31 Dec	Trading account	156,000

The account now has a nil balance, and is ready to receive the transactions for 20-2. In the trading account the balances of sales, returns in, returns out and stock accounts will be treated in the same way and be transferred from the double entry accounts in the books of the business.

Profit and Loss Account

Expenses and income items will be similarly transferred from the double entry accounts of the business. In the example below, the salaries account of Express Pasta has been transferred to profit and loss account.

Dr.		Salaries Account			Cr.
20-1		£	20-1		£
31 Dec	Balance b/d	46,000	31 Dec	Profit and Loss Account	46,000

The salaries account now has a nil balance and is ready to receive the transactions for 20-2, the next financial year.

The Use of the Trial Balance

It is important to appreciate that while the trial balance contains the basic figures necessary to draw up the trading and profit and loss accounts, the final accounts are often in practice, as in the examples above, drawn from the *double entry accounts* of the business. Nevertheless the trial balance is a useful summary from which to prepare the final accounts, and it will be used for this purpose in this book.

the balance sheet

Whereas the trading and profit and loss accounts show how the profit (or loss) has been achieved during the financial year, the balance sheet shows the state of the business on the last day of the financial year. The "balance" is between what the business owns (less current liabilities), shown in the first sections as *Net Assets*, and where the money has come from, shown in the second *Financed by* section. The balance sheet of Express Pasta is set out in full on the next page.

BALANCE SHEET OF EXPRESS PASTA AS AT 31 DECEMBER 20-1

	£	£
Fixed Assets		
Premises		78,000
Equipment		30,000
Vehicles		21,500
		129,500
Current Assets		
Stock	25,300	
Debtors	23,850	
Bank	1,239	
Cash	125	
	50,514	
Less Current Liabilities		
Creditors	28,756	
Working Capital		21,758
		151,258
Less Long-Term Liabilities		
Long term loan		35,000
NET ASSETS		116,258
FINANCED BY		
Capital		
Opening capital		62,500
Add net profit		64,200
		126,700
Less drawings		10,442
		116,258

Note the following points:

- **Assets** are items owned or owed to the business, normally listed in order of permanence:
  Fixed assets are assets held for the long term (premises, equipment, vehicles)
  Current assets are short term assets (stock, debtors, bank balance, cash).

- **Intangible assets** (not shown here) will sometimes be shown on a balance sheet, and are normally listed before fixed assets. An *intangible asset* is an asset that does not have *material*

  substance (is not *tangible*), but belongs to the business and has value. A common example is *goodwill*, which is where a business has bought another business and paid an agreed amount for the existing reputation and customer connections (the *goodwill*).

- **Liabilities** are items owed by the business:
  Long term liabilities are external borrowings, where repayment is due in over 12 months' time
  Current liabilities are amounts owed by the business and due for repayment within 12 months (and usually a great deal less), for example bank overdraft, creditors.

- **Capital** is money owed by the business to the owner, and is calculated as follows:
  owner's investment *plus* net profit for the year *less* drawings for the year.

- **Working Capital** is the excess of curent assets over current liabilities. Without working capital a business cannot continue to operate. The subject will be dealt with in Chapters 20 and 21.

Significance of the Balance Sheet

From these definitions it is possible to see that the balance sheet of a business (in this case Express Pasta) shows how the business is financed in the long term. The concept may be reduced to a formula:

Fixed Assets + Working Capital – Long Term Loans = Net Assets = Owner's Capital

preparing final accounts from a trial balance

As we have seen, final accounts may be produced either direct from the double entry account balances, or via the trial balance. It is important, when transferring figures to the final accounts, to be methodical and logical in your approach; if you are not, the balance sheet may not balance. It is a good idea to add a fourth column to the trial balance as in the illustration below, to make a note of which part of which final statement the entry will be transfered, and then tick each figure as you transfer it to the final accounts. In this way you will avoid errors and omissions such as taking a figure twice, or not at all. The trial balance of Express Pasta will then look like this:

Trial Balance of Express Pasta as at 31 December 20-1

	£	£		
Sales		250,000	Trading A/c	√
Purchases	156,000		Trading A/c	√
Returns in	5,400		Trading A/c	√
Returns out		7,200	Trading A/c	√
Discount received		2,500	Profit & Loss	√
Discount allowed	3,700		Profit & Loss	√
Stock	nil		-	-
Salaries	46,000		Profit & Loss	√
Electricity and gas	3,000		Profit & Loss	√
Rent and rates	2,000		Profit & Loss	√
Sundry expenses	4,700		Profit & Loss	√
Premises	78,000		Fixed Assets	√
Equipment	30,000		Fixed Assets	√
Vehicles	21,500		Fixed Assets	√
Debtors	23,850		Current Assets	√
Bank	1,239		Current Assets	√
Cash	125		Current Assets	√
Creditors		28,756	Current Liabs	√
Capital		62,500	Capital	√
Drawings	10,442		Capital	√
Long term loan		35,000	Long term liabs	√
	385,956	385,956		

accounting concepts

Accounting Concepts are broad assumptions which underlie the preparation of all accounting statements. The final accounts produced in this Chapter illustrate a number of basic concepts: the *business entity concept*, the *money measurement concept* and the *objectivity concept*.

The Business Entity Concept

This states that that the financial statements (including final accounts) of a business show the trading activity, assets and liabilities of that particular business, and *not* the activities of the owner or manager as individuals. The business owner or manager will not include his private assets on the balance sheet, even if they are pledged as security for bank borrowing.

Money Measurement Concept

This states that all items in the financial statements have to be expressed in terms of money values. This may seem an obvious point, but it must be borne in mind that this common standard enables different businesses to be compared, performances quantified and tax liabilities calculated.

Objectivity Concept

Financial statements should not be influenced by the opinions or biased personal expectations of the owners of the business concerned, or the accountant preparing the accounts. The financial information presented should be entirely *objective*.

CHAPTER SUMMARY

❑ A sole trader business is a very common business entity, in which the sole trader takes all the risks and all the profits.

❑ The sole trader will need to keep accounts, either on his own, or with the help of a book-keeper. He may also use a computer to assist him.

❑ Whoever keeps the accounts will extract a trial balance at the end of the financial year of the business; this, together with the account balances, will form the basis of the final accounts.

❑ The accountant will normally produce the final accounts: trading account, profit and loss account and balance sheet, which will provide the owner, the Inland Revenue and the bank manager with a clear picture of the business' performance.

❑ The final accounts are produced on the basis of fundamental accounting concepts: the business entity concept, the money measurement concept, and the objectivity concept.

In the next Chapter we will examine the year-end adjustments which have to be made to any set of final accounts in order for them to comply with further accounting concepts.

✍ STUDENT ACTIVITIES

You are working for Price Anderson & Co., a firm of Chartered Accountants (143 High Street, Greenham GR4 5TD). Your senior partner asks you to set out the trading and profit and loss accounts and balance sheet in vertical format for each of the following businesses for the year ended 31 December 20-1.

Business One

Trial Balance of Wintergreen Service Station as at 31 December 20-1

	£	£
Premises	120,000	
Long term loan		60,000
Capital		70,000
Debtors	1,900	
Creditors		1,500
Drawings	5,000	
Cash	150	
Stock:1 Jan 20-1	4,200	
Fixtures & fittings	4,000	
Vehicles	8,000	
Bank overdraft		750
Sales		195,000
Purchases	154,000	
Wages	20,500	
Sundry expenses	9,500	
	327,250	327,250

Stock at 31 December 20-1 was valued at £5,200

Business Two

Trial Balance of John Adams, antique dealer, as at 31 December 20-1

	£	£
Debtors	37,200	
Creditors		35,920
Bank	10,000	
Capital		50,500
Sales		289,620
Purchases	182,636	
Stock: 1 Jan 20-1	32,020	
Salaries	36,930	
Heat & light	3,640	
Rent & rates	11,294	
Motor Vehicles	19,640	
Office equipment	11,000	
Sundry expenses	1,690	
Motor expenses	3,368	
Drawings	26,622	
	376,040	376,040

Stock at 31 December 20-1 was valued at £34,000

Business Three
Trial Balance of Andrew Brown, fashion designer, as at 31 December 20-1

	£	£
Purchases	31,480	
Sales		65,660
Stock at 1 Jan 20-1	7,580	
Returns in	240	
Returns out		620
Discounts allowed	380	
Discounts received		1,080
Drawings	14,720	
Premises	76,000	
Fixtures & fittings	21,000	
Wages & salaries	18,620	
Advertising	2,360	
Bank	4,020	
Cash	120	
Debtors	4,480	
Creditors		3,740
Capital		109,900
	181,000	181,000

Stock at 31 December 20-1 was valued at £6,060

Business Four
Trial Balance of "Crusty Crumpets" as at 31 December 20-1

	£	£
Purchases	50,280	
Sales		87,114
Rent	3,650	
Wages	12,438	
Heat & light	1,696	
Sundry expenses	952	
Capital		34,770
Premises	40,000	
Ovens & equipment	6,560	
Vehicle	7,580	
Debtors and Creditors	2,098	2,440
Stock at 1 Jan 20-1	2,000	
Bank	2,620	
Cash	50	
Drawings	4,400	
Long term loan		10,000
Discounts	4,300	3,750
Returns	4,000	4,550
	142,624	142,624

Stock at December 20-1 was valued at £2,745

A week later, Carole Jones, owner of the bakery "Crusty Crumpets" (175 High Road, Greenham, GR3 1SZ) telephones to thank you for the accounts. She is pleased about the profit, but is puzzled by some of the terminology. She asks you to write to her explaining:

- the difference between gross profit and net profit; why, she asks, are there two figures for profit?
- the difference between capital and working capital; why are they in different parts of the balance sheet?
- why should the net profit be included in the "Financed by" section; what is it financing?

6 ADJUSTMENTS TO THE FINAL ACCOUNTS

The final accounts produced in the last Chapter represent a basic statement of the profitability of the business and its balance sheet position. There are, however, a number of adjustments which may be made to the final accounts at the year end which will give a truer and more fair view of the business. These adjustments are made in accordance with a number of accepted *accounting concepts*.

Accounting Concepts: SSAP 2

We have already seen in the last Chapter the application of the concepts of business entity, money measurement and objectivity, all fundamental assumptions underlying the preparation of financial statements. A further set of accounting concepts is set out in a document entitled SSAP 2.

SSAP 2 *Disclosure of Accounting Policies*
An SSAP (Statement of Standard Accounting Practice) is a document produced by a body called the Accounting Standards Board (ASB). All accountants are professionally bound to abide by the terms of SSAP's, which cover a wide area of accounting practice, and will be referred to where appropriate later in this book. SSAP 2 *Disclosure of Accounting Policies* sets out four main concepts which should underly the preparation of accounting statements:

The going concern concept assumes that the business will continue to operate for the foreseeable future, and that the profit and loss account and balance sheet do not reflect any measures or values which might indicate otherwise.

The consistency concept assumes a consistent accounting treatment of the financial statements from year to year.

The accruals concept requires that expenditure and income be matched to the accounting period to which they relate and not necessarily to the period in which they were incurred; in simple terms if you pay next year's rates *this year*, the expenditure must appear in *next year's* profit and loss account.

The prudence concept (also known as the concept of *conservatism*) requires that revenues and profits are not anticipated, but are only included in the profit and loss account when they are realised. The concept also requires that adequate provision is made for likely losses and likely expenses, either when the amount is known or when a reliable estimate can be made.

These concepts apply equally to the financial statements of sole traders, partnerships and limited companies; in the case of limited companies they are given legal force in the Companies Act 1985.

adjustments to the final accounts

The adjustments to the final accounts which comply with these concepts are set out in detail below:

- adjusting for *prepayments* (payments made this financial year for expenses relating to the next)
- adjusting for *accruals* (expenses due this financial year but not yet paid)
- *depreciation* of assets (to write them off over their effective life)
- *bad debts written off* (removal from the Sales Ledger of accounts that are not likely to be paid)
- *bad debts provision* (making provision for debtors who *may* not pay)

If you examine each of the items above you will see that the two main concepts which form the basis to these adjustments are the *accruals concept* (prepayments and accruals) and the *prudence concept* (depreciation and treatment of bad debts). We will now look at these in detail.

prepayments

A prepayment is a payment made in advance of the accounting period to which it relates

The accruals concept states that a payment must be matched to the appropriate accounting period. If a business pays an annual insurance premium of £800 on 1 April and its financial year end is 30 June, only £200 (three months) of the premium should be entered as an expense in the profit and loss account for the *current* financial year; the remaining £600 should be included in the following year's profit and loss account. This £600 is known as a *prepayment.*

In this book and generally in accounting exercises, details of the prepayment will normally appear as a note to the trial balance. The adjustments in the accounts will be:

1. Deduct the amount of the prepayment from the balance of the appropriate account in the trial balance and show the amended amount in the profit and loss account. In the case of the insurance premium of £800 the calculation will be:
   premium £800 less prepayment £600 = amount entered in profit and loss account £200

2. Include the prepayment, together with any other prepayments, as a single item "Prepayment(s)" in the Current Assets section of the balance sheet.

accruals

An accrual is an amount due in an accounting period which remains unpaid at the end of that period

Any accrued expenses must also be adjusted for in the accounts. For example unpaid rent of £50 at the end of a financial year must be charged to the profit and loss account for that year, but as it is an amount owing it will also appear in the balance sheet as a current liability. As with prepayments, accruals will appear as a note to the trial balance. The adjustments in the acccounts will be as follows:

1. Add the accrued amount (unpaid rent of £50) to the balance of the appropriate account as shown in the trial balance, and show the result in the profit and loss account. In the case quoted above the calculation would be:
   Rent already paid (trial balance figure, say £450) plus accrued amount (£50) = amount entered in profit and loss account (£500)

2. The £50 accrual, together with any other accruals is entered as "Accruals" in the Current Liabilities section of the balance sheet.

depreciation

Depreciation is the estimate of the amount of the fall in value of fixed assets over a stated period

Depreciation is the method of writing down the value of a fixed asset in the accounts. A consistent depreciation policy is important, not only because it reliably informs the owner what his or her assets are worth, but also because it complies with the *consistency concept,* and with the *prudence concept* which implies that an asset is only worth what someone will pay for it.

Depreciation is the subject of SSAP 12, *Accounting for Depreciation,* which requires that a business selects a method of depreciation that is "most appropriate to the type of asset" but lays down no specific guideline as to *what* method should be adopted. There are in fact two main methods of calculating depreciation: the *straight line* method and the *reducing balance* method.

Straight line depreciation reduces the value of an asset by a fixed equal amount each year. The amount is normally calculated by dividing the difference between the cost price of the asset and the amount expected to be realised when the item is resold (residual value) by the number of years the business intends to hold the asset. For example:

A van costing £12,000 is expected to be resold at £2,000 in five years' time.

Annual depreciation   = $\dfrac{£12,000\ (cost)\ less\ £2,000\ (resale\ value)}{5\ (years)}$ =   *£2,000 per year*

Of course, if an asset is not expected to be resold, annual depreciation is simply the cost price of the asset divided by the number of years it is expected to last. In the case of the van costing £12,000 and expected to last for only five years, the calculation would be:

Annual depreciation   = $\dfrac{£12,000\ (cost)}{5\ (years)}$ =   *£2,400 per year*

Reducing Balance Depreciation writes off a fixed percentage from the written down or "reduced" balance at the end of each year. Reducing balance depreciation at 20% for the van costing £12,000 for the first two years would be calculated as follows:

End of year 1: £12,000 x 20%   =   £2,400 (value of van now £12,000 less £2,400 = £9,600)
End of year 2: £9,600 x 20%   =   £1,920 (value of van now £9,600 less £1,920 = £7,680)

Adjustments are made in the profit and loss account and balance sheet for both types of depreciation as follows:

1. Depreciation for the year is deducted as an expense in the profit and loss account

2. Depreciation for the year is added to previous years' depreciation and deducted from the fixed asset value in the balance sheet. The balance sheet itself shows the workings in three columns set out in the Fixed Asset section. The following example shows a van which depreciates at £2,000 per year, at the end of the second year of its life:

	£	£	£
Fixed Assets	*Cost*	*Depreciation to date*	*Net*
Motor Van	12,000	4,000	8,000

- The left hand money column is the original cost of the vehicle.
- The middle money column (Depreciation) is the depreciation from previous years (shown as a credit balance *Provision for Depreciation* in the trial balance) added to the depreciation for this year [shown in the profit and loss account]).
- The right hand column is the net "book" value of the motor van: £12,000 (cost) *less* £4,000 (previous depreciation of £2,000 plus this year's depreciation of £2,000) *equals* £8,000 (net book value).

You should note that although depreciation is charged in the profit and loss account as an expense, it is a *non-cash expense*: the business does not suffer a £2,000 cash loss each year on account of its motor van. The reduction in profits from depreciation each year and the adjustment of the fixed asset value in the balance sheet are *prudent* measures which will give the owner and any interested parties a true and fair view of the business as it stands.

bad debts

The prudence and consistency concepts also apply to the treatment of the bad debts.

A bad debt is a debt owing to a business which it considers will never be paid

Credit control, the monitoring and collection of debts is an important function in the efficient running of a business. The prompt issue of invoices, statements and chaser letters, the sending of solicitors' letters, all bring an increasing pressure on the debtor to pay. If all these fail, and court action is not economic because of the size of the debt, the debt will be termed a "bad debt" and will be *written off*; the debtor's account will be struck out of the Sales Ledger and the amount treated as an unfortunate but unavoidable expense to the business. The double entry treatment will be to transfer the figure (a debit) to a *bad debts account* in the General Ledger which records all debts written off during the year. Thus at the end of the year there will be a bad debts figure in the debit column of the trial balance which will be entered in the profit and loss account as an expense, and a loss, to the business.

Writing off bad debts is clearly a prudent measure as it reduces the debtors figure (Sales Ledger) to a realistic level. If a large bad debt were not written off, the debtors figure in the balance sheet would give an over-optimistic picture of the net asset value and working capital position of the business.

provision for bad debts

There is sometimes confusion between writing off bad debts (as seen above) and the creation of a *provision* for bad debts. They are completely separate procedures, and should not be confused.

Provision for bad debts is the estimate by a business of the likely percentage of its debtors which may go bad during any one accounting period.

Initial creation of a Provision for Bad Debts
The procedure for provision for bad debts is very similar to that for the depreciation of assets. For example:

1. A business at the end of the financial year estimates the percentage of its debtors which may go bad, say 5%.

2. The provision is calculated (£10,000 x 5% = £500) and

    - charged to the profit and loss account as an expense "Provision for bad debts"
    - deducted from the debtors figure in the Current Assets section of the balance sheet in a separate column inset to the left from the listing of the other current assets:

Current Assets	£	£
Stock		75,000
Debtors	10,000	
Provision for bad debts	500	
		9,500
Prepayments		1,000
Bank		5,400
		90,900

It must be stressed that the £500 of debtors in question *have not gone bad*; if they did so, they would appear in the bad debts account and would already have been deducted from debtors before the balance sheet was drawn up, as we saw in the previous section. The business, in creating a *provision* for bad debts, is presenting a realistic and prudent estimate of its debtor position.

Adjustments of Provision for Bad Debts in subsequent years

Unlike depreciation of fixed assets, which is made at a fixed percentage each year, and which runs down the asset value, provision for bad debts remains as a static percentage of debtors, for example a fixed 5%. The only adjustments that need to be made to the provision *money amount* are:

- a change in provision *policy*, e.g. an increase in the fixed percentage from 5% to 10%
- *arithmetic* adjustment in the provision as a result of a change in the total of debtors (5% of £15,000 is going to be £250 more than 5% of £10,000)

It follows that if either of these two situations arises, the adjustment to the existing provision will either be

- *upwards* (increase in provision percentage or increase in debtor figure), *or*
- *downwards* (decrease in provision percentage or decrease in debtor figure)

An ***increase in the provision*** is dealt with as follows:

1. Show the increase as an expense in the profit and loss account.
2. Add the increase to the existing provision for bad debts figure and show the total on the balance sheet.

A ***decrease in the provision***, requires you to

1. Show the decrease as in income item in the profit and loss account (added to gross profit in the right hand column.
2. Subtract the decrease from the existing provision for bad debts figure, and show the total in the balance sheet.

Please note again that any provision for bad debts and the writing off of bad debts *are completely separate adjustments*. The two should never be confused. It is therefore quite common to see in a profit and loss account entries for both *bad debts* (bad debts written off) and *provision for bad debts* (creation or adjustment of provision for bad debts).

Case Problem: Adjustments to the Accounts of Express Pasta

If you turn back to pages 45 and 47 you will see the final accounts of Express Pasta. The owner has now decided to make adjustments in order to make these final accounts present a more true and fair view of his business. He notes the following items:
- rates of £500 have been prepaid
- an electricity bill of £250 has not been paid
- he wants to depreciate his equipment and vehicles by 20% (straight line method)
- he needs to write off £350 of bad debts from his debtors figure
- he wishes to create a bad debts provision of 5%

We will now consider each of these adjustments in turn and examine the way in which they are treated in the accounts. We will then produce an amended set of final accounts. First, however, it is important to bear in mind the two rules for making adjustments:

1. *Each adjustment involves **two** entries in the final accounts*

2. *One entry will be in either the trading account or the profit and loss account, the other in the balance sheet*

Prepayment: Prepaid rates of £500

As rates of £500 have been prepaid they should be included in the following year's accounts.
Profit and loss: Deduct £500 from rent and rates of £2,000 to give rent and rates of £1,500.
Balance sheet: Enter prepayments of £500 in the Current Assets section after debtors.

Accruals: Electricity owing of £250

As this remained unpaid at the end of 20-1, it should be included in the expenses for that year.
Profit and loss: Add £250 to electricity & gas of £3,000 to give a total of £3,250.
Balance sheet: Enter accruals of £250 in the Current Liabilities section after creditors.

Note: It is easy to remember by their initial letters that you <u>a</u>dd <u>a</u>ccruals in the profit and loss account and you therefore *deduct* prepayments, when dealing with expenses.

Depreciation of Equipment and Vehicles at 20%

Assuming the straight line method and no previous years' depreciation, the calculation will be:

Equipment £30,000 x 20% = £6,000
Vehicles £21,500 x 20% = £4,300

The entries will therefore be:
Profit and loss: "Depreciation of equipment £6,000" and "Depreciation of vehicles £4,300" as separate items among the expenses.
Balance sheet: Enter the depreciation amounts of £6,000 and £4,300 in the depreciation column in the Fixed Asset section. As there is no previous years' depreciation, this year's amounts represent the total depreciation to date.

Bad Debts Written Off £350

These are bad debts which are to be written off as an expense to the business.
Profit and loss: Enter £350 as "Bad debts written off" among the expenses.
Balance Sheet: Reduce debtors figure of £23,850 by £350 *before* entering it in the Current Assets section. Do not show your workings in the balance sheet.

Provision for Bad Debts of 5%

Provision for bad debts is created *after* the writing off of actual bad debts. In this case the calculation will be: debtors £23,500 x 5% = £1,175.
Profit and loss: Enter "Provision for bad debts" of £1,175 among the expenses
Balance Sheet: Deduct the provision of £1,175 from debtors in an *inset* column in the Current Asset section. The net debtor position then shows as £23,500 less £1,175 = £22,325.

The adjusted final accounts of Express Pasta will then appear as follows (with calculations for prepayments and accruals shown in italics):

TRADING AND PROFIT AND LOSS ACCOUNT OF EXPRESS PASTA
FOR THE YEAR ENDED 31 DECEMBER 20-1

	£	£	£
Sales			250,000
Less Returns in			5,400
			244,600
Opening stock			-
Purchases	156,000		
Less Returns out	7,200		
		148,800	
Less Closing stock		25,300	
Cost of Goods Sold			123,500
Gross Profit			121,100
Add Discounts received			2,500
			123,600

	£	£	£
Less			
Salaries		46,000	
Electricity and gas	*3,000 + 250* ----	3,250	
Rent and rates	*2,000 - 500* ----	1,500	
Sundry expenses		4,700	
Discounts allowed		3,700	
Depreciation (equipment)		6,000	
Depreciation (vehicles)		4,300	
Bad debts written off		350	
Provision for Bad Debts		1,175	
			70,975
Net Profit			52,625

BALANCE SHEET OF EXPRESS PASTA AS AT 31 DECEMBER 20-1

	£	£	£
	Cost	Depreciation	Net
Fixed Assets			
Premises	78,000	-	78,000
Equipment	30,000	6,000	24,000
Vehicles	21,500	4,300	17,200
	129,500	10,300	119,200
Current Assets			
Stock		25,300	
Debtors	23,500		
Provision for bad debts	1,175		
		22,235	
Prepayments		500	
Bank		1,239	
Cash		125	
		49,489	
Less Current Liabilities			
Creditors	28,756		
Accruals	250		
		29,006	
Working Capital			20,483
			139,683
Less Long-Term Liabilities			
Long term loan			35,000
NET ASSETS			104,683

FINANCED BY

Capital			
Opening Capital			62,500
Add net profit			52,625
			115,125
Less drawings			10,442
			104,683

preparation of the adjusted final accounts from the trial balance

At the end of this Chapter are a number of exercises which require you to prepare final accounts from a trial balance and make the adjustments discussed in this Chapter. A methodical and logical approach to this process is *essential*. Set out below are some guidelines to assist you.

The Trial Balance
Examine the trial balance and decide in which of the final accounts to insert each figure.

Notes to the Trial Balance
Next deal with the notes to the trial balance. Remember that each item (including closing stock) will be needed twice in the final accounts: once in either the trading account or the profit and loss account, and once in the balance sheet. Make a note of where the adjustments are to be made. It is suggested that you deal with the adjustments in the following order:

Accruals: add to the appropriate figure in the profit and loss account, and insert in the Current Liabilities section of the balance sheet.

Prepayments: deduct from the appropriate figure in the profit and loss account, insert in the Current Assets section of the balance sheet.

Depreciation:
- calculate the annual amount first (noting whether straight line or reducing balance)
- show the year's depreciation in the expenses section of the profit and loss account
- check to see if there is an existing provision for depreciation in the trial balance (credit side)
- construct the Fixed Asset section in three columns, remembering to add any existing provision for depreciation in the middle "Depreciation" column

Bad Debts:
Charge *any* bad debts to the profit and loss account. Bad debts can be indicated in *two* ways: if they are already recorded in a double entry account shown as a debit balance in the trial balance, *no adjustment* need be made to the debtors figure. If bad debts are shown in a note to the trial balance, *they should be deducted from the debtors figure* before it is transferred to the balance sheet.

Provision for Bad Debts:
- calculate the required percentage of provision from the debtors figure after writing off any bad debts (see item above); deduct this figure from the debtors in the balance sheet in an inset column
- check to see if there is an existing provision
- if there is, and it is *higher* than the new provision, show the difference on the income side of the profit and loss account (right hand column)
- if the existing provision is *lower* than the new provision, charge the difference between the two to the expenses side of the profit and loss account

CHAPTER SUMMARY

❏ The accounting concepts of going concern, consistency, accruals and prudence, set out in SSAP 2 are fundamental to the presentation of accounting statements.

❏ In order to comply with these concepts, certain adjustments need to be made to the figures contained in the trial balance when constructing the final accounts. These are:
- prepayments and accruals
- depreciation (straight line and reducing balance)
- writing off bad debts
- creation of a provision for bad debts

✍ STUDENT ACTIVITIES

You are working for Price Anderson & Co., a firm of Chartered accountants. You are asked to set out the trading and profit and loss accounts and balance sheets in vertical format for the following businesses for the year ended 31 December 20-1. Some of the accounts you may already have processed. He asks you to take particular care, this time, over the adjustments which had not been indicated earlier.

Business One
Trial Balance of Wintergreen Service Station as at 31 December 20-1

	£	£
Premises	120,000	
Long term loan		60,000
Capital		70,000
Debtors	1,900	
Creditors		1,500
Drawings	5,000	
Cash	150	
Stock at 1 Jan 20-1	4,200	
Fixtures & fittings	5,000	
Provision for depreciation (fixtures and fittings)		1,000
Vehicles	10,000	
Provision for depreciation (vehicles)		2,000
Bank overdraft		750
Sales		195,000
Purchases	154,000	
Wages	20,500	
Sundry expenses	9,500	
	330,250	330,250

The following notes are provided by the business:
- Stock at 31 December 20-1 was £5,200
- Vehicles and fixtures and fittings are to be depreciated at 20% (straight line)
- Bad debts, amounting to £200, are to be written off
- Wages prepaid are £560, and sundry expenses accrued are £500

Business Two
Trial Balance of John Adams, antique dealer, as at 31 December 20-1

	£	£
Debtors	37,200	
Creditors		35,920
Bank	10,000	
Capital		50,500
Sales		289,620
Purchases	182,636	
Stock at 1 Jan 20-1	32,020	
Salaries	36,930	
Heat & light	3,640	
Rent & rates	11,294	
Vehicles	21,640	
Provision for depreciation (vehicles)		2,000
Equipment	13,000	
Provision for depreciation (equipment)		2,000
Sundry expenses	1,690	

	£	£
Motor expenses	3,368	
Drawings	26,622	
	380,040	380,040

The following notes were provided by John Adams:
- Stock at 31 December was valued at £34,000
- Bad debts of £2,200 are to be written off and a provision for bad debts of 5% is to be created
- Vehicles are to be depreciated at 20% p.a. and equipment at 10% p.a. (both reducing balance)
- There are sundry expenses accruals of £270, and rates prepayments of £2,190

Business Three
Trial Balance of Andrew Brown, fashion designer, as at 31 December 20-1

	£	£
Purchases	31,480	
Sales		65,660
Stock at 1 Jan 20-1	7,580	
Returns	240	620
Discounts	380	1,080
Drawings	14,720	
Premises	76,000	
Fixtures and fittings	24,000	
Provision for depreciation (fixtures and fittings)		3,000
Wages and salaries	18,620	
Advertising	2,260	
Bank	4,020	
Cash	120	
Debtors	5,000	
Bad debts written off	100	
Provision for bad debts		520
Creditors		3,740
Capital		109,900
	184,520	184,520

The following notes to the accounts are provided:
- Stock at 31 December 20-1 was valued at £6,060
- Depreciation is to be provided on fixtures and fittings at 12.5% p.a. (straight line method)
- Provision for bad debts is to be 5% of debtors
- Wages accrued are £500, and advertising prepaid is £350

Your last task is to reply to the following letter from Mr Brown dated 30 March 20-2 and addressed to Victor Price, your senior partner. The reply should be for Mr Price's signature. Mr Brown's address is 12 Blenheim Close, Greenham GR4 3ES

```
Dear Mr Price,

Thank you for the recent set of accounts received today.  There are a number of
queries I have, and as I cannot easily see you soon, I shall be grateful if you
will write to me explaining them. The first   item I find confusing is the
"provision for bad debts"; there appears to be an income item in the profit and
loss account, and yet there is a deduction in the balance sheet with the same
description.  This is all very confusing, considering the fact that bad debts were
only £100 last year!  The second item is depreciation:  the figure in the profit
and loss account differs from the figure in the balance sheet.  As you appreciate,
I am not an accountant, and I need help in understanding these accounts.
Yours sincerely,

Andrew Brown.
```

7 INCOMPLETE RECORDS

In our examination of accounting records, we have concentrated on the double entry system, and have seen how one can prepare final accounts from the trial balance. But what is the situation when there is no trial balance because the double entry system has not been adopted?

There are two sets of circumstances when this can happen:

1. When the business has a *single entry system,* recording receipts and payments through a Cash Book, and maintaining separate records of debtors, creditors, assets and liabilities.

2. When the owner of the business keeps very little in the way of accounting records, possibly only a Cash Book for "money in" and "money out".

In both instances the accountant has the task of constructing the final accounts - the trading and profit and loss accounts and balance sheet - from *incomplete records.* In the case of the single entry system, the task is comparatively straightforward; in the case of working from the cash book only or even scantier records, it can be time consuming for the accountant and costly for the owner in terms of the accountant's fees.

information available to the accountant

The financial records which may be available to the accountant dealing with incomplete records in either circumstance are:

*   banking details - statements, chequebook counterfoils, paying-in books
*   Cash Book - the central record for any single entry system
*   invoices - relating to purchases and sales
*   fixed assets and long term liability records – details of items purchased and liabilities incurred (e.g. receipts for assets purchased, documentation for bank loans), both at the beginning and the end of the year

The information which may *not* be available, and will need to be calculated includes:

*   capital at the beginning and end of the financial year
*   gross and net profit for the year
*   purchases and sales for the year

In this Chapter we will examine the way in which the accountant of a small bakery business, "Anne's Cookies" (run by Anne Jones) constructs the final accounts from a *single entry* system. The same method would be used when dealing with a less complete system, but clearly the accountant's task would be more difficult.

Case Problem "Anne's Cookies": The Statement of Affairs

The construction of a Statement of Affairs, or summary balance sheet, at the beginning and end of any financial year is a useful short cut method of calculating the change in the capital position for that financial year, and hence the retained profit for the year (net profit after drawings). The basis of the calculation is the two formulae:

- *Assets **less** liabilities* = *capital*
- *Capital at the end of the year **less** capital at the beginning of the year* = *retained profit*

Anne's Cookies has the following assets and liabilities at 1 January 20-1, the beginning of its financial year :

Assets	*Liabilities*
Premises £75,000	Creditors £ 5,950
Equipment £30,000 at cost (depreciation to date £10,000)	Long term loan £40,000
Stock £10,000	
Debtors £1,750	
Bank £3,291	

A *Statement of Affairs,* or summary balance sheet, will be drawn up to calculate the capital figure at the beginning of the year:

STATEMENT OF AFFAIRS OF ANNE'S COOKIES AS AT 1 JANUARY 20-1

	£	£
Assets		
Premises		75,000
Equipment (after depreciation)		20,000
Stock		10,000
Debtors		1,750
Bank		3,291
		110,041
Less Liabilities		
Creditors	5,950	
Long term loan	40,000	
		45,950
Capital at 1 Jan 20-1		64,091

If the figures for the assets and liabilities of Anne's Cookies at the end of the financial year were similarly set out in a Statement of Affairs, the year-end capital could be calculated, and consequently the retained profit (net profit less drawings by the owner):

Capital at the end of the year *less* capital at the beginning of the year = retained profit

This formula is a useful and quick method of arriving at a profit figure, but it has the disadvantage that it does not reconstruct the full set of final accounts of the business. The principal shortcoming of the method is that it bypasses and ignores the workings of the trading and profit and loss accounts: the owner of Anne's Cookies will have no precise figure for sales, purchases, or gross profit for the year. Nevertheless the Statement of Affairs *at the beginning of the year* is essential for the accountant, as it will provide the opening capital figure for the balance sheet which he is going to construct.

Having drawn up the opening Statement of Affairs, the accountant will next:
- draw up a *Cash Book summary*
- calculate sales and purchases for the year using *control accounts*

This will enable the accountant to obtain the figures for the trading and profit and loss accounts and balance sheet. You will note that it is not necessary to draw up a trial balance.

cash book summary

Assuming that all transactions pass through the bank account, the accountant will examine the bank column in the Cash Book and reconcile the entries in the bank statement to produce a summary of receipts and payments for the year. In the case of Anne's Cookies they are as follows:

Receipts from debtors	£95,500
Payments to creditors	£53,200
Drawings by owner	£13,000
Business expenses	£17,000

These receipts, payments and expenses form the basis of the trading and profit and loss accounts. But first it is important to appreciate that total receipts from debtors, and payments to creditors, *are not the same as sales and purchases for the year.* If one takes the 'receipts from debtors' figure, for instance, this will *include* receipts from sales made at the end of the previous year, and will *exclude* sales made this year and paid for next year. To arrive at a true sales figure, in arithmetic terms,

*sales for the year = receipts from debtors in the year **less** debtors at the beginning of the year (receipts from last year's sales) **plus** debtors at the end of the year (sales made in the year but not yet paid for)*

A purchases figure for the year is arrived at by a similar calculation:

*purchases for the year = payments to creditors in the year **less** the creditors at the beginning of the year **plus** the creditors at the end of the year*

These calculations to find the sales and purchases figures for year are worked out in the books of a business by means of *control accounts.*

control accounts

A control account is a summary account or master account which records the totals of entries to a particular set of accounts, but does not form part of the double entry system. The Sales Ledger control account, for instance, shows the total of all debtors' accounts in the Sales Ledger, and will provide at the year-end the *debtors* figure which appears on the balance sheet; the Purchases Ledger control account shows the total of all the creditors' accounts in the Purchases Ledger and will provide the creditors figure for the balance sheet.

Calculation of Sales: Sales Ledger Control Account

The following information is available to the accountant from the books of Anne's Cookies:

Debtors at 1 January 20-1	£1,750
Debtors at 31 December 20-1	£2,250
Receipts from debtors in 20-1	£95,500

Remember that the Sales Ledger control account is a summary of debtors, and that therefore any balance in its columns will refer to the total of debtors at that particular date. The Sales Ledger control account for Anne's Cookies for the year 20-1will be set out as follows:

Dr.			**Sales Ledger Control Account**			Cr.
20-1		£	20-1			£
1 Jan	Balance b/d	1,750		Receipts (bank)		95,500
	Sales *(missing figure)*	?	31 Dec	Balance c/d		2,250
		97,750				97,750
20-2						
1 Jan	Balance b/d	2,250				

The figure for sales for 20-1 can be worked out arithmetically from the debit figure column as it is the missing figure:

Sales = *£97,750* - *£1,750* = <u>*£96,000*</u>

The advantage of using a control account is that if any one of the four constituent figures is missing, it can be calculated from the remaining information. A Purchase Ledger control account works in the same way.

Calculation of Purchases: Purchases Ledger Control Account
The information relating to purchases taken by the accountant from the books of Anne' Cookies is:

Creditors at 1 January 20-1	£5,950
Creditors at 31 December 20-1	£6,720
Payments to creditors in 20-1	£53,200

The control account will then appear as follows:

Dr.			**Purchases Ledger Control Account**		Cr.
20-1		£	20-1		£
	Payments to creditors	53,200	1 Jan	Balance b/d	5,950
31 Dec	Balance c/d	6,720		Purchases *(missing figure)*	?
		59,920			59,920
			20-2		
			1 Jan	Balance b/d	6,720

The missing figure for purchases for 20-1 can be worked out from the credit column:
Purchases = £59,920 - £5,950 = <u>£53,970.</u>

construction of the final accounts: Anne's Cookies

The accountant has now extracted the following figures:

Statement of Affairs at 1 January 20-1
Opening Capital	£64,091

Cash Book Summary
Drawings	£13,000
Business Expenses	£17,000

Sales	£96,000
Purchases	£53,970

The next step is to extract a schedule of assets and liabilities as at the end of the year from the business records. Depreciation on equipment is charged at 10% of cost.

Schedule of Assets and Liabilities as at 31 December 20-1
Premises	£75,000
Equipment at cost	£30,000
(depreciation to date £13,000)	
Stock	£12,000
Debtors	£2,250
Bank	£15,591
Creditors	£6,720
Long term loan	£40,000

The accountant now has all the figures needed to draw up the final accounts of Anne's Cookies:

ANNE JONES TRADING AS "ANNE'S COOKIES"
TRADING AND PROFIT AND LOSS ACCOUNTS FOR THE YEAR ENDED 31 DEC 20-1

	£	£
Sales		96,000
Opening Stock	10,000	
Purchases	53,970	
Less Closing Stock	12,000	
Cost of Sales		51,970
Gross Profit		44,030
Less		
Business Expenses	17,000	
Depreciation	3,000	
		20,000
Net Profit		24,030

BALANCE SHEET OF ANNE JONES TRADING AS "ANNE'S COOKIES"
AS AT 31 DECEMBER 20-1

	£ Cost	£ Depreciation	£ Net
Fixed Assets			
Premises	75,000	-	75,000
Equipment	30,000	13,000	17,000
	105,000	13,000	92,000
Current Assets			
Stock		12,000	
Debtors		2,250	
Bank		15,591	
		29,841	
Less Current Liabilities			
Creditors		6,720	
Working Capital			23,121
			115,121
Less Long-Term Liabilities			
Long term loan			40,000
NET ASSETS			75,121
FINANCED BY			
Capital			
Opening Capital			64,091
Add net profit			24,030
			88,121
Less drawings			13,000
			75,121

The following points should be noted about the process of drawing up the final accounts from incomplete records:

Trial Balance

The construction of final accounts from incomplete records does not use a trial balance. This is logical because a trial balance is drawn up from *double entry accounts* whereas incomplete records are based on a *single entry* system.

Reconciliation of Closing Bank Balance

A useful check on the accuracy of one's calculations is to reconcile the closing bank balance with the opening bank balance and the summary of the banking transactions for the year:

	£	£
Opening balance (1 Jan 20-1)		3,291
Add receipts from debtors		95,500
		98,791
Less		
Payments to creditors	53,200	
Business expenses	17,000	
Drawings	13,000	
		83,200
Closing balance (31 Dec 20-1)		15,591

CHAPTER SUMMARY

❏ When a business does not operate a full double entry book-keeping system, the records are said to be incomplete; the accountant will have to make further calculations to construct the final accounts.

❏ This situation can arise either when the business keeps an efficient single entry system, or when the business owner keeps accounts that are incomplete in every sense of the word.

❏ The calculations will involve the drawing up of

- a Statement of Affairs at the beginning of the financial year listing assets and liabilities
- a Cash Book summary categorizing payments to creditors, receipts from debtors, drawings and business expenses
- control accounts for Sales and Purchases Ledgers to extract the sales and purchases figures
- a schedule of assets and liabilities at the end of the financial year

❏ On the basis of these calculations the accountant can then construct the trading and profit and loss accounts and balance sheet without recourse to a trial balance.

In the next Chapter we will examine a specialised form of final accounts: partnership accounts.

✍ STUDENT ACTIVITIES

You work as an accountant in the firm of Clark, Cruikshank & Co., and have been drafted into the section dealing with small business audit. Many of your clients use single entry systems and therefore do not provide you with a trial balance from which to work. During the course of a week you encounter the following four sets of accounts and have to deal with them as instructed.

Business One: Colin Smith, Electrical Supplier

Colin Smith has just submitted his financial records for the year ended 31 December 20-5. All that you can extract from them is a statement of assets and liabilities and a bank transaction summary:

Statement of Assets and Liabilities

	1 Jan 20-5	31 Dec 20-5
	£	£
Stock	25,000	27,500
Premises (at cost)	50,000	50,000
Debtors	36,000	35,000
Bank	1,500	1,210
Creditors	32,500	30,000

Bank Summary	£
Balance at 1 Jan 19-5	1,500
Business expenses	30,000
Drawings	8,790
Receipts from debtors	101,000
Paid to suppliers	62,500

You are to:

• calculate the opening and closing capital

• calculate the retained profit figure, sales and purchases

• draw up trading and profit and loss accounts for the year ended 31 December 20-5 and a balance sheet at that date. Ignore depreciation.

Business Two: Jane Price, owner of a fashion shop, "Trendsetter"

You have in front of you the accounting records for the first year of trading of "Trendsetter". All that is available is a list of assets and liabilities at the year end and a summary of bank transactions gleaned from bank statements, cheque book counterfoils and paying-in book details.

Summary of Assets and Liabilities as at 31 December 20-5

	£
Shop fittings at cost	50,000
Stock	73,900
Debtors	2,500
Creditors	65,000

Summary of Bank Transactions for 20-5

	£
Capital introduced	60,000
Receipts from sales	153,500
Paid to suppliers	95,000
Advertising	9,830
Wages	15,000
Rent and rates	3,750
General expenses	5,000
Shop fittings	50,000
Drawings	15,020

You are to:

- calculate the closing capital

- calculate the net profit

- draw up trading and profit and loss accounts for the year ended 31 December 20-5 and a balance sheet at that date. Ignore depreciation.

Business Three: William Penny, stationery wholesaler

William Penny keeps a small one-man business in the town which provides him with a moderate but adequate income. He only uses a Cash Book to record his bank transactions and relies on your firm to draw up his annual accounts for tax purposes. This year he provides you with the following information:

Statement of Assets and Liabilities

	1 Jan 20-5	31 Dec 20-5
	£	£
Shop fittings	8,000	8,000
Stock	25,600	29,800
Bank	14,000	18,000
Cash	1,000	1,600
Debtors	29,200	20,400
Creditors	20,800	16,000

Bank Summary for 20-5

	£
Receipts from sales	127,800
Payments to suppliers	82,600
Drawings	10,000
Business expenses	30,600

You are to:

- calculate the opening and closing capital

- calculate the net profit

- draw up a trading and profit and loss accounts for the year ended 31 December 20-5 and a balance sheet as at that date. Ignore depreciation.

Business Four: Owen Hughes, toy retailer
Owen Hughes runs a chain of toy shops in the area under the trade name "Bright and Beautiful".   He buys on credit, importing mostly from overseas, but all his sales are cash sales which he pays into his bank account. He keeps a minimum of accounting records, but you are able to extract the following information from his records for 20-5:

Summary of Assets and Liabilities

	1 Jan 20-5 £	31 Dec 20-5 £
Creditors	48,000	60,000
Stock	60,000	54,000
Shop fittings	12,000	10,800
Premises	150,000	150,000
Bank	14,400	*not known*

Summary of Bank Account

	£
Sales receipts	996,800
Payments to creditors	744,000
Rent	9,000
Drawings	50,000
Salaries	55,000
Expenses	75,720

You are to:

- calculate the closing bank balance

- calculate opening and closing capital

- calculate the net profit figure

- draw up a trading and profit and loss accounts for the year ended 31 December 20-5 and a balance sheet as at that date.

Note: Mr Hughes has depreciated his shop fittings by 10% over the year.

ASSIGNMENT

3 *Joan Pearce: Incomplete Records*

covering
books of account, choice of systems, final accounts, incomplete records

SITUATION

You are an accountant working for the firm of Porterhouse & Co., 78 High Road, Greenham GR1 29Z. Miss Joan Pearce, one of your clients, keeps a wool and knitting accessories shop "The Wool Shop" in Greenham. Book-keeping is not one of Miss Pearce's strong points. She has called you in to sort out her accounts for the year; all she has in her office are bank statements, chequebook stubs and paying-in book counterfoils, a disorderly pile of invoices and bills, and a wages book she keeps for two part-time staff who work on Saturdays. You are able, after much work, to piece together the following information from her records for the financial year ended 30 June 20-7:

1. **Details of assets and liabilities at 1 July 20-6**

		£
	Bank	8,115
	Debtors	2,910
	Shop fittings (cost £5,250)	3,750
	Stock	14,835
	Vehicles (cost £13,000)	9,000
	Creditors	18,975

2. **Invoices in a box file marked "Invoices and bills"**

    *   unpaid invoices she has issued for credit sales amount to £2,040 at 30 June 20-7.
    *   unpaid invoices from suppliers amount to £23,550 at 30 June 20-7
    *   an electricity bill for £155 for the quarter ending 30 June 20-7 remains unpaid
    *   a rates bill of £1,250 has been paid on 1 April 20-7, but 60% of it relates to the financial year ending 30 June 20-8

3. **Stock Records**

    Her stocks, after a stock-take on 30 June 20-7, were valued at £13,650.

4. **Banking Records**

Her banking records reveal that receipts from cash sales for the year were £104,145, and receipts from debtors were £18,540.

Payments were:

		£
Suppliers		89,820
Drawings		13,500
Rent and rates		5,100
Heat and light		630
Wages		3,390
General expenses		1,515
New shop fittings		750

5. **Depreciation of Fixed Assets**

From an examination of Miss Pearce's records you decide to depreciate both vehicles and shop fittings by 20% per annum on a reducing balance basis.

Note: you have already assumed a certain amount of depreciation for prior years in your schedule of assets and liabilities as at 1 July 20-6, the beginning of the financial year in question.

TASKS

1. Draw up a schedule of assets and liabilities in order to calculate Miss Pearce's capital at 1 July 20-6.

2. Calculate, by means of control accounts, Miss Pearce's purchases and sales figures for the year to 30 June 20-7.

3. Calculate Miss Pearce's bank balance at 30 June 20-7.

4. Draw up trading and profit and loss accounts for Miss Pearce for the year ended 30 June 20-7, and a balance sheet at that date.

5. Write a letter to Miss Pearce ("The Wool Shop", 108 The Broadway, Greenham, GR4 9UX) enclosing the final accounts. You are to explain in simple terms what the financial statements tell her, and more importantly, suggest diplomatically to Miss Pearce how she could improve her book-keeping system, using a single entry system.

8 PARTNERSHIP ACCOUNTS

The partnership is a common form of business enterprise, and can be found in the form of:

- sole traders who have joined forces with others in order to raise finance and expand operations
- established family firms such as manufacturers, traders and builders
- professional firms such as solicitors, accountants, estate agents, doctors and dentists

The Partnership Act 1890 sets out a legal definition of a partnership as

the relation which subsists between people carrying on a business with a view of profit

constitution of a partnership

A partnership:

- is an association of two to twenty partners (some professional firms may exceed this limit)

- is often known as "the firm" and may be described as "& Co." or "& Sons" in the case of a family firm

- involves all of the partners being personally liable for the debts of the partnership (except in the very rare case of a Limited Partnership set up under the Limited Partnership Act 1907)

- can be formed by oral agreement (i.e. with no written agreement), or

- can be formed by a written Partnership Agreement or by a Deed of Partnership (a more formal sealed written document)

It must be stressed that a partnership is a very different business organization from a limited company, which we will deal with in Chapter 9. The two should never be confused, despite the misleading "& Co." designation of some partnerships.

the partnership agreement: financial arrangements

In this Chapter we will examine the constitution and accounting requirements of Charles and Andrew Oak, two brothers who own two antique shops in a county area and trade under the name of "The Collectors". Following an earlier dispute over the distribution of profits - a not uncommon feature in the running of partnerships - a Partnership Agreement agreement has been drawn up with the help of the local solicitor and signed by the two brothers.

Reasons for drawing up the Partnership Agreement

Disputes apart, another good reason for a Partnership Agreement, which sets out the financial arrangements of the partnership, is the restrictive nature of the financial provisions of the Partnership Act 1890. This provides that, in the absence of any Partnership Agreement:

- profits and losses are to be shared equally between the partners
- no partner is entitled to a salary
- partners are not entitled to receive interest on their capital
- interest is not to be charged on partners' drawings
- when a partner contributes more capital *than the amount agreed,* he or she is entitled to receive interest at 5% per annum on the excess

The Financial Provisions of "The Collectors" Partnership Agreement

The Partnership Agreement in the case of the Oak brothers goes well beyond the terms of the Partnership Act, and provides for the following:

Amount of capital contributed	Charles Oak £15,000 Andrew Oak £25,000 These are unequal amounts. Andrew is the elder brother, but takes a less active part in the business.
Division of profits/losses	Shared in proportion to the capital in the firm: Charles 37.5% (Capital £15,000) Andrew 62.5% (Capital £25,000)
Rate of interest allowed on capital	7.5% Equivalent to a rate obtainable on an alternative investment of capital, a common arrangment where capital contributions are unequal.
Rate of interest charged on partners' drawings	5% Interest is charged on money taken out of the business by each partner, and is chargeable from the date of withdrawal.
Salary	Charles £9,000 per annum. A partner will often be paid a salary for extra work carried out. In this case Charles receives £9,000 for managing the second shop in a nearby town. His work load is far greater than that of Andrew who prefers his golf and fishing.

financial statements of partnerships

The basic format of the final accounts of a partnership is the same as that of a sole trader: thetrading account and profit and loss account, and the balance sheet.

There are, however, additional points to note:

- The *appropriation account,* which follows the profit and loss account and distributes the net profit (or loss) among the partners after adjusting for interest on drawings, interest on capital and any salaries due to partners

- The *capital accounts* and *current accounts* in the Capital section of the balance sheet, showing the capital contributed by each partner (capital account) and the distribution of profits, interest and drawings for each individual partner (current accounts).

Case Study: the appropriation account: "The Collectors"

The appropriation account for Charles and Andrew Oak, set out below is typical of an arrangement where the partners have unequal capital. The interest rates quoted and details of capital are taken from the terms laid down in their Partnership Agreement. As you will see from the layout, the account first calculates what is due to the partners, and then distributes all of it. The layout is in vertical format, as in the profit and loss account. In the year ended 31 December 20-1, net profit was £ 45,000, and Charles and Andrew drew £5,000 and £12,000 respectively on 30 June.

APPROPRIATION ACCOUNT OF C & A OAK, TRADING AS "THE COLLECTORS"
FOR THE YEAR ENDED 31 DECEMBER 20-1

	£	£	£
Net profit brought down			45,000
Interest charged on drawings			
Charles Oak		125	
Andrew Oak		300	
			425
			45,425
Less			
Interest allowed on capital			
Charles Oak	1,125		
Andrew Oak	1,875		
		3,000	
Salary			
Charles Oak		9,000	
			12,000
			33,425
Balance of profits shared			
Charles Oak 37.5%			12,534
Andrew Oak 62.5%			20,891
			33,425

You should note the following points about the appropriation account:

Net profit distribution
The net profit figure of £45,000 is brought straight down from the profit and loss account. In practice the appropriation account will follow on from, and be merged into the profit and loss account. It will not necessarily have a separate heading as in the example above.

Interest charged on Drawings
Interest on drawings is here calculated on drawings made by the partners exactly half way through the financial year, i.e. on 30 June 20-1:
Charles: £5,000   drawings x 5% x 0.5 year = £125
Andrew: £12,000 drawings x 5% x 0.5 year = £300
Interest charged on drawings is *added* to the net profit, as it represents income from the partners, and will form part of the distribution.

Interest allowed on Capital
Charles: £15,000 x 7.5% = £1,125
Andrew: £25,000 x 7.5% = £1,875
Interest allowed on capital forms part of the distribution and is *deducted* from the appropriation account.

Salaries
Charles' salary of £9,000 is deducted as part of the distribution.

Share of Profits
The remaining distribution   (£33,425) will be allocated to the partners according to the percentage of capital they have contributed. Nothing will then be left in the account.
Charles' share of profit: £33,425 x 37.5% [capital £15,000]   =   £12,534
Andrew's share of profit: £33,425 x 62.5% [capital £25,000]   =   £20,891

capital accounts and current accounts

It is usual for partnerships to maintain a *capital account* and a *current account* for each partner. The capital account is *fixed*, and the balance only alters if there is a permanent increase or decrease in the capital contribution of the partner. The current account, however, fluctuates, and it is to this account that the following transactions are passed:

- share of profits (or losses)
- salaries for salaried partners
- interest allowed on capital
- interest charged on drawings
- drawings made

The term "current account" is also used by the banks, and the concept is very similar. A partnership current account is a running account maintained to show the net credit or net debit position of each partner in relation to the partnership. The balance of each partner's current account at the end of the financial year will show either

- *a credit balance*, where the amount of the distribution (share of net profit, any salary and interest allowed on capital) exceeds drawings and interest charged on drawings, or
- *a debit balance,* where drawings and interest on drawings exceed the partner's distribution

The capital and current accounts (summaries of the double entry accounts in the partnership's General Ledger) appear in the balance sheet in the same position as a sole trader's capital/net profit/drawings section, which they replace.

BALANCE SHEET (EXTRACT) OF C & A OAK TRADING AS "THE COLLECTORS"
AS AT 31 DECEMBER 20-1

	£	£	£
Capital Accounts			
Charles Oak		15,000	
Andrew Oak		25,000	
			40,000
Current Accounts	*Charles Oak*	*Andrew Oak*	
Balance b/d	3,500	2,100	
Share of profits	12,534	20,891	
Salary	9,000	-	
Interest on capital	1,125	1,875	
	26,159	24,866	
Less			
Interest on drawings	125	300	
Drawings	5,000	12,000	
Balance c/d	21,034	12,566	
			33,600
			73,600

The following points should be noted:
- Drawings are taken from the partners' current accounts on the balance sheet, not from the appropriation account, which merely allocates the share of profits.

- Both partners in this case have retained a healthy proportion of their profit in the business. They themselves constitute the partnership and therefore the balance of their individual current accounts is still available to them. It may not however be lying idle as cash balances; it may have been invested in fixed assets, or more likely in the antique trade, in stock. This profit retention is an indication of a well managed and prosperous business.

- It would be possible for a partner's current account to be in debit, i.e. he would owe the partnership money. For example, supposing Andrew had drawn out £25,000 during the year, the final section of his current account would show an overdrawn balance of £734:

	£
Share of distribution	24,866
less interest on drawings	600
less drawings	25,000
	(734)

Note: in this case, interest charged on drawings has increased from £300 to £600, reflecting Andrew's greater indebtedness to the partnership. One would imagine that Charles would not have approved of this high level of drawings, as it would be drawing cash out of the business.

preparation of partnership accounts from the trial balance

The preparation of partnership accounts from the trial balance is dealt with in exactly the same way as the preparation of sole traders' accounts. The only differences to note are:

- charging of partners' salaries appears in the appropriation account, not in the profit and loss account where their employees' salaries would be shown

- current accounts of partners appear in the Capital section of the balance sheet, whether they are in debit or in credit; debit current accounts are deducted from the total and are shown in brackets

CHAPTER SUMMARY

❑   A partnership is formed when two or more people set up in business together.

❑   The Partnership Act 1890 sets out certain accounting rules which tend to be restrictive.

❑   Many partnerships draw up Partnership Agreements which over-ride the Partnership Act by allowing flexibility in the contribution of capital and the distribution of profits.

❑   The final accounts of partnerships are similar to those of a sole trader, but incorporate
  - an appropriation account as a continuation of the profit and loss account
  - individual capital and current accounts for each partner in the balance sheet.

In the following Chapters we will examine in detail the accounts of limited companies, which, as we will see, are business entities quite unlike partnerships: they are separate legal entities, regulated by the Companies Act 1985, and required to make their accounts available to the public.

✍ STUDENT ACTIVITIES

You are an accountant in the firm of Capel Masters, 150 Old Market Street, London EC1N 2HR. You have to undertake a number of tasks in the course of a day's work (28 February 20-2).

Task One
Answer in your own name the following letter from your client Harry Morgan, an antiquarian bookseller, 170 Compton Road, London N17 2LO.

```
20 February 20-2

Dear Sirs

As you know from our past dealings, I  run a small bookshop which does
reasonably well.  I now have the opportunity of going into partnership
with a trading colleague of mine, Jim Hawker, who runs a second-hand book
stall which he takes around the street markets, and does a nice brisk
trade.  I shall be grateful if you could give me an idea of what forming a
partnership will entail in terms of formalities.  Do I need a written
agreement, and what will happen to my accounts that you have been looking
after?  Will they be the same?  I shall be very grateful for your advice.

Yours sincerely   Harry Morgan
```

Task Two
Stan Hardy and Oliver Laurel run an odd-job business. They have presented you with their books of account and have already drafted the trading account for the year ended 31 December 20-1, but seem to have got into a 'fine mess' at that point. They ask you to draw up their profit and loss account, and capital and current accounts. The balances they give you are at 31 December 20-1:

	£	
Capital accounts:		
Hardy	27,000	Cr
Laurel	27,000	Cr
Current accounts:		
Hardy	448	Cr
Laurel	1,520	Cr
Drawings:		
Hardy	2,256	Dr
Laurel	1,016	Dr
Gross profit	16,000	Cr
Advertising	1,000	Dr
Salaries	3,088	Dr
Rent and rates	1,200	Dr
Insurance	2,400	Dr
Discounts received	1,216	Cr
Discounts allowed	384	Dr

The partners are to receive 5% interest on capital and share profits equally.

Task Three
Henry James and Stephen Ramsay run a wine emporium, "The Grapes", in the Portobello Road. They have drawn up a trial balance at 31 December 20-1, from which they have extracted the trading account.

	£	£
Capital accounts:		
James		16,000
Ramsay		14,000
Current Accounts:		
James		8,000
Ramsay	4,000	

Drawings:

James	7,000	
Ramsay	9,000	
Gross profit		72,000
Rent and rates	4,000	
Advertising	4,000	
Heat and light	3,000	
Sundry expenses	10,000	
Salaries	17,000	
Equipment	25,000	
Bank	15,000	
Debtors	16,000	
Creditors		4,000
	114,000	114,000

You are required to draw up a profit and loss account and appropriation account for the year ended 31 December 20-1 and a balance sheet as at that date, incorporating capital and current accounts. You note the following:

- profits and losses are to be shared equally
- interest on capital is to be paid at 5% per annum
- depreciation is to be charged on the equipment at 10% per annum

Task Four

Simon Lamb and Sarah Penny run a catering service in Putney. They draw up a trial balance at 31 December 20-1.

	£	£
Capital accounts:		
Lamb		10,000
Penny		6,000
Current accounts:		
Lamb		480
Penny		380
Drawings:		
Lamb	2,400	
Penny	1,400	
Purchases and sales	15,260	27,980
Stock at 1 Jan 20-1	3,560	
Salaries	5,720	
Debtors and creditors	7,660	3,820
Equipment	1,320	
Bank	9,120	
Cash	600	
Rent and rates	880	
Expenses	740	
	48,660	48,660

You are to draw up a full set of final accounts, incorporating appropriation, capital and current accounts. You are also provided with the following notes:

- stock at 31 December 20-1 was valued at £4,000
- expenses of £117 were accrued
- depreciation of 10% per annum is to be charged on the equipment
- interest of 7% per annum is to be paid on partners' capital; they share profits in proportion to capital
- the partners' drawings were made on 30 September 20-1; interest is to be charged at 5% per annum.

9 | LIMITED COMPANY ACCOUNTS

In the last Chapter we examined the constitution and accounting requirements of the partnership, a business entity which is a collection of individuals with *unlimited* liability who own and *are* the firm. In this Chapter we will turn to the *limited liability company,* which has its own *corporate* identity in law, and more stringent accounting requirements.

A limited liability company is a legal entity which has a separate identity from its shareholder owners, whose liability for the company's debts is strictly limited.

The shareholder owners (sometimes known as 'members') receive shares in return for their capital contribution. The directors, who manage the company, are strictly speaking the employees of the company, although they will also be shareholders, and in the case of smaller companies will probably own the majority of the shares.

advantages of forming a limited company

Individuals setting up in business, or partners considering changing the constitution of their partnership may *incorporate* (form a limited liability company), for a number of reasons:

Limited Liability
The liability of shareholders (members) for the debts of the company is limited to the amount of share capital they have not yet contributed (uncalled capital). In other words, if the company concerned became insolvent, shareholders would have to pay any unpaid instalments to pay off the creditors. As this is an extremely unlikely occurance, shareholders are in a very safe position: their personal assets, unless pledged as security to a lender, *are not available to the company's creditors.* Contrast this with the partnership, where *every partner is personally liable for the whole debt of the partnership.*

Ability to raise Finance
A limited company can raise substantial funds from outside sources by the issue of shares, either privately, for the smaller company, or from the public on the Stock Exchange, or Alternative Investment Market, for the larger company.

Membership
Whereas most partnerships are restricted to twenty partners, there is no limit on the membership of a limited company, except that it cannot be greater than the number of shares issued.

Status
For some reason there is considerable status attaching to limited companies. Being a company director has traditionally sounded more appealing than being a sole trader or partner. In effect, of course, there is very little difference between these roles in the smaller business.

the Companies Acts 1985 and 1989

All limited companies incorporated since 1 July 1985 are regulated by the Companies Act 1985 which consolidated and amended earlier Acts. The Companies Act 1989 amended some of the provisions of the 1985 Act. Under the terms of the 1985 Act there are two types of limited company: the larger *public limited company* (abbreviated to "plc"), which is defined in the Act, and the smaller company, traditionally known as a *private limited company* (abbreviated to "ltd.").

Public Limited Company (plc)
A company may become a public limited company if it has

- issued share capital of over £50,000
- at least two members (shareholders) and at least two directors

A public limited company may raise capital from the public on the Stock Exchange or related markets, and the many new issues and privatizations are examples of this. A public limited company does *not have to* raise funds on the Stock Markets, and not all do so.

Private Limited Company (ltd.)
The private limited company is the most common form of limited company. The term *private* is not set out in the Companies Act 1985, but it is a traditional description, and well describes the smaller company, often in family ownership. A private limited company has

- no minimum requirement for issued share capital
- at least two members (shareholders) and at least one director

The shares are not traded publicly, but are freely transferable, although valuation will be more difficult for shares not quoted on the Stock Markets.

accounting requirements of the Companies Acts

The Companies Acts requires that all limited companies should have their accounts audited and filed within nine months of the financial year-end on a central register at Companies House in Cardiff. These accounts are then available for public inspection. The accounting requirements will be dealt with in more detail in Chapter 11 *Introduction to Published Accounts of Limited Companies*. The accounts will be audited by *external* auditors; this is a costly and time consuming exercise, and may be a deterrent to someone wishing to form a limited company.

Case Problem: Griffin Gloves - forming a limited company

Griffin Gloves is a thriving glove manufacturing business, an old family firm run on the basis of a partnership. It has a capital of £75,000 but wishes to raise a further £75,000 to finance an expansion plan; it also wishes to keep open an option to raise a further £50,000 at a later date. There is no problem over raising the funds: family and business associates are willing to invest in the business, but do not want to become partners, partly because of the risk, and partly because they do not want to play an active role in running the business. Their accountant and solicitor advise them to form a limited company, to *incorporate*. They will take the following steps:

To Buy a Company or to Incorporate?
Their solicitor and accountant will tell them that it is possible to buy an existing company 'off the shelf' from specialist agencies, and change the name of the company to Griffin Gloves Limited. Another route, taken in their case, is to establish a new company by application to Companies House in Cardiff. The solicitor will be required to draft two documents: the *Memorandum of Association* and the *Articles of Association*, often referred to collectively as the *Memorandum and Articles*.

Memorandum of Association

The Memorandum sets out the powers and constitution of the company. The most important clauses, required by law, are:

Share Capital. A statement of the amount and the division of the authorised share capital of the company. *Authorised share capital* is the amount of share capital the company is allowed to issue, whereas another term, *issued share capital,* refers to the amount of share capital actually issued. In the case of Griffin Gloves Limited the situation is:

- authorised share capital of 200,000 shares of £1 each (the amount they can issue)
- issued share capital of £150,000 (the amount they wish to issue initially)

Each of the former partners and the investors in the new company will therefore receive a £1 share for every £1 invested in the business. The partners will become directors and, at the same time, substantial shareholders. Note that the amount of issued share capital is *not* set out in the Memorandum, but is decided upon by the company in the normal course of its business.

Name of the Company, in this example Griffin Gloves Limited.

Limited Liability. A statement to the effect that the liability of the members (shareholders) of the company is limited.

Objects Clause. A clause will be included stating what operations the business intends to undertake. The 1989 Companies Act allows a company to state in the Objects Clause that it is a "general trading company", which means that it can do anything, as long as it is legal.

Address of the Registered Office of the company. The law requires the company to state whether its registered office is in England and Wales or in Scotland (which has a different code of law).

Articles of Association

The Articles of Association are the rules of the company and set out regulations for the conduct and powers of the shareholders and directors; they regulate the day-to-day running of the business. The Companies Act obligingly sets out a model set of Articles, known as *Table A.*

After these two documents have been sent to Companies House by Griffin Gloves for approval and registration, a *Certificate of Incorporation* will be issued by Companies House. This important document is a simple certificate, often known as the 'birth certificate' of a company, evidencing the date of incorporation and the company name, in this case "Griffin Gloves Limited". If you visit a company you will often see the Certificate of Incorporation hanging on the office wall.

Before considering the final accounts of Griffin Gloves Limited in detail it is important to look at the areas in which final accounts of limited companies differ from those of sole traders and partnerships. These areas are

- the issue of shares and debentures
- the inclusion of a limited company appropriation account after the profit and loss account

financing of limited companies: shares and debentures

Shares

The authorised and issued share capital of a company is divided into a number of classes of shares, the most common of which are *ordinary shares* and *preference shares*. Each share has a face value, or *nominal* value, of say 25p or £1, which will be stated (as in the case of Griffin Gloves) in the Memorandum of Association. The nominal value is rarely the true or market value of the shares: if you look in the financial press you will see that well-known quoted bank shares, for instance, often have a nominal value of £1 and a market value many times that amount.

Shareholders receive dividends on their shares; this being a distribution of the company's profits for:
- part of the year, (the *interim* dividend)
- the rest of the year, (the *final* dividend)

Ordinary Shares

This is the most common type of share and is in fact the type of share issued by Griffin Gloves Limited. Ordinary shares take a share of the profits available for distribution after allowance has been made for all expenses of the business, including taxation, and after preference dividends (if any). The ordinary share dividend may vary from year to year, depending on the level of profits. Not all the profits of the company will be distributed as dividend, a proportion is usually retained as a *reserve*, shown on the balance sheet as "profit and loss account" or "retained profits".

Preference Shares

Preference shares, which normally pay a fixed rate of dividend, are paid in *preference to* the ordinary shareholders. Preference shares may be *cumulative* or *non-cumulative:*

- *cumulative* preference shares, if the dividend is not paid in one year because there is no profit, will accumulate the amount due, and pay it in a later year: the dividend will not be lost
- *non-cumulative* preference shares, if the dividend is not paid in one year, will not pay that amount in a later year: the dividend is lost

All preference shares are assumed to be cumulative unless otherwise stated.

Debentures

There are two forms of debenture seen in practice: the traditional long term funding *fixed rate debenture* issued by public limited companies, and the *bank debenture* which is effectively a loan secured on the assets of the company. Griffin Gloves Limited, as you will see from the balance sheet later in the Chapter, is borrowing by way of a bank debenture.

Fixed Rate Debenture

Traditionally a debenture is a formal certificate issued by a company acknowledging that a sum of money is borrowed, at a fixed interest rate, and is due to be repaid on fixed dates. A number of plc's issue *Debenture Stock*, as a study of the stock prices in the financial press will show. The debentures may be secured against company assets, ensuring that debenture holders will be recompensed if the company goes into liquidation; or they may be unsecured *naked* debentures.

Bank Debenture

The debenture that many companies issue is the bank debenture. If a company borrows from a bank, the borrowing will inevitably be secured, either against the directors' personal guarantees, or against company assets (or both). If the company pledges its assets as security it will do so by means of a *Debenture mortgage deed* known as a *fixed and floating charge* against the fixed assets and floating (current) assets of the company.

The form of borrowing under a bank debenture is very flexible: Griffin Gloves Limited, for example, has an overdraft limit of £10,000, repayable on demand, and a medium term loan of £20,000 repayable at the end of seven years. As the company assets are considerable - the premises are valued at £150,000 in the balance sheet - the bank is happy to rely on its debenture, the fixed and floating charge, to secure its lending.

profit and loss and appropriation accounts of limited companies

Profit and loss account

A limited company uses the same type of year-end financial statements as a sole trader and a partnership, but includes two items in the profit and loss account which are not to be found elsewhere: *directors' salaries and other remuneration*, and *debenture interest*, which are deducted in the profit and loss account.

Appropriation Account

A limited company, like a partnership distributes its profits in an appropriation account which follows the profit and loss account. The profit of a limited company is allocated to meet:

- corporation tax payable by the company, based on net profit
- preference dividends (if any)
- ordinary dividends
- transfers to reserves (profits retained within the company)

It should be noted that a company will not usually dispose of all of its after-tax profits as dividends. Undistributed profits may be left in the appropriation account; they will be recorded in the year-end balance sheet as *retained profits* or *profit and loss account*. Many companies also transfer part of their profits to a *general reserve* account, recorded as such on the balance sheet. Retained profits, whether kept in the appropriation account or transferred to general reserve, form the *revenue reserves* of the company.

If we move forward three years in time from the incorporation of Griffin Gloves Limited, we can examine the appropriation account of the company. Griffin Gloves Limited has made a net profit of £45,000 for the year ended 31 December 20-3, the third year of trading. It has also accumulated revenue reserves of undistributed profits amounting to £35,000.

APPROPRIATION ACCOUNT OF GRIFFIN GLOVES LIMITED FOR THE YEAR ENDED 31 DECEMBER 20-3	£	£
Net profit for the year before taxation		45,000
Less corporation tax		15,600
Profit for year after taxation		29,400
Less proposed ordinary dividend		12,000
		17,400
Less transfer to General Reserve		12,400
		5,000
Add balance of retained profit at beginning of the year		35,000
Balance of retained profit at end of year		40,000

The following points should be noted:

- net profit of £45,000 is brought down from the profit and loss account to the appropriation account
- the company expects to pay £15,600 Corporation tax on the year's profits
- an ordinary dividend of £12,000 is proposed and will be paid in the following year
- the sum of £12,400 has been transferred to the General Reserve
- the balance of £35,000 retained profit from previous years is added
- the final balance of the account of £40,000 will appear in the balance sheet as *Profit and loss account* among shareholders' funds, and will be carried down into the appropriation account for the following year (20-4).

Availability of Reserves

A common misconception, and an understandable one, is to assume that the Revenue Reserves, including the General Reserve, as they are generated from profits, are some sort of cash reserve which the company can draw upon when it needs to. This is, of course, not true. The reserves are shareholders' funds in the *Financed by* section of the balance sheet, and they are represented by a wide range of assets in the *Net Assets* section. It is possible, for instance, that the company has invested its profits in new machinery. In short, reserves are *not* cash balances.

balance sheets of limited companies

Balance sheets of limited companies follow essentially the same layout as those of sole traders and partnerships. The difference lies in the capital section, which is more complex because of the different classes of shares that may be issued, and the various reserves that may accumulate. Set out below is the balance sheet of Griffin Gloves Limited at the end of its third year of trading. Note in particular where the various items from the appropriation account have been shown.

BALANCE SHEET OF GRIFFIN GLOVES LIMITED AS AT 31 DECEMBER 20-3

	£ Cost	£ Depreciation	£ Net
Fixed Assets			
Premises at revaluation (cost £100,000)	150,000	-	150,000
Machinery	95,000	25,000	70,000
Fixtures and fittings	50,000	30,000	20,000
	295,000	55,000	240,000
Current Assets			
Stock		80,000	
Debtors	40,000		
Less provision for bad debts	2,000		
		38,000	
Cash		1,250	
		119,250	
Less Current Liabilities			
Creditors	26,000		
Proposed dividends	12,000		
Corporation tax	15,600		
Bank	1,300		
		54,900	
Working Capital			64,350
			304,350
Less Long-Term Liabilities			
Bank medium term loan			20,000
NET ASSETS			284,350
FINANCED BY			
Authorised Share Capital			
200,000 Ordinary shares of £1 each			200,000
Issued Share Capital			
150,000 Ordinary shares of £1 each fully paid			150,000
Capital Reserve			
Revaluation Reserve		50,000	
Revenue Reserves			
Profit and loss	40,000		
General Reserve	44,350		
		84,350	
			134,350
Shareholders' Funds			284,350

The following points should be noted about the balance sheet of Griffin Gloves Limited:

Fixed Assets

Following the revaluation of the premises from £100,000 to £150,000 in 20-2, a corresponding *Revaluation Reserve* of £50,000 was created and listed under the heading "Capital Reserve". A capital reserve differs from a revenue reserve in that it cannot be used to pay dividends.

Current Liabilities

The proposed dividend of £12,000 and the Corporation tax due of £15,600, which both appeared in the appropriation account, are due for payment within twelve months, and are therefore classed as current liabilities.

Authorised Share Capital

This separate section sets out the share capital authorised in the company's Memorandum of Association, 200,000 shares of £1 in the case of Griffin Gloves Limited. The amount is not added into the balance sheet total, but appears for information only, and may, as in this case, differ from the figure for shares issued. Griffin Gloves Limited has only issued Ordinary shares. If the company decided to authorise the issue of Preference shares, these would be listed in exactly the same way.

Issued Share Capital

The 150,000 shares issued by Griffin Gloves Limited are fully paid and no further call can be made on the shareholders by the company. The amount shown in the balance sheet is therefore £150,000. If Griffin Gloves Limited decided to issue the remaining 50,000 shares authorised in the Memorandum of Association, a further £50,000 would be added to the issued share capital figure in the balance sheet. Again, if Griffin Gloves Limited decided to issue Preference shares, after amending the Memorandum of Association, these would be included in this section.

Revenue Reserves

Profit and loss account and *General Reserve* represent funds which have been retained from the profits of the company and have not been distributed as dividends to the shareholders. Clearly, the greater the figure for reserves, the greater the actual value placed on the shares by the shareholders.

Capital Reserves

The Revaluation Reserve of £50,000, as was mentioned when examining the fixed asset section, represents the rise in value of the company's premises, an amount which increases the value of the shareholders' investment in the company. This is purely a 'book' adjustment, no cash has changed hands, and the reserve cannot be used to fund the payment of dividends.

Share Premium Account is classed as a *capital* reserve because it derives from non-trading activity. It does not appear in the balance sheet of Griffin Gloves Limited as yet, but it could do so if and when the remaining 50,000 Ordinary shares are issued. The reason for this is that the price asked for the new shares may well be more than the £1 nominal value set out in the Memorandum of Association. The company has been trading successfully and accumulated substantial reserves; the value of the existing £1 shares could be, say, £1.75. In fairness to existing shareholders, the new shares might be issued at £1.75 rather than £1.

This creates a problem on the balance sheet because only £1 per share can be recorded in the Issued Share Capital section, and £1.75 cash will be received for each share. The extra 75p cash per share will therefore be recorded in a Share Premium Account. The balance sheet entries will be:

- an increase in cash (or bank) in the Current Assets of 50,000 (shares) x £1.75 = £87,500 from the sale of the shares
- an increase in the issued share capital figure of £50,000 (nominal value only), *plus* a new item, Share Premium Account of 50,000 (shares) x 75p = £37,500.

Shareholders' Funds

Any shareholder or person interested in the *value* of shares in a limited company will examine what is known as the "Shareholders' Funds" of a company. This comprises the issued share capital *plus* reserves. Clearly the higher this figure is in relation to any external liabilities such as bank debentures, the stronger the company will be.

further reading

The accounts of Griffin Gloves are an introduction to the format and the workings of limited company accounts. They are typical of a smaller company, but, as you will be aware, companies vary as much in activity as in size, and you are strongly recommended to investigate further sets of accounts and see how they compare with Griffin Gloves Limited. As limited companies are obliged by law to make their accounts public, there should be no difficulty in obtaining copies or making them available to fellow students.

One specific type of company accounts will be dealt with in full in Chapter 11, *Published Accounts of Public Limited Companies.* Before reading that Chapter you should first study Chapter 10, which examines another accounting statement found in published company accounts, the *Cash Flow Statement.*

CHAPTER SUMMARY

❏ A limited company, unlike a sole trader or a partnership, is a separate legal entity, regulated by the Companies Act 1985, owned by shareholders and managed by directors.

❏ A limited company may be either a public limited company or a private limited company.

❏ The liability of the shareholder is strictly limited to the unpaid portion of the shares held.

❏ A limited company raises finance by means of the issue of different classes of share capital and by borrowing from external sources, often by means of debentures.

❏ The final accounts of a limited company must be prepared in accordance with the Companies Acts and must be filed for public inspection at Companies House.

❏ The final accounts of a limited company include:

  • an appropriation account which follows the profit and loss account
  • a statement of the authorised and issued share capital in the balance sheet
  • details of Capital Reserves and General Reserves.

✍ STUDENT ACTIVITIES

You are an accountant in the firm of Britton Verity & Co., 20 The Close, Greenham, GR7 2OB, and encounter the following tasks during the course of your work on 30 March 20-2.

Task One

Wendy and Henry Fletcher run as partners a highly successful gift shop "Greenham Giftstore" situated at 109 The Broadway, Greenham GR2 1OS.   They are considering incorporating the business into a limited company. They have a number of queries, however, and telephone you for advice. In particular they want to know the following:

* Is it possible to buy a limited company?
* Is there much paperwork involved in setting up a limited company?
* Who can hold the shares? Can directors hold shares?
* What is the difference between a partner and a director in terms of liability for the business?
* What is the accountant's role in running a limited company?
* Are the final accounts different for a limited company when compared with those of a partnership?
* They have heard that the accounts will have to be "filed". What does this mean?

You are to write them a suitable letter of advice to go out under your own signature.

Task Two

Mason Motors Limited is a second-hand car business in the town. The business started ten years ago as a partnership of two brothers, James and Stuart Mason. It incorporated three years ago, and has continued to prosper. The Mason brothers are able salesmen, but less gifted (James in particular) when it comes to figures.   You are working on the accounts for the year ended 31 December 20-1 (which has been a bumper year for profit) and have the following information to hand:

* balance of unappropriated profits from previous years stands at £150,000
* net profit for the year was £75,000
* it has been agreed that a transfer to a general reserve of £50,000 is to be made
* corporation tax of £20,050 is to be paid on the year's profit
* it has been agreed that a dividend of 10% is to be paid on the issued share capital of £100,000

You are to set out the appropriation account for Mason Motors Limited, and append notes explaining exactly what you have done. James telephones you the week following receipt of the figures, and asks if they could use the £50,000 being transferred to General Reserve to rebuild their forecourt. What would be your reply?

Task Three

You are working on the accounts of Peter Whiteman Limited, an engineering company. You are to prepare the appropriate final accounts from the trial balance and attached notes.

Trial Balance of Peter Whiteman Limited as at 31 December 20-1

	£	£
Share capital		480,000
Premises at cost	284,000	
Vehicles at cost	110,000	
Provision for depreciation (vehicles)		43,600
Stock at 1 Jan 20-1	85,200	
Purchases and sales	378,546	594,918
Rent and rates	8,000	
Wages and salaries	68,860	
General expenses	20,000	

	£	£
Bad debts written off	2,000	
Directors' salaries	49,896	
Debtors and creditors	102,964	36,100
Profit and loss account		36,800
Bank	81,952	
	1,191,418	1,191,418

Notes to the accounts:
- stock at 31 December 20-1 was valued at £95,000
- authorised share capital is 600,000 ordinary shares of £1 each and all issued share capital is fully paid
- general expenses accrued amount to £250 and rent of £950 is prepaid
- the directors have proposed a dividend of 5% on the ordinary shares
- depreciation on vehicles is to be charged at 15% per annum using the straight line method

Task Four

You are working on the accounts of Tempus Limited, an exporter of reproduction antique clocks.
The company's authorised and issued share capital is 100,000 ordinary shares of £1 each, fully paid, and 20,000 10% preference shares of £1 each, fully paid. The trial balance you have available is as follows:

Trial Balance of Tempus Limited as at 31 December 20-1

	£	£
Ordinary share capital		100,000
10% Preference share capital		20,000
Machinery at cost	60,000	
Provision for depreciation (machinery)		32,000
Vehicles at cost	40,000	
Provision for depreciation (vehicles)		14,400
Debtors and creditors	69,960	31,740
Bank	29,010	
Medium term loan		20,000
Stock at 1 Jan 20-1	50,400	
Rent and rates	10,040	
Heat and light	12,000	
Purchases and sales	329,528	464,768
Bad debts written off	6,600	
Discounts	650	1,280
Wages and salaries	48,420	
Loan interest	600	
Directors' salaries	34,640	
Profit and loss account		6,600
Provision for bad debts		1,060
	691,848	691,848

Notes to the accounts:

- stock at 31 December 20-1 was valued at £50,500
- depreciation on machinery and vehicles is to be charged at 10% per annum using the straight line method
- provision for bad debts is to be increased to 5% of debtors
- at 31 December 20-1 rates prepaid were £3,501, and a heating oil bill of £752 remained unpaid
- the directors have proposed a dividend of 5% to holders of ordinary shares; 10% will be payable to preference shareholders.
- Make a provision for corporation tax of £2,500

You are to prepare trading and profit and loss accounts (including appropriation account) for Tempus Limited for the year ended 31 December 20-1, together with a balance sheet as at that date.

Task Five

You are working on the accounts of Bacchus Limited, a local wine merchant. The authorised share capital is 200,000 ordinary shares of £1 each, of which 150,000 have been issued fully paid. The trial balance you have available is as follows:

Trial Balance of Bacchus Limited as at 31 December 20-1

	£	£
Ordinary share capital		150,000
Share premium account		50,000
Bank debenture		100,000
Premises at cost	240,000	
Equipment at cost	60,000	
Vehicles at cost	130,000	
Provision for depreciation:		
Equipment		36,000
Vehicles		20,000
Purchases and Sales	417,400	626,500
Debtors and Creditors	35,600	20,700
Bad debts	1,900	
Provision for bad debts		1,600
Wages and salaries	45,200	
Rates	8,100	
Loan interest	15,000	
Directors' salaries	36,000	
Motor expenses	11,300	
General expenses	5,500	
Advertising expenses	1,200	
Stock at 1 Jan 20-1	74,500	
Bank		1,800
Profit and loss account		75,100
	1,081,700	1,081,700

Notes to the accounting records:

- stock at 31 December 20-1 was valued at £ 82,760
- provision for bad debts is to be 5% of debtors
- unpaid advertising expenses at 31 December 20-1 amounted to £456
- rates paid in advance at 31 December 20-1 amounted to £985
- equipment is to be depreciated by 10% per annum on a straight line basis
- vehicles are to be depreciated by 20% per annum on a reducing balance basis
- a dividend of 6% on ordinary shares is proposed
- corporation tax of £15,000 is to be provided for

You are to prepare trading and profit and loss accounts (including appropriation account) for Bacchus Limited for the year ended 31 December 20-1, together with a balance sheet as at that date.

10 CASH FLOW STATEMENTS

A balance sheet shows the financial state of a business at a particular date and is usually only prepared once a year. While it is possible to obtain a great deal of information on the progress of the business by comparing one year's balance sheet with that of the next year, it is more difficult to see what has gone on during the period between the two balance sheet dates.

A cash flow statement uses information from the accounting records (including profit and loss account) and balance sheet, and shows an overall view of money flowing in and out of a business during an accounting period.

Such a statement concentrates on the liquidity of a business and explains to the owner or shareholders why, after a year of good profits for example, there is a reduced balance at the bank or a larger bank overdraft, at the year-end than there was at the beginning of the year.

Cash flow statements are especially important because they deal with flows of money. It is invariably a shortage of money that causes most businesses to fail, rather than a poor quality product or service. The importance of the cash flow statement is such that Financial Reporting Standard No 1 (FRS 1) – see also page 113 – requires all but small companies to include this statement as a part of their accounts which they publish and send to shareholders. For sole traders and partnerships, the information that the statement contains is of considerable interest to the owner(s) and to a lender, such as a bank.

A cash flow statement can look either at what has gone on in a past accounting period, or it can, based on a forecast trading and profit and loss account and balance sheet, demonstrate the effect on cash flow of future alternative courses of action.

format of the cash flow statement

Cash flow statements are divided into eight sections:
1. Operating activities
2. Returns on investments and servicing of finance
3. Taxation
4. Capital expenditure and financial investment
5. Acquisition and disposals
6. Equity dividends paid
7. Management of liquid resources
8. Financing

The cash flows for the year affecting each of these main areas of business activity are shown in the statement, although not every business will have cash flows under each of the eight sections.

The diagram on the next page shows the format of the cash flow statement, with the main cash inflows and outflows under each heading. There is also further explanation of the first section – operating activities – the main source of cash flow for most businesses.

operating activities

The net cash inflow from operating activities is calculated by using figures from the profit and loss account and balance sheet as follows:

- operating profit (ie net profit, before deduction of interest)
- add depreciation for the year (added to profit because depreciation is a non-cash expense, that is, no money is paid out by the business in respect of depreciation charged to profit and loss account)
- add decrease in debtors, or deduct increase in debtors
- add increase in creditors, or deduct decrease in creditors
- add decrease in stock, or deduct increase in stock

FORMAT OF THE CASH FLOW STATEMENT

Operating activities
- Operating profit (ie net profit, before deduction of interest)
- Depreciation charge for the year (see page 98) for treatment of a profit or a loss on sale of fixed assets)
- Changes in debtors, creditors and stock

Returns on investments and servicing of finance
- *Inflows:* interest received, dividends received
- *Outflows:* interest paid, dividends paid on preference shares (but not ordinary shares – see below)

Taxation
- *Outflow:* corporation tax paid by limited companies during the year

Capital expenditure and financial investment
- *Inflows:* sale proceeds from fixed assets and investments
- *Outflows:* purchase cost of fixed assets and investments

Acquisitions and disposals
- *Inflows:* sale proceeds from investments and interests in
  - subsidiary companies (where more than 50 per cent of the shares in another company is owned)
  - associated companies (where between 20 per cent and 50 per cent of the shares in another company is owned)
  - joint ventures (where a project is undertaken jointly with another company)
- *Outflows:* purchase cost of investments in subsidiary companies, associated companies, and of interests in joint ventures

Equity dividends paid
- *Outflow:* the amount of dividends paid to equity (ordinary) shareholders during the year (where the cash flow statement is for a sole trader or partnership, the amount of drawings will be shown here)

Management of liquid resources
- *Inflows:* sale proceeds from short-term investments that are almost as good as cash – such as treasury bills (a form of government debt), and term deposits of up to a year with a bank
- *Outflows:* purchase of short-term liquid investments

Financing
- *Inflows:* receipts from increase in capital /share capital, raising/increase of loans
- *Outflows:* repayment of capital/share capital/loans

---

layout of a cash flow statement

A cash flow statement uses a common layout which can be amended to suit the particular needs of the business for which it is being prepared. The following layout – with specimen figures included – is commonly used:

ABC LIMITED
CASH FLOW STATEMENT FOR THE YEAR ENDED 31 DECEMBER 20-1

	£	£
Operating activities:		
Operating profit (note: before tax and interest)	75,000	
Depreciation for year	10,000	
Decrease in stock	2,000	
Increase in debtors	(5,000)	
Increase in creditors	7,000	
Net cash inflow from operating activities		89,000
Returns on investments and servicing of finance:		
Interest received	10,000	
Interest paid	(5,000)	
		5,000
Taxation:		
Corporation tax paid (note: amount *paid* during year)		(6,000)
Capital expenditure and financial investment		
Payments to acquire fixed assets	(125,000)	
Receipts from sales of fixed assets	15,000	
		(110,000)
Acquisitions and disposals		
Purchase of subsidiary undertakings	(–)	
Sale of a business	–	–
Equity dividends paid: (note: amount *paid* during year)		(22,000)
Cash outflow before use of liquid resources and financing		(44,000)
Management of liquid resources:		
Purchase of treasury bills	(250,000)	
Sale of treasury bills	200,000	
		(50,000)
Financing:		
Issue of share capital	275,000	
Repayment of capital/share capital	(–)	
Increase in loans	–	
Repayment of loans	(90,000)	
		185,000
Increase in cash		91,000

Notes:
- The separate amounts shown for each section can, if preferred, be detailed in a note to the cash flow statement.

- Money amounts shown in brackets indicate a deduction or, where the figure is a sub-total, a negative figure.

- The changes in the main working capital items of stock, debtors and creditors have an effect on cash balances. For example, a decrease in stock increases cash, while an increase in debtors reduces cash.

- The cash flow statement concludes with a figure for the *increase or decrease in cash*. This is calculated from the subtotals of each of eight sections of the statement.

Case Study: Mrs Green, a sole trader

Question

Mrs Green runs a children's clothes shop in rented premises in a small market town. Her balance sheets for the last two years are as follows:

BALANCE SHEET AS AT 31 DECEMBER

	20-1 £ Cost	20-1 £ Dep'n	20-1 £ Net	20-2 £ Cost	20-2 £ Dep'n	20-2 £ Net
Fixed assets						
Shop fittings	1,500	500	1,000	2,000	750	1,250
Current assets						
Stock		3,750			4,850	
Debtors		625			1,040	
Bank		220			–	
		4,595			5,890	
Less Current liabilities						
Creditors	2,020			4,360		
Bank	–			725		
		2,020			5,085	
Working capital			2,575			805
			3,575			2,055
Less Long-term liabilities						
Loan from husband			–			1,000
NET ASSETS			3,575			1,055
FINANCED BY						
Capital						
Opening capital			3,300			3,575
Add net profit for year			5,450			4,080
			8,750			7,655
Less drawings			5,175			6,600
			3,575			1,055

Note: Interest paid on the loan and bank overdraft in 20-2 was £450.

Mrs Green says to you: "I cannot understand why I am overdrawn at the bank by £725 on 31 December 20-2 when I made a profit of £4,080 during the year". She asks for your assistance in seeking an explanation.

Answer

A cash flow statement will give Mrs Green the answer:

CASH FLOW STATEMENT FOR THE YEAR ENDED 31 DECEMBER 20-2

	£	£
Operating activities:		
Operating profit (before interest)	4,530	
Depreciation for year	250	
Increase in stock	(1,100)	
Increase in debtors	(415)	
Increase in creditors	2,340	
Net cash inflow from operating activities		5,605
Returns on investments and servicing of finance:		
Interest paid		(450)
Taxation:		
Corporation tax paid		n/a
Capital expenditure and financial investment:		
Payments to acquire fixed assets		(500)
Equity dividends paid: (drawings)		(6,600)
Cash outflow before use of liquid resources and financing		(1,945)
Financing:		
Loan from husband		1,000
Decrease in cash		(945)

Points to note:

- Net profit for the year (before interest) is calculated as:

net profit for 20-2	£4,080
interest for 20-2	£ 450
	£4,530

- Depreciation for the year of £250 is the amount of the increase in depreciation to date shown on the balance sheets, that is, £750 minus £500.

- An increase in stock and debtors reduces the cash available to the business (because stock is being bought, debtors are being allowed more time to pay). In contrast, an increase in creditors gives an increase in cash (because creditors are allowing Mrs Green more time to pay).

- In this example there is no tax paid (because Mrs Green is a sole trader who will be taxed as an individual, unlike a company which pays tax on its profits); however, the place where tax would appear is indicated on the cash flow statement.

- As this is a sole trader busines, drawings are shown on the cash flow statement in place of equity dividends.

- The change in the bank balance is summarised as follows: from a balance of £220 in the bank to an overdraft of £725 is a 'swing' in the bank of minus £945, which is the amount of the decrease in cash shown by the cash flow statement.

Explanation to Mrs Green

In this example, the statement highlights the following points for the owner of the business:

- net cash inflow from operating activities is £5,605, whereas owner's drawings are £6,600; this state of affairs cannot continue for long

- fixed assets costing £500 have been purchased

- a long-term loan of £1,000 has been raised from her husband

- there has been a decrease in cash of £945; this trend cannot be continued for long

- by the end of 20-2 the business has an overdraft of £725, caused mainly by the excessive drawings of the owner

- in conclusion, the position of this business has deteriorated over the two years, and corrective action will be necessary

Case Study: Newtown Trading, a limited company

Question

The balance sheets of Newtown Trading Company Limited for 20-6 and 20-7 are as follows:

BALANCE SHEET AS AT 31 DECEMBER						
		20-6			20-7	
	£	£	£	£	£	£
	Cost	Dep'n	Net	Cost	Dep'n	Net
Fixed assets	47,200	6,200	41,000	64,000	8,900	55,100
Current assets						
Stock		7,000			11,000	
Debtors		5,000			3,700	
Bank		1,000			500	
		13,000			15,200	
Less Current liabilities						
Creditors	3,500			4,800		
Proposed dividends	2,000			2,500		
Corporation tax	1,000			1,500		
		6,500			8,800	
Working capital			6,500			6,400
			47,500			61,500
Less Long-term liabilities						
Debentures			5,000			3,000
NET ASSETS			42,500			58,500
FINANCED BY						
Ordinary share capital			30,000			40,000
Share premium account			1,500			2,500
Retained profits			11,000			16,000
SHAREHOLDERS' FUNDS			42,500			58,500

Note: Interest paid on the loan in 20-7 was £400.

Prepare a cash flow statement for the year ended 31 December 20-7 and comment on the main points highlighted by the statement.

Answer

NEWTOWN TRADING COMPANY LIMITED
CASH FLOW STATEMENT FOR THE YEAR ENDED 31 DECEMBER 20-7

	£	£
Operating activities:		
Operating profit (before interest)*	9,400	
Depreciation for year§	2,700	
Increase in stock	(4,000)	
Decrease in debtors	1,300	
Increase in creditors	1,300	
Net cash inflow from operating activities		10,700
Returns on investments and servicing of finance:		
Interest paid		(400)
Taxation:		
Corporation tax paid		(1,000)
Capital expenditure and financial investment:		
Payments to acquire fixed assets		(16,800)
Equity dividends paid:		(2,000)
Cash outflow before use of liquid resources and financing		(9,500)
Financing:		
Issue of ordinary shares at a premium		
ie £10,000 + £1,000 =	11,000	
Repayment of debentures	(2,000)	
		9,000
Decrease in cash		(500)

Notes:
* Calculation of the operating profit for 20-7 before interest, tax and dividends:

	£
increase in retained profits	5,000
interest paid in 20-7	400
proposed dividends, 20-7	2,500
corporation tax, 20-7	1,500
operating profit before interest, tax and dividends	9,400

§ Depreciation charged: £8,900 – £6,200 = £2,700

Both proposed dividends and corporation tax (which are current liabilities at 31 December 20-6) are paid in 20-7. Likewise, the current liabilities for dividends and tax at 31 December 20-7 will be paid in 20-8 (and will appear on that year's cash flow statement).

How useful is the statement?

The following points are highlighted by the statement:

- net cash inflow from operating activities is £10,700

- a purchase of fixed assets of £16,800 has been made, financed partly by operating activities, and partly by an issue of shares at a premium

- the bank balance during the year has fallen by £500, ie from £1,000 to £500

- in conclusion, the picture shown by the cash flow statement is that of a business which is generating cash from its operating activities and using them to build for the future

profit or loss on sale of fixed assets

When a business sells fixed assets it is most unlikely that the resultant sale proceeds will equal the net book value (cost price, less depreciation to date). The accounting solution is to transfer any small profit or loss on sale – *non-cash* items – to profit and loss account. However, such a profit or loss on sale must be handled with care when preparing a cash flow statement because, in such a statement we have to adjust for non-cash items when calculating the *net cash inflow from operating activities*; at the same time we must separately identify the amount of the sale proceeds of fixed assets in the *capital expenditure* section.

Example showing profit or loss on sale of fixed assets in a cash flow statement

H & J Wells are electrical contractors. For the year ended 30 June 20-2 their profit and loss account is as follows:

	£	£
Gross profit		37,500
Less expenses:		
General expenses	23,000	
Provision for depreciation: machinery	2,000	
vehicles	3,000	
		28,000
Net profit		9,500

Profit on sale

During the course of the year, but not yet recorded in their profit and loss account, they have sold the following fixed asset:

		£
Machine	cost price	1,000
	depreciation to date	750
	net book value	250
	sale proceeds	350

As the machine has been sold for £100 more than book value, this sum is shown in profit and loss account, as follows:

	£	£
Gross profit		37,500
Profit on sale of fixed assets		100
		37,600
Less expenses:		
General expenses	23,000	
Provision for depreciation: machinery	2,000	
vehicles	3,000	
		28,000
Net profit		9,600

The cash flow statement, based on the amended profit and loss account, will include the following figures:

CASHFLOW STATEMENT (EXTRACT) OF H & J WELLS
FOR THE YEAR ENDED 30 JUNE 20-2

	£	£
Operating activities:		
Operating profit (before interest)	9,600	
Depreciation	5,000	
Profit on sale of fixed assets	(100)	
(Increase)/decrease in stock	. . .	
(Increase)/decrease in debtors	. . .	
Increase/(decrease) in creditors	. . .	
Net cash inflow from operating activities		14,500
Capital expenditure and financial investment:		
Payments to acquire fixed assets	(. . .)	
Receipts from sales of fixed assets	350	
		350

Note that profit on sale of fixed assets is deducted in the operating activities section because it is non-cash income. (Only the sections of the cash flow statement affected by the sale are shown above.)

Loss on sale
If the machine had been sold for £150, this would have given a 'loss on sale' of £100. this amount would be debited to profit and loss account, to give an amended net profit of £9,400.

The effect on the cash flow statement would be twofold:

- In the operating activities section, loss on sale of fixed assets of £100 would be *added*; the net cash inflow from operating activities remains at £14,500 (which proves that both profit and loss on sale of fixed assets are non-cash items)

- In the capital expenditure section, receipts from sales of fixed assets would be £150

Conclusion
The rule for dealing with a profit or a loss on sale of fixed assets in cash flow statements is:

- *add* the amount of the loss on sale, or *deduct* the amount of the profit on sale, to or from the net profit when calculating the net cash flow from operating activities

- show the *total* sale proceeds, ie the amount of the cheque received, as receipts from sales of fixed assets in the capital expenditure section

CHAPTER SUMMARY

❏   The objective of a cash flow statement is to show an overall view of money flowing in and out of a business during an accounting period.

❏   A cashflow statement is divided into eight sections:
1   operating activities
2   returns on investments and servicing of finance
3   taxation
4   capital expenditure and financial investment
5   acquisitions and disposals
6   equity dividends paid
7   management of liquid resources
8   financing

❏   The Financial Reporting Standard No 1 on cash flow statements provides a specimen layout.

❏   Most limited companies are required to include a cash flow statement as a part of their published accounts. They are also useful statements for sole traders and partnerships.

STUDENT ACTIVITIES

10.1   John Smith has been in business for two years. He is puzzled by his balance sheets because, although they show a profit for each year, his bank balance has fallen and is now an overdraft. He asks for your assistance to explain what has happened. The balance sheets are as follows:

BALANCE SHEETS AS AT 31 DECEMBER

	20-1			20-2		
	£	£	£	£	£	£
	Cost	*Dep'n*	*Net*	*Cost*	*Dep'n*	*Net*
Fixed Assets						
Fixtures and fittings	3,000	600	2,400	5,000	1,600	3,400
Current Assets						
Stock		5,500			9,000	
Debtors		750			1,550	
Bank		850			-	
		7,100			10,550	
Current Liabilities						
Creditors	2,500			2,750		
Bank overdraft	-			2,200		
		2,500			4,950	
Working Capital			4,600			5,600
NET ASSETS			7,000			9,000
FINANCED BY						
Capital			5,000			7,000
Add Net profit for year			8,750			11,000
			13,750			18,000
Less Drawings			6,750			9,000
			7,000			9,000

Note: Interest paid on the bank overdraft in 20-2 was £250.

You are to prepare a cash flow statement for the year-ended 31 December 20-2.

10.2 Richard Williams runs a stationery supplies shop; his balance sheets for the last two years are:

BALANCE SHEETS AS AT 30 SEPTEMBER						
		20-5			**20-6**	
	£	£	£	£	£	£
	Cost	*Dep'n*	*Net*	*Cost*	*Dep'n*	*Net*
Fixed Assets	60,000	12,000	48,000	70,000	23,600	46,400
Current Assets						
Stock		9,800			13,600	
Debtors		10,800			15,000	
		20,600			28,600	
Less Current Liabilities						
Creditors	7,200			14,600		
Bank overdraft	1,000			4,700		
		8,200			19,300	
Working Capital			12,400			9,300
			60,400			55,700
Less Long-term Liabilities						
Bank loan			10,000			15,000
NET ASSETS			50,400			40,700
FINANCED BY						
Capital			50,000			50,400
Add Net profit/(loss)			10,800			(1,500)
			60,800			48,900
Less Drawings			10,400			8,200
			50,400			40,700

Note: Loan and overdraft interest paid in 20-6 was £2,200.

You are to prepare a cash flow statement for the year-ended 30 September 20-6.

10.3 Using the balance sheets of Richard Williams in question 10.2 (above), prepare revised cash flow statements for the year to 30 September 20-6, to take note of the following:

Situation 1
A fixed asset with a cost price of £5,000 and depreciation to date of £3,000 was sold for £2,500.

Situation 2
A fixed asset with a cost price of £5,000 and depreciation to date of £3,000 was sold for £1,500.

Notes

- two separate cash flow statements for the year ended 30 September 20-6 are required
- assume that the balance sheet for 20-6 already includes the sale transactions, ie do *not* adjust the net loss by the amount of the profit or loss on sale, or the bank account by the sale proceeds

10.4 Martin Jackson is a shareholder in Retail News Limited, a company that operates a chain of newsagents throughout the West Midlands. Martin comments that, whilst the company is making reasonable profits, the bank balance has fallen quite considerably. He provides you with the following information for Retail News Limited:

BALANCE SHEETS AS AT 31 DECEMBER

	20-4 £000	20-4 £000	20-5 £000	20-5 £000	20-6 £000	20-6 £000
Fixed Assets at cost		252		274		298
Add Additions during year		22		24		26
		274		298		324
Less Depreciation to date		74		98		118
		200		200		206
Current Assets						
Stock	50		64		70	
Debtors	80		120		160	
Bank	10		-		-	
	140		184		230	
Less Current Liabilities						
Creditors	56		72		78	
Bank	-		10		46	
Proposed dividends	16		20		16	
Corporation tax	4		5		8	
	76		107		148	
Working Capital		64		77		82
NET ASSETS		264		277		288
FINANCED BY						
Share Capital		200		210		210
Retained profits		64		67		78
		264		277		288

Note
Interest paid on the bank overdraft was: £3,000 in 20-5, and £15,000 in 20-6.

You are to prepare a cash flow statement for the years ended for 20-5 and 20-6.

10.5 The balance sheets of Simplex Limited are shown below.

BALANCE SHEETS AS AT 31 DECEMBER

	20-6			20-7		
	£	£	£	£	£	£
	Cost	*Dep'n*	*Net*	*Cost*	*Dep'n*	*Net*
Fixed Assets						
Land and buildings	100,000	-	100,000	100,000	-	100,000
Plant and equipment	51,400	8,400	43,000	70,300	14,300	56,000
	151,400	8,400	143,000	170,300	14,300	156,000
Current Assets						
Stocks		44,000			61,000	
Debtors		28,000			32,000	
Bank		-			5,000	
		72,000			98,000	
Less Current Liabilities						
Creditors	23,000			27,500		
Bank overdraft	6,500			-		
Corporation tax	13,500			16,000		
Dividend proposed	10,500			15,000		
	53,500			58,500		
Working Capital			18,500			39,500
			161,500			195,500
Less Long-term Liabilities						
Debentures			30,000			40,000
NET ASSETS			131,500			155,500
FINANCED BY						
Shareholders' Funds						
Share capital			110,000			130,000
Retained profits			21,500			25,500
			131,500			155,500

Notes
- interest paid on the debentures and bank overdraft in 20-7 was £2,850
* you should show your calculation of profit (before tax and interest)

You are to prepare a cash flow statement for 20-7:

10.6 The balance sheets of Jason Limited at 31 December 20-7 and 20-8 are shown below.

BALANCE SHEETS AS AT 31 DECEMBER

	20-7 £000 Cost	20-7 £000 Dep'n	20-7 £000 Net	20-8 £000 Cost	20-8 £000 Dep'n	20-8 £000 Net
Fixed Assets (see note)	2,000	770	1,230	3,980	1,100	2,880
Current Assets						
Stocks		1,600			2,800	
Debtors		920			1,520	
Bank		-			350	
		2,520			4,670	
Less Current Liabilities						
Creditors	800			900		
Bank overdraft	250			-		
		1,050			900	
Working Capital			1,470			3,770
			2,700			6,650
Less Long-term Liabilities						
Debentures			500			1,500
NET ASSETS			2,200			5,150
FINANCED BY						
Shareholders' Funds						
Share capital			500			2,000
Share premium account			-			500
Retained profits			1,700			2,650
			2,200			5,150

Notes

- The net profit for 20-8 was £950,000, and interest paid on the debentures and bank overdraft was £20,000. There will be no proposed final dividend, and taxation is to be ignored.

- During 20-8 fixed assets, which had originally cost £500,000 and had been depreciated by £200,000, were sold for £270,000.

You are to prepare a cash flow statement for 20-8.

11 PUBLISHED ACCOUNTS OF LIMITED COMPANIES

All limited companies have shareholders and many of the largest companies have many thousands of shareholders. Each shareholder owns a part of the company and, although they do not take part in the day-to-day running of the company (unless they are also directors), each is entitled to know the financial results of the company.

Every limited company, whether public or private, is required by law to publish financial statements, which are also available for anyone to inspect if they so wish. We need to distinguish between the statutory accounts and the report and accounts. The statutory accounts are those which are required to be produced under company law, and a copy of these is filed at Companies House. Smaller companies can file abbreviated accounts. The report and accounts, a copy of which is available to every shareholder, must include the statutory accounts, but usually also contains more information about the activities of the company. The report and accounts of large well-known companies are often presented in the form of a glossy booklet, well illustrated with photographs and diagrammatic presentations. Some companies, with the agreement of the shareholders, issue a simpler form of annual review, including a summary financial statement, the full report and accounts being available on request.

Company law not only requires the production of financial statements, but also states the detailed information that must be disclosed. The financial statements of all public limited companies and larger private companies must be audited (ie professionally checked) and the Auditors' Report included in the statements. All these legal requirements are detailed in the relevant sections of the Companies Act 1985 (as amended by the Companies Act 1989).

statements required by the Companies Act

The financial statements required by the Companies Act are:
- profit and loss account
- balance sheet
- directors' report

When producing financial statements, companies also have to bear in mind the requirements of the various Statements of Standard Accounting Practice (SSAPs) and Financial Reporting Standards (FRSs). These are issued by the Accounting Standards Board and lay down acceptable accounting methods for various topics. Of particular note is FRS1, which requires larger limited companies to include a cash flow statement as part of the published accounts.

The reporting procedures of smaller companies call for simpler and less detailed disclosure requirements.

profit and loss account

The profit and loss account does not detail every single expense incurred by the company but, instead, summarises the main items. However, the Companies Act requires that certain items must be detailed either in the profit and loss account itself, or in separate notes.

The profit and loss account must follow one of two standard formats set out in the Act, and the example which follows shows the one that is most commonly used by trading companies. (The other format is appropriate for manufacturing companies.) Specimen figures have been shown – amounts in brackets are deducted and the presentation is in vertical style.

XYZ PLC

Profit and loss account
for the year ended 31 December 20-1

	£000s
Turnover (sales)	27,000
Cost of sales	(16,500)
Gross profit	10,500
Distribution costs	(3,250)
Administrative expenses	(3,000)
Other operating income (eg rent received)	500
Income from investments	100
Interest payable	(200)
Profit on ordinary activities before tax	4,650
Tax on profit on ordinary activities	(2,000)
Profit on ordinary activities after tax	2,650
Dividends paid and proposed	(1,350)
Transfer to reserves	(500)
Retained profit for the financial year	800

notes to the accounts
In the notes to the profit and loss account must be disclosed details of:
- hire charges of plant and machinery
- auditors' fees
- rent receivable
- depreciation amounts
- the total of directors' emoluments (ie earnings)
- the highest paid director's emoluments (only required to be shown by companies quoted on the Stock Exchange, and where total directors' emoluments exceed £200,000 per year)
- the average number of employees, together with details of costs of wages and salaries, national insurance and pensions.

Fig 11.1 on the next page shows a profit and loss account for The Body Shop International PLC.

Consolidated Profit and Loss Account

for the 53 weeks ended 2 March 1996

	Note	1996 (53 weeks) £m	1995 (52 weeks) £m
Turnover	2	256.5	219.7
Cost of sales		107.6	89.6
Gross profit		148.9	130.1
Operating expenses	3	115.2	95.6
Operating profit	2,5	33.7	34.5
Interest payable (net)	4	1.0	1.0
Profit on ordinary activities before tax		32.7	33.5
Tax on profit on ordinary activities	8	14.1	11.7
Profit for the financial year	9	18.6	21.8
Dividends paid and proposed	10	6.5	4.5
Retained profit	21	12.1	17.3
Earnings per ordinary share	11	9.8p	11.5p

*Fig 11.1 Profit and loss account of The Body Shop International PLC
(note that, for comparison, figures for both the current year and the previous year are shown)*

continuing and discontinued operations, extraordinary and exceptional items

Limited company profit and loss accounts are also required (by Financial Reporting Standard No 3, entitled "Reporting Financial Performance") to show the financial results of any changes to the structure of the company, eg the purchase of another company, or the disposal of a section of the business. To this end the company must distinguish between:

- *continuing operations* – the profit and loss amounts relating to those activities of the company which continue in business at the end of the year; shown separately under this heading will be amounts relating to any acquisitions, ie businesses bought during the year

- *discontinued operations* – the amounts relating to activities which have now been sold or terminated during the year

As well as the above, there must be disclosed any *exceptional items* – large, usually one-off transactions, but which form part of normal trading activities. The following such transactions must be disclosed under FRS3:

- profits or losses on the sale or termination of part of the business

- costs of a fundamental reorganisation or restructuring

- profits or losses on the disposal of fixed assets

Finally, there must be disclosed any *extraordinary items* – large, one-off transactions which are outside normal trading activities.

The objective of these requirements is to give more information to users and to encourage them to seek a deeper understanding of the accounts.

balance sheet

The Companies Act 1985 sets out the standard formats for balance sheets. The example below is presented in the layout most commonly used. As with the profit and loss account, extra detail is often shown in the notes to the balance sheet.

	£000s	£000s
XYZ PLC		
Balance sheet		
as at 31 December 20-1		
Fixed assets		
Intangible assets (eg goodwill)		50
Tangible assets (eg buildings, machinery)		3,750
Investments		1,000
		4,800
Current assets		
Stock	900	
Debtors	1,300	
Bank/cash	100	
	2,300	
Current liabilities		
Creditors	(800)	
Working capital		1,500
		6,300
Less Long-term liabilities		
Bank loan		1,500
NET ASSETS		4,800
FINANCED BY		
Capital and reserves		
Called up share capital		2,800
Reserves		1,200
Profit and loss account		800
SHAREHOLDERS' FUNDS		4,800

The notes to the balance sheet must include:
- fixed assets: cost, depreciation to date, net book value
- when fixed assets have been revalued, the date of revaluation and valuation amount
- investments: current market value and book value
- stock: where appropriate, amounts of raw materials, work in progress and finished goods
- creditors: amount payable within one year shown as a current liability
- creditors: amount payable in more than one year shown as a long-term liability, details to include repayment terms, interest rates, and security, if any given
- share capital, showing authorised and issued share capital and giving details of number of shares, nominal values (eg 25p, 50p, £1), and types of shares (ordinary, preference)
- reserves: details and movements on reserves

Fig 11.2 shows a balance sheet for The Body Shop International PLC.

Balance Sheets

as at 2 March 1996

	Note	Group 2 March 1996 £m	Group 25 February 1995 £m	Company 2 March 1996 £m	Company 25 February 1995 £m
Fixed assets					
Intangible assets	12	0.7	2.2	0.7	2.2
Tangible assets	13	78.2	73.6	51.2	50.5
Investments	14	0.5	0.5	13.0	13.0
		79.4	76.3	64.9	65.7
Current assets					
Stocks	15	37.6	38.6	20.3	21.1
Debtors	16	44.0	44.5	64.4	52.5
Cash at bank and in hand		30.1	29.0	24.9	24.3
		111.7	112.1	109.6	97.9
Creditors: amounts falling due within one year	17	49.1	51.2	32.7	41.1
Net current assets		62.6	60.9	76.9	56.8
Total assets less current liabilities		142.0	137.2	141.8	122.5
Creditors: amounts falling due after more than one year	18	17.7	23.7	0.1	0.7
Provisions for liabilities and charges					
Deferred tax	19	1.7	2.9	3.1	3.9
		122.6	110.6	138.6	117.9
Capital and reserves					
Called up share capital	20	9.5	9.5	9.5	9.5
Share premium account	21	37.2	37.0	37.2	37.0
Profit and loss account	21	75.9	64.1	91.9	71.4
		122.6	110.6	138.6	117.9

These financial statements were approved by the Board on 8 May 1996 and signed on its behalf by:

TG Roddick
Director

Fig 11.2 Balance Sheet of The Body Shop International PLC
(note that both the 'group' and 'company' balance sheets are shown – see also page 113)

cash flow statements

All but the smaller limited companies must include, as part of their published accounts, a cash flow statement, which we described in detail in Chapter 10. Such a statement shows where the funds (money) have come from during the course of a financial year, and how such funds have been used. The statement also provides a direct link between the previous year's balance sheet and the current one. The Cash Flow Statement of The Body Shop International PLC is shown in Fig. 11.3 on the next page.

Consolidated Cash Flow Statement

for the 53 weeks ended 2 March 1996

	Note	1996 (53 weeks) £m	1996 (53 weeks) £m	1995 (52 weeks) £m	1995 (52 weeks) £m
Net cash inflow from operating activities	22a		45.1		41.6
Returns on investments and servicing of finance					
Interest received		1.4		1.4	
Interest paid		(2.4)		(2.4)	
Dividends paid		(4.9)		(4.1)	
Net cash outflow from returns on investments and servicing of finance			(5.9)		(5.1)
Taxation					
UK corporation tax paid		(11.3)		(9.9)	
Overseas tax paid		(0.5)		(0.2)	
Tax paid			(11.8)		(10.1)
Investing activities					
Purchase of tangible fixed assets		(15.2)		(16.4)	
Purchase of external investments		–		(0.5)	
Goodwill acquired		(4.2)		(2.0)	
Sale of tangible fixed assets		0.5		0.1	
Disposal of subsidiary undertaking	22b	–		0.3	
Net cash outflow from investing activities			(18.9)		(18.5)
Net cash inflow before financing			8.5		7.9
Financing					
Issue of ordinary share capital		0.2		1.4	
Other loans		–		(2.0)	
Loan repayments		(6.7)		(1.7)	
Capital element of finance lease rental payments		–		(0.1)	
Net cash outflow from financing	22c		(6.5)		(2.4)
Increase in cash and cash equivalents	22d		2.0		5.5

Fig 11.3 Cash Flow Statement of The Body Shop International PLC

directors' report

The directors' report must contain details of the following:
- review of the activities of the company over the past year and in the future
- directors' names and their shareholdings
- proposed dividends
- transfers to reserves
- significant changes in fixed assets
- political and charitable contributions
- policy on employment of disabled people
- health and safety at work of employees

auditors' report

Larger companies must have their accounts audited by external auditors, who are appointed by the shareholders to check the accounts. The audit report, which is printed in the published accounts, is the culmination of their work. The three main sections of the auditors' report are:
- *respective responsibilities of directors and auditors,* ie the directors are responsible for preparing the accounts, while the auditors are responsible for forming an opinion on the accounts
- *basis of opinion*, ie the framework of Auditing Standards (issued by the Auditing Practices Board) within which the audit was conducted, other assessments, and the way in which the audit was planned and performed
- *opinion*, ie the auditors' view of the company's accounts

An *'unqualified'* auditors' opinion will read as follows:

> *"In our opinion the financial statements give a true and fair view of the state of affairs of the Company at .... 20.., and of the profit, and cash flows of the Company for the year then ended, and have been properly prepared in accordance with the Companies Act 1985."*

A *qualified* auditors' report will raise points that the auditors consider have not been dealt with correctly in the accounts. Where such points are not too serious, the auditors will use phrases such as "except for ...." or "subject to .... the financial statements give a true and fair view." Much more serious is where the auditors' statement says that the accounts "do not show a true and fair view" or "we are unable to form an opinion ....".

These indicate a major disagreement between the company and the auditors, and a person involved with the company – such as an investor or a creditor - should take serious note.

Note that companies are exempt from audit requirements if their turnover (sales) for the year is below a certain figure (£350,000 at the time of writing).

accounting policies

Accounting policies are the specific accounting bases that the directors of a company choose to follow; for example, whether to depreciate fixed assets using the straight-line method or the reducing balance method, and at what rate. Companies include a statement of their accounting policies in the published accounts. Fig 11.4 on the next page shows an extract from the accounting policies of The Body Shop International PLC.

Notes to the Accounts
for the 53 weeks ended 2 March 1996

Accounting policies

The financial statements have been prepared under the historical cost convention and in accordance with applicable accounting standards. The Company has taken advantage of the exemption from presenting its own profit and loss account.

Accounts are prepared to the Saturday nearest to the end of February in each year. On that basis the 1996 Accounts are for a 53 week period ended 2 March 1996 and the 1995 Accounts were for a 52 week period ended 25 February 1995. The principal accounting policies, which have not changed in the year, are:

Basis of consolidation   The consolidated accounts incorporate the financial statements of The Body Shop International PLC and all of its subsidiary undertakings made up to 2 March 1996. The Group uses the acquisition method of accounting to consolidate the results of subsidiary undertakings and the results of subsidiary undertakings are included from the date of acquisition to the date of disposal. The holding company's accounting policies have been applied consistently in dealing with items which are considered material in relation to the consolidated accounts.

Goodwill   Goodwill arising on the acquisition of a subsidiary or business is the difference between the consideration paid and the fair value of the assets and liabilities acquired. Goodwill is written off immediately to reserves.

Valuation of investments   Investments held as fixed assets are stated at cost less any provision for a permanent diminution in value.

Depreciation   Depreciation is provided to write off the cost, less estimated residual values, of all tangible fixed assets, except for freehold land, over their expected useful lives.

It is calculated using the following rates:
Freehold buildings   – Over 50 years
Leasehold property   – Over the period of the respective leases
Plant and equipment – Over 3 to 10 years.

Intangible fixed assets   The intangible fixed assets represent industrial property rights and "know how" and are amortised through the profit and loss account over four years, being the Directors' estimate of their useful economic lives.

Stocks   Stocks are valued at the lower of cost and net realisable value. Cost is calculated as follows:

Raw materials	– Cost of purchase on a first-in first-out basis
Work in progress and finished goods	– Cost of raw materials and labour together with attributable overheads.

Net realisable value is based on estimated selling price less further costs to completion and disposal.

Fig 11.4 Extract from the Accounting Policies of The Body Shop International PLC

accounting standards

A number of *accounting standards* have been produced to provide the rules, or framework, of accounting. The intention has been to reduce the variety of alternative accounting treatments. At present the rules of accounting are represented by:
- Statements of Standard Accounting Practice
- Financial Reporting Standards

Statements of Standard Accounting Practice
Statements of Standard Accounting Practice – or SSAPs as they are more usually known – are issued by the Accounting Standards Board. This Board requires accountants to observe the applicable accounting standards, and to disclose and explain significant departures from the

standards. A number of SSAPs have been replaced by Financial Reporting Standards (see below) as part of an attempt to reduce the number of permissable accounting treatments.

An example of a Statement of Standard Accounting Practice is SSAP2 'Disclosure of accounting policies', which includes the four accounting concepts (see page 52) which apply to all final accounts, and are given legal force to company accounts by the Companies Act.

Financial Reporting Standards (FRSs)

Financial Reporting Standards (FRSs) are issued by the Accounting Standards Board which wishes to ensure that standards are consistent, and that there are few options allowed in the preparation of final accounts. Examples of FRSs include FRS1 'Cash Flow Statements' (see below and Chapter 10) and FRS3 'Reporting Financial Performance' (see page 107).

statutory support for accounting standards

The Companies Act 1989 requires that limited company accounts must state that they have been prepared in accordance with applicable accounting standards and, if there have been any material departures, must give details and the reasons for such departures.

To enforce this part of the Act, the Secretary of State for Trade and Industry, and other authorised bodies (principally the Financial Reporting Review Panel) are able to apply to the courts for an order requiring the directors of the company to make revisions to defective accounts.

consolidated accounts

Over the last twenty or thirty years many companies have been taken over by other companies to form groups. Each company within a group maintains its separate legal entity, and so a group of companies may take the following form:

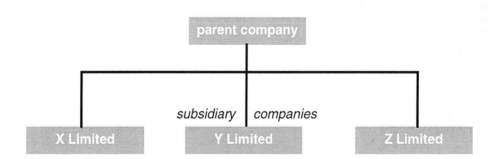

The Companies Act 1985 makes various provisions concerning groups of companies, including:

- A parent company and subsidiary company relationship exists where a parent company owns more than 50% of another company's share capital, or controls the composition of its board of directors.
- A parent company is required to produce group published accounts.
- Group accounts must include a consolidated profit and loss account and a consolidated balance sheet. (Such consolidated accounts are designed to show the position of the group as a whole to the outside world.)
- A parent company, which produces a consolidated profit and loss account, is not legally obliged to produce its own profit and loss account.

It is quite likely that, when you are studying a set of published accounts, you will find that you need to use the consolidated accounts for the group.

CHAPTER SUMMARY

❏ The Companies Act 1985 requires a considerable amount of detail to be disclosed in the published accounts of limited companies.

❏ The Acts require all limited companies to produce:
  • a profit and loss account
  • a balance sheet
  • a directors' report

❏ The Act lays down formats for profit and loss account and balance sheet.

❏ Besides the requirements of the Companies Acts, companies must also abide by the Statements of Standard Accounting Practice (SSAPs) and Financial Reporting Standards (FRSs) as laid down by the Accounting Standards Board.

❏ Many companies also include in their published accounts a cash flow statement which shows where the funds (money) has come from during the course of the financial year, and how it has been used.

❏ External auditors report to the shareholders on the state of affairs of the company.

❏ The directors establish the accounting policies which the company will follow.

❏ Consolidated accounts are prepared for groups of companies.

✍ STUDENT ACTIVITIES

11.1 The local College is running a day course for local business people, entitled 'Understanding Business Accounts'. A number of students, including yourself, have been invited to sit in on the lecture sessions. During the coffee break you overhear the following 'snippets' of conversation:

"I never bother with accruals and prepayments. It is money in and money out that matters."

"We have decided to change our depreciation method so that we show higher profits: that should impress the bank manager."

"I am going to have the factory revalued; that will help us to show a healthy profit for this year."

"We are likely to have some bad debts this year, but we won't show anything in the accounts because we are going to keep chasing the amounts due."

Later on you mention what you have heard to your tutor who then asks you what you think is the correct accounting treatment in each case. State your answer in each case.

11.2 Describe the main accounting statements required by the Companies Act to be produced by companies.

11.3 From a set of published company accounts, give an example of an unqualified auditors' report. What factors are likely to make the auditors qualify their report?

ASSIGNMENT

4 *Published accounts of public limited companies*

> ***covering***
> financial accounts of different organisations, cash flow statements, ratio analysis

SITUATION AND AIMS

Those who take financial decisions within a business need to understand the implications of their decision-making. They need to be aware of internal and external influences which affect the financial management of organizations.

This Assignment enables you to demonstrate an ability to study the financial reports of a public limited company, and to show an understanding of accounting conventions and methodology. It will also enable you to interpret the influences exerted by national and international economic policies and by political climates on an individual organization.

The assignment is designed for group work: two or three is the optimum size.

TASKS

1. Select a public limited company of your choice. (It is suggested that a fairly large plc is chosen, and one whose share price is listed in the 'Financial Times', or similar newspaper).

2. Obtain the latest set of published accounts. Many companies publish their year-end results in the financial pages of newspapers and, often, the address is given to which one can write to for accounts. Alternatively you can telephone the company for the accounts.

3. Monitor the plc chosen for a minimum period of one term; noting once per week the share price quoted on the Stock Exchange. Also make a note of one of the Stock Exchange indices quoted in the financial press. It is best to choose one of the FTSE 100 (Financial Times/Stock Exchange 100 top shares) known as the 'FOOTSIE'. Plot on separate graphs the share price and the chosen index in order to highlight any changes that take place over the period.

4.   During the period of this Assignment, study the financial press and other relevant publications for mention of the company; these may give reasons for changes in the company's share price and may also help you to assess changes in government policy, and international affairs, and how they have affected the organisation being studied.

Some of the major newspapers are now published on CD ROM which are often purchased by resource centres. You may be able to find useful data from these sources.

Prepare a summary of events relating to the chosen company and comment on significant influences which may have affected the company's performance and the share price's performance.

5.   From a study of the published accounts, extract the following information for the past two years:

Profit and loss account*
(a)   Turnover
(b)   Profit before tax
(c)   Earnings per share

Balance sheet*
(a)   Total of fixed assets
(b)   Total of current assets
(c)   Total of current liabilities (often shown as 'creditors: amounts falling due within one year')
(d)   Capital employed

Cash flow statement*
(a)   Total cash inflows for the year (noting any significant amounts)
(b)   Total cash outflows (noting any significant amounts)

Auditors' report (current year only)
(a)   Does it state that the accounts show a 'true and fair view'?
(b)   Are there any 'qualifications' to the report?

Accounting policies (current year only)
(a)   What method is used for valuing stocks?
(b)   What depreciation policies are used?

* if there is a choice, use the group (consolidated) figures

6.   Compile a report to be presented to your student group which incorporates tasks 1 - 5, and contains:

• An introduction to the selected plc; its structure, size, products, position in its own industry.

• A summary of share price movements over the period studied.

• The information extracted from the published accounts.

• A portfolio of your observations over the period assessing the influence of external factors on the selected plc and other significant developments.

3

cost and management accounting

12 COST ACCOUNTING AND MANUFACTURING ACCOUNTS

Most of the accounting that we have studied up until now has been concerned with *financial accounting*, which involves recording business transactions and providing the owners of the business with financial information about what has already happened. *Cost accounting*, by contrast, is concerned with helping the owners of the business to make financial decisions which will affect what the business does in the future, e.g.

- to manufacture more of one product than another
- to reduce selling prices
- to manufacture a new product
- to close one department or division of the business.

Closely linked to cost accounting is *management accounting* and, in practice, there is no clear dividing line between the two, except in larger businesses and organizations. Technically, the cost accountant is the person who obtains information about costs, e.g. unit costs of materials, labour, and overheads, which is then interpreted by the management accountant for the benefit of the owners of the business.

differences between financial accounting and cost accounting

Financial Accounting

Historical
Records past accounting transactions; covers previous year's trading; looks backwards.

For outsiders
Year-end accounts prepared for shareholders, creditors, bank, Inland Revenue, Registrar of Companies.

Outsiders make the rules
The Companies Act 1985 specifies the accounting information that must be prepared; also the Inland Revenue has requirements; the accountancy professional bodies agree Statements of Standard Accounting Practice.

A 'true and fair' view
Financial accounting is required to present a 'true and fair' view of the financial affairs of the business.

Cost (including Management) Accounting

Recent past and future
Performance reports containing financial information on recent past, and projections for future.

For insiders
Available only to managers, directors, and owners (but not to shareholders generally); may be made available to bank.

Insiders make the rules
The content of reports and the principles used can be suited to the activities of the business and the requirements of its managers.

A useful report
The requirement of cost and management accounting is to produce information that will enable the business to conduct its operations more effectively.

Timing
Generally there is little urgency to produce financial accounts; the statutory requirement is to prepare final accounts once a year.

Timing
Cost and management information is prepared as frequently as circumstances demand; speed is often vital as information may go out of date very quickly.

the manufacturing process

Cost accounting is certainly not confined to manufacturing businesses and many service industries, for example banks, make use of costing information in their decision-making. However, it is probably easier to see the usefulness of costing, in the first place, by considering the costs incurred by a manufacturer, as shown below.

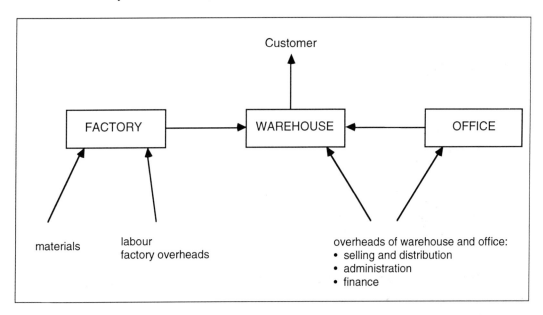

elements of cost

The diagram shown above indicates that there are *three* elements of total cost:

- materials
- labour
- expenses (broadly the overheads - see below)

This classification is only a starting point for the cost accountant and we must take each cost and categorise it into:

- *direct costs* - those costs that can be directly identified with each unit of production
- *indirect costs* - all other costs, i.e. those that cannot be identified with each unit of production

The elements of cost now appear as:

MATERIALS
- **Direct**: materials from which the finished product is made.
- **Indirect**: other materials used in the factory, e.g. grease for machines, cleaning materials, etc.

LABOUR

Direct: wages paid to those who work the machinery on the production line or who are involved in assembly of the product.

Indirect: wages and salaries paid to those who are not directly involved in production, e.g. supervisors, maintenance staff, etc.

EXPENSES

Direct: expenses which can be attributed to units of production, e.g. royalties payable to the designer of a product, special items bought in for a particular product.

Indirect: other expenses, such as rent, rates, telephone, lighting, heating, etc., which cannot be attributed directly to production.

case problem: identifying the costs

Severn Manufacturing Co. Ltd. makes chairs for school and college use. The chairs have plastic seats, and tubular steel legs. The firm's cost accountant asks you to help her classify the manufacturing costs into:

- direct materials
- indirect materials
- direct labour
- indirect labour
- direct expenses
- indirect expenses

The costs to be classified are:

COST	CLASSIFICATION (write your answer here)
(a) Tubular steel	
(b) Factory foreman's salary	
(c) Wages of employee operating the moulding machine which produces the chair seats	
(d) Works canteen assistant's wages	
(e) Rates of factory	
(f) Power to operate machines	
(g) Factory heating and lighting	
(h) Plastic for making chair seats	
(i) Hire of special machinery for one particular order	
(j) Cost of oil for the moulding machine	
(k) Rent of administrative office	
(l) Depreciation of factory machinery	
(m) Depreciation of office equipment	

Answers:
(a) direct materials, (b) indirect labour, (c) direct labour, (d) indirect labour, (e) indirect expenses, (f) indirect expenses, (g) indirect expenses, (h) direct materials, (i) direct expenses, (j) indirect materials, (k) indirect expenses, (l) indirect expenses, (m) indirect expenses.

Note: In the above, the cost of power to operate machinery was classified as an indirect expense. This is often the case because it is not worthwhile for the cost accountant to analyse the cost of power for each unit of production. An industry that uses a lot of power might well have meters fitted to each machine so that costs can be identified. Other, lesser users of power, are unlikely to calculate the separate cost and will consider power to be an indirect expense.

overheads

The indirect costs of materials, labour and expenses form the *overheads* of the business:

indirect materials + indirect labour + indirect expenses = total overheads

The overheads are subdivided amongst the main sections of the business, commonly:

- Factory, or production, overheads
- Selling and distribution overheads
- Administration overheads
- Finance overheads

Other headings can be used to suit the needs of a particular business.

manufacturing account

For cost accounting purposes, a statement of manufacturing costs is used which takes the following form:

	Direct materials
Add	Direct labour
Add	Direct expenses
Equals	PRIME COST
Add	Factory overheads
Equals	PRODUCTION COST
Add	Selling and distribution costs ⎤
Add	Administration costs ├── Office overheads
Add	Finance costs ⎦
Equals	TOTAL COST
	Sales
Less	Total cost
Equals	NET PROFIT

This format is used to prepare:

- *manufacturing account,* which shows production cost
- *trading account,* which shows gross profit
- *profit and loss account,* which shows net profit, after allowing for office overheads, including finance costs.

The layout of a manufacturing, trading, and profit and loss account (with sample figures for Severn Manufacturing Co. Ltd.) is as follows:

Manufacturing, trading, and profit and loss accounts for the year ended 31 December 20-1

	£	£
Opening stock of raw materials		5 000
Add Purchases of raw materials		50,000
		55,000
Less Closing stock of raw materials		6,000
COST OF RAW MATERIALS USED		49,000
Direct labour		26,000
Direct expenses		2,500
PRIME COST		77,500
Factory overheads		
Indirect materials	2,000	
Indirect labour	16,000	
Rent of factory	5,000	
Depreciation of factory machinery	10,000	
Factory light and heat	4,000	
		37,000
		114,500
Add Opening stock of work-in-progress		4,000
		118,500
Less Closing stock of work-in-progress		3,000
PRODUCTION COST OF GOODS COMPLETED		115,500
Sales		195,500
Opening stock of finished goods	6,500	
Production cost of goods completed	115,500	
	122,000	
Less Closing stock of finished goods	7,500	
COST OF GOODS SOLD		114,500
GROSS PROFIT		81,000
Office overheads		
Selling and distribution costs	38,500	
Administration costs	32,000	
Finance costs	3,500	
		74,000
NET PROFIT		7,000

Points to note:
- Gross profit is calculated as: *SALES - COST OF GOODS SOLD = GROSS PROFIT*
- A manufacturing business, at any one time, usually has stock in three different forms:
  raw materials, work-in-progress (or partly manufactured goods), finished goods
  The closing valuation of each of these must be included in the firm's balance sheet at the year-end.

nature of costs

It is important in cost accounting to appreciate the nature of costs and, in particular, to appreciate that not all costs increase or decrease directly in line with production increases or decreases. Certain costs are *fixed;* others are *variable,* while others are *semi-variable.*

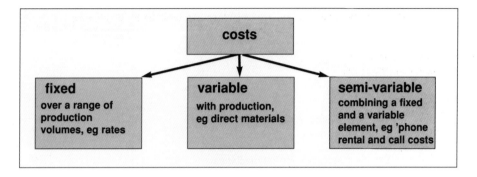

We shall see in Chapter 15, *Break-Even; Marginal and Absorption Costing,* how a knowledge of the nature of costs can help in decision-making.

CHAPTER SUMMARY

❑   The role of the financial accountant is rather different from that of the cost or management accountant: the former is concerned with recording past transactions, while the latter produces financial information to help the managers of a business in their decision-making.

❑   For manufacturing businesses there are three elements of total cost:

- materials
- labour
- expenses

Each of these can be *direct* or *indirect..*

❑   The total of all the indirect costs is known as *overhead:*   this is divided amongst the main sections of the business, commonly:

- factory (or production)
- selling and distribution
- administration
- finance

❑   The manufacturing account brings together all the elements of cost which make up production cost; the trading and profit and loss accounts deal with warehouse and office costs.

The next two Chapters look more closely at material costs, labour costs, and overheads, while later chapters in this section of the book investigate the role of cost accounting as an aid to management decision-making.

✍ STUDENT ACTIVITIES

12.1   Eveshore Pottery Co. Ltd. manufactures a range of 'souvenir' mugs, cups and saucers, plates, etc., which sell well to visitors from abroad who are seeking a reminder of 'Olde England'. A number of different costs have been incurred during the last month, and you are asked to assist the cost accountant by classifying them into:

(1)	Direct materials
(2)	Indirect materials
(3)	Direct labour
(4)	Indirect labour
(5)	Direct expenses
(6)	Indirect expenses

The costs are:

(a)	Cleaning materials for the machines
(b)	Wages of factory foreman
(c)	Clay from which the 'pots' are made
(d)	5p royalties payable to the designer for each 'Eveshore Plate' made
(e)	Salary of office typist
(f)	Electricity used to heat the kilns
(g)	Rates of factory
(h)	Depreciation of office typewriters
(i)	Wages of production-line workers
(j)	Salesman's salary
(k)	Interest charged on bank overdraft

Of the overhead costs, i.e. indirect materials, indirect labour, and indirect expenses, you are to indicate which would be:

- Factory overheads
- Selling and distribution overheads
- Administration overheads
- Finance overheads

12.2   The following figures relate to the accounts of Hughes Ltd., a manufacturing business, for the year ended 31 December 20-1:

	£
Stocks of raw materials at 1 January 20-1	15,930
Stocks of raw materials at 31 December 20-1	22,395
Stocks of work-in-progress at 1 January 20-1	6,250
Stocks of work-in-progress at 31 December 20-1	6,980
Stocks of finished goods at 1 January 20-1	21,320
Stocks of finished goods at 31 December 20-1	48,255
Purchases of raw materials	118,830
Sales of finished goods	398,475
Rent and rates	16,460
Manufacturing wages	117,315
Manufacturing power	3,825
Manufacturing heat and light	1,185
Manufacturing expenses and maintenance	4,095
Salaries and wages	69,350
Advertising	11,085
Office expenses	3,930
Depreciation of plant and machinery	3,725

One-half of 'salaries and wages' and three-quarters of the 'rent and rates' are to be treated as a manufacturing charge.

You are to prepare manufacturing, trading and profit and loss accounts for the year to show clearly :

(1) prime cost
(2) production cost of goods completed
(3) cost of goods sold
(4) gross profit for the year
(5) net profit for the year

12.3 From the following figures, which relate to Martley Manufacturing Ltd. for the year-ended 31 December 20-1, prepare accounts in such a form as to show clearly:

(a) cost of raw materials used
(b) prime cost
(c) production cost of goods completed
(d) cost of goods sold
(e) gross profit
(f) net profit

	£
Stocks at beginning of year:	
Raw materials	105,000
Work-in-progress	24,000
Finished goods	43,000
Stocks at end of year:	
Raw materials	102,000
Work-in-progress	29,000
Finished goods	32,000
Expenditure during year:	
Purchases of raw materials	272,000
Direct factory wages	126,000
Rent and rates	12,000
Factory power	20,000
Depreciation of factory machinery	9,000
Repairs to factory buildings	3,000
Sundry factory expenses	9,000
Indirect wages and salaries	84,000
Advertising	38,000
Office expenses	31,000
Depreciation of office equipment	7,500
Sales during year	704,000

Additional information:

(a) indirect wages and salaries owing at year-end £4,000
(b) office expenses prepaid at year-end £2,000
(c) one-half of indirect wages and salaries to be treated as a manufacturing charge
(d) three-quarters of rent and rates to be treated as a manufacturing charge

12.4 The following figures relate to John Smith's manufacturing business for the year ended 31 March 20-7:

	£
Capital	184,440
Light and heat	16,500
Manufacturing wages	99,010
Bank overdraft	50,870
Drawings	15,500
Office salaries	21,160
Royalties (paid to owners of patents)	42,930
Advertising	8,560
Stocks (1 April 20-6):	
Raw materials	71,020
Finished goods	72,780
Commission paid to salesman	18,100
Premises (at cost)	58,750
Machinery and plant (cost £125,000)	76,000
Sales	715,800
Debtors	75,000
Provision for bad debts	2,000
Office Machinery (cost £10,000)	5,000
Rates	1,700
Creditors	78,330
Purchases of raw materials	449,430

You are also given the following information at 31 March 20-7:

(1) Stocks: raw materials £70,640.
finished goods £74,480.

(2) Light and heat is to be apportioned two-thirds to the factory, one-third to the office.

(3) Rates are to be divided equally between factory and office.

(4) The provision for bad debts is to be maintained at 4% of debtors.

(5) Salaries due but unpaid amount to £490.

(6) Depreciation: machinery and plant - 15% on reducing balance.
office equipment - 10% on cost.

You are to prepare:

1. Accounts for the year ended 31 March 20-7 to show clearly:
   (a) Prime cost
   (b) Production cost of goods completed
   (c) Cost of goods sold
   (d) Gross profit
   (e) Net profit

2. Balance sheet at 31 March 20-7.

12.5 The following balances have been extracted from the accounting system of Eresham Manufacturing Co. Ltd. and relate to the year-ended 31 December 20-3:

	£
Share capital (£1 ordinary shares)	410,000
Retained profits at 1 January 20-3	24,650
10% Debentures	100,000
Freehold premises at cost	425,000
Factory machinery at cost	250,000
Office equipment at cost	45,000
Depreciation on factory machinery to 31 December 20-2	68,500
Depreciation on office equipment to 31 December 20-2	17,500
Sales	824,500
Purchases of raw materials	326,250
Manufacturing wages	236,650
Factory rates and insurance	17,285
Office rates and insurance	6,390
Factory power	12,250
Office heating and lighting	2,755
Factory expenses	3,210
Office expenses	4,865
Bank interest	2,315
Office salaries	65,950
Debtors	84,690
Creditors	47,610
Bank overdraft	80,740
Stocks at 1 January 20-3:	
Raw materials	41,250
Work-in-progress	17,860
Finished goods	31,780

The following additional information is available:

(a) Debenture interest for the year has not yet been paid and is to be provided for.

(b) Depreciation on factory machinery and on office equipment is to be calculated at 10% per annum on cost.

(c) Provision is to be made for an ordinary share dividend of 10p per share.

(d) Office expenses owing at 31 December 20-3 amount to £375.

(e) Factory insurance prepaid at 31 December 20-3 amounts to £510.

(f) Stocks at 31 December 20-3 amount to:
Raw materials	47,680
Work-in-progress	24,310
Finished goods	30,620

You are to prepare:

1. Manufacturing, trading and profit and loss accounts for the year-ended 31 December 20-3.

2. Balance sheet at 31 December 20-3.

ASSIGNMENT

5 *Manufacturing accounts*

> *covering*
> final accounts of different organisations, performance indicators

SITUATION

You are a trainee accountant working for the Alpha Manufacturing Co Ltd. The company manufactures domestic electrical switches to a standard design. These are sold to wholesalers, retailers (including several large DIY superstores), and to the building trade. The company's offices and factory are located in Wolverhampton.

The following list of balances has been extracted by the book-keeper from the accounting system and relates to the year which has just ended on 31 December 20-2:

	£
Share capital, fully paid (£1 ordinary shares)	350,000
8% Debentures	100,000
Freehold premises at valuation	550,000
Machinery at cost	120,000
Office equipment at cost	33,000
Depreciation on machinery to 31 December 20-1	68,000
Depreciation on office equipment to 31 December 20-1	8,700
Sales	841,500
Purchases of raw materials	260,150
Manufacturing wages	335,310
Factory fuel and power	68,715
Factory rates and insurance	32,175
Sundry factory expenses	21,065
Office rates and insurance	15,210
Office expenses	20,385
Office salaries	104,860
Bank interest	5,210
Debenture interest	8,000
Bank overdraft	89,425
Debtors	20,285
Creditors	17,865

	£
Retained profits to 31 December 20-1	65,795
Property revaluation reserve	150,000
Stocks at 1 January 20-2:	
raw materials	50,655
work-in-progress	19,725
finished goods	26,540

The following additional information has been provided by the book-keeper:

(a) Depreciation on machinery, and on office equipment is calculated at 10% per annum on cost.

(b) At 31 December 20-2, factory rates and insurance paid in advance amount to £450.

(c) At 31 December 20-2, office expenses owing amount to £150.

(d) Stocks at 31 December 20-2 were valued as follows:
 raw materials £46,835
 work-in-progress £21,740
 finished goods £30,280

(e) The directors are proposing that no dividend on the ordinary shares will be paid for the year, because poor results are expected.

The number of switches produced during the year was 487,180.

The management of Alpha Manufacturing Co Ltd is expecting that the company will have produced poor financial results during the past year. They are of the opinion that the problem lies in the factory which is equipped with old machinery. One of the accounts staff has been given the task of investigating two possible courses of action:

• To replace the old machinery with up-to-date, computer controlled equipment manufactured in Germany. The new equipment will cost £750,000, but the factory workforce will be reduced from 65 to 25 employees. With this course of action the factory cost per switch is calculated to be £1.10.

• To close down the factory, and make all the factory workforce redundant. Manufacture will be sub-contracted to a factory in Taiwan which will supply switches at a delivered price of £1.15 each. If this course of action is taken, the factory will be sold for an estimated £350,000, but the part of the site which contains the offices and warehouse will be retained. There will be no effect on the number of staff employed in the office.

TASKS

1. You are required to prepare manufacturing, trading, profit and loss accounts, and an appropriation account for the year-ended 31 December 20-2. A balance sheet is also to be prepared at the above date.

2. You are to help your colleague who is investigating the future of the company. He asks you to prepare the part of the report that assesses the social and economic implications of both decisions. In particular, you should identify the costs and revenues (both to the company and the local community) that will change with the proposed courses of action. (You can assume such other information as is necessary for the completion of this Task; detailed accounting calculations are not needed.)

13 ACCOUNTING FOR MATERIALS AND LABOUR

"How much did that cost?" An easy question to answer, it would seem. For a business though, it is not that easy to answer. For example, supposing a shop bought in 100 tins of baked beans at a cost of 25p each; a week later another 100 tins are purchased but the price has increased to 30p a tin. They are identical tins and, if you now ask the question, "How much did this particular tin cost?" the reply will be "it depends." It depends on how the business has chosen to account for its stocks. This Chapter will look at three main methods of accounting for stocks of materials: FIFO, LIFO and AVCO.

Also in the Chapter we will look at a number of ways in which labour can be remunerated, so as to link output with costs.

stock valuation

At the end of a financial year, a business must value its stocks of materials so that the closing stock figure can be entered in the accounts.

The usual method of stock valuation is at the lower of cost and net realizable value.

This definition is taken from Statement of Standard Accounting Practice No 9, entitled 'Stocks and long-term contracts'. Using this method of stock valuation, two different values have to be examined - *cost,* and *net realizable value,* i.e. the amount the stock will sell for. The lower of these two values is taken, and *different items or categories of stock are compared separately.*

Case Problem: Clothing Extra Limited

This shop bought in a range of 'designer' beachwear in the Spring, with each item costing £15 and retailing for £30. Most of the stock is sold but, by Autumn, ten items remain unsold. These are put onto the 'bargain rail' at £18 each. On 31 December, at the end of the shop's financial year, five items remain unsold. At what price will they be included in the year-end stock valuation?

Answer: They will be valued at cost of £15 each, ie 5 x £15 = £75.

Twelve months later three items still remain unsold, and have just been further reduced to £10 each. At what price will they now be valued in the year-end stock valuation?

Answer: they will now be valued at net realizable value of £10 each, i.e. 3 x £10 = £30.

Important Note: Stock is *never* valued at selling price when selling price is above cost price. The reason for this is that selling price includes profit, and to value stock in this way would bring the profit into the accounts before it has been earned.

Case Problem: Smith & Jones (Paints & Wallpapers) Limited

The year-end stocks for the two main categories of stock of this business are found to be:

	Cost	Net Realizable Value
	£	£
Paints	1,250	1,150
Wallpapers	2,500	3,750
	3,750	4,900

Which of the following valuations do you think is correct?
- (a) £3,750
- (b) £4,900
- (c) £3,650
- (d) £5,000

Answer:
Stock valuation (c) is correct, because it has taken the 'lower of cost and net realizable value' for each *category* of stock, ie

Paints (at net realizable value)	£1,150
Wallpapers (at cost)	£2,500
	£3,650

You will also note that this valuation is the lowest of the four possible choices, indicating that stock valuation follows the *prudence (conservatism) concept* (see Chapter 6) of accounting.

commonly used stock valuation methods

As we saw at the very beginning of this chapter, calculating the cost of stock of materials can be a more involved process than at first appears. There are three commonly used methods of recording and valuing stock; these are:

FIFO (first in, first out) This method assumes that the first stocks acquired are the first to be disposed of, so that the valuation of stock on hand at any time consists of the most recently acquired stock.

LIFO (last in, first out) Here it is assumed that the last stocks acquired are the first to be used, so that the stock on hand is made up of earlier purchases.

AVCO (average cost) Here the average cost of items held at the beginning of the period is calculated; as new stocks are acquired a new average cost is calculated (usually based on a weighted average, using the number of units acquired as the weighting).

These methods are used to ascertain:

- the price at which materials are to be issued to the production department;
- the year-end valuation of stocks.

The use of a particular method does not necessarily correspond with the method of physical distribution adopted in a firm's stores. For example, in a car factory one starter motor of type X is the same as another, and no-one will be concerned if the storekeeper issues one from the last batch received, even if the FIFO system has been adopted. However, perishable goods are always physically handled on the basis of first in, first out, even if the accounting stock records use another method.

Having chosen a suitable stock valuation method, a business would continue to use that method unless there were good reasons for making the change. This is in line with the *consistency concept* of accounting.

Case Problem: The Corner Stores

Let us go back to the situation of the shop buying tins of baked beans which we considered at the very beginning of this Chapter. Let us suppose that:

Week 1:   100 tins of beans bought at a cost of 25p per tin
            50 tins sold at 40p per tin

Week 2:   100 tins of beans bought at a cost of 30p per tin
            75 tins sold at 40p per tin

What will the stock valuation be at the end of week 2, using
- FIFO
- LIFO
- AVCO
and what gross profit has been made on beans over the two week period?

Answer:
At the end of week 2 there are 75 tins of beans in stock.

FIFO
Using FIFO, the week 2 closing stock consists of 75 tins at the
latest price, i.e. 30p. Therefore the stock valuation is 75 x 30p   = £22.50

LIFO
With LIFO the closing stock consists of:

50 tins from week 1 at 25p each	= £12.50
25 tins from week 2 at 30p each	= £ 7.50
75	= £20.00

AVCO
We must calculate the average cost as follows:

50 tins in stock at end of week 1 at 25p	= £12.50
100 tins received in week 2 at 30p	= £30.00
150 tins at an average cost of 28.33p (£42.50 ÷ 150)	= £42.50
75 tins sold in week 2	= £21.25
75 tins at 28.33p each	= £21.25

The conclusion here is that, even with tins of baked beans, there is a difference in closing stock valuation depending on the method used:

FIFO	£22.50
LIFO	£20.00
AVCO	£21.25

From these results we can draw a general conclusion that, in times of rising prices, FIFO always gives the highest valuation, LIFO the lowest, and AVCO comes somewhere between the two (although not necessarily exactly half-way between the two).

You may be saying to yourself, "Why spend so much time on looking at different stock valuation methods?" The answer to this is that the method adopted for stock valuation is important because of the effect it has on the profits of the business. Let us now see how much profit this business made on its sales of baked beans:

Trading account (baked beans) for the two weeks ended ....

		£
Sales: 50 tins at 40p		20.00
75 tins at 40p		30.00
		50.00

	FIFO	LIFO	AVCO
	£	£	£
Purchases: 100 tins at 25p	25.00	25.00	25.00
100 tins at 30p	30.00	30.00	30.00
	55.00	55.00	55.00
Less closing stock	22.50	20.00	21.25
COST OF GOODS SOLD	32.50	35.00	33.75
GROSS PROFIT	17.50	15.00	16.25
	50.00	50.00	50.00

As a result of using different stock valuations, the gross profit is different, with FIFO giving the highest profit, LIFO the lowest, and AVCO between the two. Do not forget, also, that the closing stock for one accounting period becomes the opening stock for the next, and so the following accounting period will also be affected.

a suitable stock valuation record

In order to be able to calculate accurately the price at which stocks of materials are issued to production, and to ascertain quickly a valuation of closing stock, the following method of recording stock data is suggested.

DATE	RECEIPTS		ISSUES		BALANCE		
20..	Quantity	Price	Quantity	Price*	Quantity	Price	Total

* Note that this price is the cost price to the business, not the selling price - virtually all stock records are kept at cost price.

Case Problem: Stock Records

In order to show how the stock records would appear under FIFO, LIFO and AVCO, the following data has been used for each:

20-1

January	Bought 40 units at a cost of £3.00 each
February	Bought 20 units at a cost of £3.60 each
March	Used 36 units in production
April	Bought 20 units at a cost of £3.75 each
May	Used 25 units in production

Answers:

FIFO

Date	Receipts			Issues			Balance			
20-1	Quantity		Price	Quantity		Price	Quantity		Price	Total
January	40	@	£3.00				40	x	£3.00 =	£120.00
February	20	@	£3.60				40	x	£3.00 =	£120.00
							20	x	£3.60 =	£72.00
							60			£192.00
March				36	@	£3.00	4	x	£3.00 =	£12.00
							20	x	£3.60 =	£72.00
							24			£84.00
April	20	@	£3.75				4	x	£3.00 =	£12.00
							20	x	£3.60 =	£72.00
							20	x	£3.75 =	£75.00
							44			£159.00
May				4	@	£3.00				
				20	@	£3.60				
				1	@	£3.75	19	x	£3.75 =	£71.25

LIFO

Date	Receipts			Issues			Balance			
20-1	Quantity		Price	Quantity		Price	Quantity		Price	Total
January	40	@	£3.00				40	x	£3.00 =	£120.00
February	20	@	£3.60				40	x	£3.00 =	£120.00
							20	x	£3.60 =	£72.00
							60			£192.00
March				20	@	£3.60				
				16	@	£3.00	24	x	£3.00 =	£72.00
April	20	@	£3.75				24	x	£3.00 =	£72.00
							20	x	£3.75 =	£75.00
							44			£147.00
May				20	@	£3.75				
				5	@	£3.00	19	x	£3.00 =	£57.00

AVCO

Date	Receipts			Issues			Balance			
20-1	Quantity		Price	Quantity		Price	Quantity		Price	Total
January	40	@	£3.00				40	x	£3.00 =	£120.00
February	20	@	£3.60				40	x	£3.00	= £120.00
							20	x	£3.60	= £72.00
							60	x	£3.20	= £192.00
March				36	@	£3.20	24	x	£3.20	= £76.80
April	20	@	£3.75				24	x	£3.20	= £76.80
							20	x	£3.75	= £75.00
							44	x	£3.45	= £151.80
May				25	@	£3.45	19	x	£3.45	= £65.55

The closing stock valuations at the end of May under each method are:
FIFO   £71.25
LIFO   £57.00
AVCO £65.55

There is quite a difference, and only because different stock methods have been used.

advantages and disadvantages of FIFO, LIFO and AVCO

FIFO (first in, first out)
Advantages:
- realistic, i.e. it assumes that goods are issued in order of receipt;
- it is easy to calculate;
- stock valuation comprises actual prices at which items have been bought;
- it is an acceptable stock valuation under Statement of Standard Accounting Practice No 9;
- the closing stock valuation is close to the most recent prices.

Disadvantages:
- prices at which goods are issued to production are not necessarily the latest prices;
- in times of rising prices, profits will be higher than with other methods.

LIFO (last in, first out)
Advantages:
- goods are issued to production at the latest prices;
- it is easy to calculate.

Disadvantages:
- illogical, i.e. it assumes goods are issued in reverse order from that in which they are received;
- the closing stock valuation is not usually at most recent prices;
- not recommended under SSAP 9 and not normally acceptable in the UK for tax purposes;
- when stocks are being run down, issues will 'dip into' old stock at out-of-date prices.

AVCO (average cost)

Advantages:
* over a number of accounting periods reported profits are smoothed, i.e. both high and low profits are avoided;
* fluctuations in purchase price are evened out so that issues to production do not vary greatly;
* logical, i.e. it assumes that identical units, even when purchased at different times, have the same value;
* acceptable under SSAP 9;
* closing stock valuation is close to current market values (in times of rising prices, it will be below current market values).

Disadvantages:
* difficult to calculate, and calculations may be to several decimal places;
* issues and stock valuation are usually at prices which never existed;
* issues may not be at current prices and, in times of rising prices, will be below current prices.

labour costs

We shall now look at ways in which the direct labour of a business can be remunerated. You will remember from Chapter 12 that the direct labour cost is the wages paid to those who work the machinery on the production line, or who are involved in assembly of the product.

There are three main ways in which direct labour can be remunerated:

1. Time-rate, where the employee is paid on the basis of time spent at work.
2. Piecework rate, where the employee is paid a certain sum for each unit of production completed, or on which is carried out his or her task.
3. Bonus systems, under which the employee is paid a time rate and then receives a bonus if output beyond a certain level is achieved within a set time. Such systems are often referred to as a measured day rate.

Note: Most other employees, e.g. factory supervisors, office staff, etc, are usually paid on the basis of a weekly or monthly wage, which may be increased by bonus payments, e.g. salespersons' commission, production bonus for factory supervisors, profit-sharing schemes etc.

There are many variations on these three methods and it is not our place to go into these in great detail: a book on industrial relations, or on personnel would give further information. The case problem which follows indicates how each of the three methods mentioned can be applied.

Case Problem: ABC Manufacturing Co.

The ABC Manufacturing Co. has three factories in the West Midlands making parts for the car industry. Each factory was bought as a going-concern business from the previous owners and, as a result, each factory has a different method for remunerating its direct labour workforce. The details of the method of remuneration in each factory, together with data on two employees from each factory, is as follows:

Factory A

In this factory, which is involved in heavy engineering, employees are paid on the basis of a time-rate. Employees are required to 'clock in' and 'clock out' each day.

John Brown is a machine operator and his clock card for last week shows that he worked 39 hours; his hourly rate of pay is £8 per hour.
Stefan Wozniak is a skilled lathe operator and his clock card shows that he worked 42 hours; his hourly rate of pay is £10 per hour, with overtime for hours worked beyond 40 hours at 'time-and-a-half'.

Factory B

This factory operates a number of light engineering production lines making such car components as windscreen wiper blades, headlamp surrounds, radiator grilles etc. The production line employees are all paid on a piecework basis; however, each employee receives a guaranteed time-rate which is paid if the piecework earnings are less than the time-rate. (This may happen if, for example, there are machine breakdowns and the production line has to be halted.)

Tracey Johnson works on the line making headlamp surrounds. For each one that passes through her part of the process, she is paid 20p; her guaranteed time-rate is 37 hours each week at £4 per hour. Last week's production records show that she processed 870 units.

Pete Bronyah is on the line which makes radiator grilles. For his part of the process he receives 50p for each one, with a guaranteed time rate of 37 hours at £5 per hour. Last week there was a machine failure and he was only able to process 300 units.

Factory C

In this factory a number of skilled engineering production lines are operated. The direct labour force is paid on a time-rate basis, but a bonus is paid if a set amount of work can be completed faster. Thus a time allowance is given for each task and, if it can be completed in less time, a bonus is paid: the bonus in this factory is to share equally the savings achieved between employee and employer. Wages are, therefore, paid on the following basis: time rate + 50% of (time saved x time-rate). If no bonus is due, then the time-rate applies.

Martin Lee worked a 38 hour work last week; his time rate is £10 per hour. He is allowed a time of 30 minutes to carry out his work on each unit of production; last week he completed 71 units.

Henry King has a time rate of £11 per hour; last week he worked 40 hours. He is allowed a time of 15 minutes to carry out his work on each unit of production; last week he completed 184 units.

What were the gross earnings of each employee?

Answer:

Factory A

John Brown:	39 hours x £8.00 per hour	= £312.00
Stefan Wozniak:	40 hours x £10.00 per hour = £400	
	2 hours x £15.00 per hour = £ 30	= £430.00

Factory B

Tracey Johnson: Piecework rate, 870 units x 20p per unit = £174.00
Guaranteed time-rate, 37 hours x £4.00 per hour = £128.00
Therefore piecework rate of £174.00 is paid.

Pete Bronyah: Piecework rate, 300 units x 50p per unit = £150.00
Guaranteed time-rate, 37 hours x £5.00 per hour = £185.00
Therefore guaranteed time-rate of £185.00 is paid.

Factory C

Martin Lee: Time-rate, 38 hours x £10.00 per hour = £380.00
Bonus, time allowed 71 units x 30 minutes each = 35 hours 30 minutes
Therefore no time saved, so no bonus payable.
Time-rate of £380 paid.

Henry King: Time-rate, 40 hours x £11.00 per hour = £440.00
Bonus, time allowed 184 x 15 minutes each = 46 hours
Therefore time saved is 6 hours
Bonus is 50% of (6 hours x £11.00) = £33.00
Therefore wages are £440.00 + £33.00 = £473.00

The above case problem illustrates some of the labour remuneration methods in use, and it should be appreciated that there are many variations on these to be found.

advantages and disadvantages to a business of different labour remuneration methods

Time-Rate

Advantages:
- easy to understand and to calculate;
- the employee receives a regular wage, unaffected by production fluctuations;
- can be used for all direct labour employees;
- quality of the finished produce does not suffer as a result of rushed work.

Disadvantages:
- both efficient and inefficient employees receive the same wage;
- no incentive is given to employees to work harder;
- slower working will not affect basic wage, but may lead to overtime;
- more supervisors will be needed to ensure that production is maintained.

Piecework Rate

Advantages:
- payment of wages is directly linked to output;
- the more efficient workers earn more than those who are less efficient;
- work is done quicker and less time is wasted.

Disadvantages:
- not suitable for all direct labour employees;
- pay will be reduced if there is a machine breakdown or a shortage of raw materials (this can be overcome if there is a guaranteed time-rate);
- quality of the finished product may be low;
- more inspectors may be needed;
- control systems needed to check the amount produced by each worker;
- more complex pay calculations;
- may be difficulty in agreeing piecework rates with unions.

Bonus Systems

Advantages:
- wages linked to output, but minimum wage is guaranteed each week;
- work is done quicker and less time is wasted;
- more efficient workers earn more;
- a bonus system can often be applied to the entire workforce.

Disadvantages:
- bonus will not be paid if circumstances beyond employee's control prevent work, e.g. machine breakdown, shortage of raw materials;
- quality of finished product may be low;
- more inspectors may be needed;
- control procedures needed/more complex pay calculations;
- may be difficulty in agreeing bonus rates with unions.

CHAPTER SUMMARY

❏ The usual valuation for stock is *at the lower of cost and net realizable value* (SSAP9).

❏ Common methods of accounting for stock include:
FIFO (first in, first out)
LIFO (last in, first out)
AVCO (average cost, based on a weighted average)

❏ Common methods of remunerating direct labour include:
Time-rate
Piecework rate
Bonus systems

❏ Time-rate wages are *hours worked* x *rate per hour*.

❏ Piecework rate wages are *units produced* x *rate per unit*. (Often with piecework rate there is a minimum guaranteed time rate.)

❏ Bonus systems are added to the time rate. One common method of calculating a bonus is *50% of (time saved* x *time rate)*.

In this Chapter we have looked at two of the main elements of cost, i.e. materials and labour; in the next Chapter we shall look at the third element, overheads, and see how this is charged to the units produced.

✍ STUDENT ACTIVITIES

13.1 A business buys twenty units of a product in January at a cost of £3 each; it buys ten more in February at £3.50 each, and ten in April at £4 each. Eight units are sold in March, and sixteen are sold in May. Calculate the value of closing stock at the end of May using:
(a) FIFO, (b) AVCO, (c) LIFO.
(Where appropriate, work to two decimal places).

13.2 XY Ltd. is formed on 1 January 20-1 and, at the end of its first half-year of trading, the stock record cards show the following

20-1	TYPE X		TYPE Y	
	Receipts (units)	Issues (units)	Receipts (units)	Issues (units)
January	100 @ £4.00		200 @ £10.00	
February		80	100 @ £9.50	
March	140 @ £4.20			
				240
April	100 @ £3.80		100 @ £10.50	
May		140	140 @ £10.00	
June	80 @ £4.50			
				100

At 30 June 20-1, the net realizable value of each type of stock is:

type X	£1,750
type Y	£1,950
	£3,700

You are to:

(a)   Calculate the value of closing stock at 30 June 20-1 using (a) FIFO, (b) AVCO, (c) LIFO. (Where appropriate, work to two decimal places.)

(b)   The business has decided to use the FIFO method. Show the amount at which stock should be valued in the balance sheet at 30 June 20-1 in order to conform with accepted accountancy practice.

13.3   Leep Ltd. was incorporated in December 20-3 to trade in a single produce called 'Peel'. The company began trading on 1 January 20-4. Purchases and sales for the five years to 31 December 20-8 when the company discontinued 'Peel' in favour of a more profitable line, were as follows:

	PURCHASES			SALES	
	Units	Price per unit		Units	Price per unit
		£			£
20-4	100	400	80	500	
20-5	100	450	80	550	
20-6	100	500	80	600	
20-7	100	550	80	650	
20-8	-	-	80	700	

You are to:

(a)   Use the FIFO basis in order to calculate the gross profit of Leep Ltd for each of the five years to 31 December 20-8.

(b)   Use the LIFO basis in order to calculate the gross profit for each of the five years to 31 December 20-8.

(c)   Compare the results of your calculations and consider the relative merits of FIFO and LIFO as bases for valuing stock during a period of inflation.

13.4   Your friend, Gerry Gallagher, has recently set up in business selling plastic toys. The transactions for his first month of trading are:

1 April	Bought 500 toys at £1.50 each
3 April	Sold 250 toys at £2.50 each
7 April	Bought 1,000 toys at £1.40 each
14 April	Sold 600 toys at £2.60 each
20 April	Sold 300 toys at £2.70 each
27 April	Bought 1,000 toys at £1.60 each

At the end of April he asks you to help him to value his closing stock. He has heard that other firms in the toy trade value their stock on one of three methods: FIFO, LIFO or AVCO. He asks you to do the calculations for him, and also to work out his gross profit using each stock valuation method. He comments that he "will use the stock valuation that gives the highest profit" because he wants to impress his bank manager.

You are to:

(a)   Calculate his closing stock valuation using each of the three methods.

(b)   Calculate the gross profit for the month, using each method.

(c)   Respond to his comment.

13.5   A manufacturing business pays its production workers on a time-rate basis. A bonus is paid where production is completed faster than the time allowed; the bonus is paid at half of the time-rate for production time saved. How much will each of the following employees earn for the week?

Employee	Time-rate	Hours worked	Time allowed	Actual production (minutes per unit)
N. Ball	£8.00 per hour	35	2 mins per unit	1,010 units
T. Smith	£9.00 per hour	37	1.5 mins per unit	1,560 units
L. Lewis	£10.00 per hour	40	3 mins per unit	855 units
M. Wilson	£7.00 per hour	38	2.5 mins per unit	940 units

13.6   Harrison & Co. is a manufacturing business. Currently it pays its production workers on a time-rate basis. Recently the union representatives have approached the management of the company with a view to seeking alternative methods of remuneration. Suggestions have been made that either a piecework system, or a time-rate with a production bonus system would be more appropriate.

You have been asked to draft a memorandum to the management giving advantages and disadvantages of:

- time-rate
- piecework
- time-rate, plus production bonus

as methods of remunerating production-line employees. In particular, you are asked to describe two circumstances under which the piecework basis would not be in the interests of employees.

13.7   (a)   A company pays its production-line employees on a piecework basis, but with a guaranteed time-rate. How much will each of the following employees earn during the week?

Employee	Time-rate	Hours worked	Production	Piecework rate
L. Fry	£10.00 per hour	40	1,200 units	30p per unit
R. Williams	£8.00 per hour	37	450 units	70p per unit
P. Grant	£9.50 per hour	36	725 units	50p per unit

(b)   What are the problems a company might face in operating a piecework system of remuneration?

14 OVERHEAD COSTS

In the previous Chapter, we looked at direct materials and direct labour - two of the three main elements of cost. Both direct materials and direct labour can be charged directly to the product in which they are involved, e.g. the materials used for making product 'A' are charged directly in the costing to that product. However, overheads cannot be charged directly to particular units of production but must, instead, be shared between all units to which they relate.

In this Chapter we shall look at ways in which overheads are charged to production, and some of the problems that may occur. Firstly though, there are two costing terms to define: *cost units* and *cost centres.*

cost units

Cost units are units of production to which costs can be charged .

Thus a cost unit can be a *unit of production,* such as a car, an item of furniture, a television, etc, or it can be a *unit of service,* such as a passenger-mile on a bus, a transaction on a bank statement, an attendance at a swimming pool, etc.

cost centres

Cost centres are sections of a business to which costs can be charged.

For example, a cost centre in a manufacturing business, is a particular department of a factory, even a whole factory, or a particular stage in the production process.

a classification of overheads

With overheads the important point to remember is that all the overheads of a business, together with the direct costs of materials and labour, must be covered by money flowing in from sales made. For example, a business makes a product which sells for £20 per unit, and the cost of direct materials is £5 and direct labour is £6.50. Taking the cost of direct materials and direct labour from the selling price gives:

$$£20 - (£5 + £6.50) = £8.50$$

The £8.50 from each unit sold is a *contribution* to covering the overheads and providing a profit for the owner(s) of the business. In other words, sufficient units have to be sold to produce a total contribution to meet the total overheads of the business and to contribute to the profits of the business. We shall look further at this concept of contribution in the next Chapter, when it will be used to help in calculating the break-even point of a business.

Overheads are usually classified *by function* under headings such as:

* *factory or production,* e.g. factory rent and rates, indirect labour, indirect materials, heating and lighting of factory
* *selling and distribution,* e.g. salesmen's salaries, packing costs, vehicle costs
* *administration,* e.g. office rent and rates, office salaries, heating and lighting of office
* *finance,* e.g. bank interest, discount allowed

In order to determine how much has been spent on overheads, it will be necessary to use the financial accounting records: for example, the expenses accounts will show the amount for rent, rates, salaries, wages, heating, lighting, vehicle costs, etc. Some figures, such as those for wages, and for purchases, will need to be analysed to see which part of the total cost is a direct expense (to be charged directly to the appropriate cost units), and which is the indirect expense (to be charged to overheads).

Once the various overheads have been classified, they are then either *allocated* or *apportioned* to cost centres.

allocation of overheads

Allocation of overheads is the charging to a cost centre of those overheads that have been directly incurred by that cost centre.

For example, in a large organization a whole factory might be a cost centre and so the rent and rates of that factory will be allocated to it as a separate cost centre. Another example would be where a department is the cost centre; here the costs of a supervisor working solely within one department would be allocated to that department.

apportionment of overheads

Apportionment is where cost centres are charged with a proportion of overheads.

For example, a department which is a cost centre within a factory will be charged a proportion of the factory rent and rates. Another example is where a supervisor works within two departments, both of which are separate cost centres: the indirect labour cost of employing the supervisor will be charged between the two cost centres.

With apportionment, a suitable basis must be found to apportion overheads between cost centres. Different methods might be used for each overhead.

Case Problem: Laser Engineering

A friend of yours, Natalie Wood, has recently established a 'hi-tech' engineering business which uses some of the latest laser equipment in one department, while another section of the business continues to use traditional machinery. You have been helping her with various aspects of the business and she now asks you which overheads of the business should be allocated or apportioned. Details of the factory are as follows:

> *Department A* is a 'hi-tech' machine shop equipped with machinery which has cost £40,000. This department has 400 square metres of floor area. There are three machine operators supervised by the foreman who spends one-third of his time in this department.

> *Department B* is a 'low-tech' part of the factory equipped with machinery which has cost £10,000. The floor area is 600 square metres. There are two workers who spend all their time in this department, supervised by the foreman for two-thirds of his time.

The overheads to be allocated or apportioned are as follows:

1.	Factory rates	£12,000
2.	Wages of the foreman	£15,000
3.	Factory heating and lighting	£2,500
4.	Depreciation of machinery	£10,000
5.	Buildings insurance	£2,000
6.	Insurance of machinery	£1,500
7.	Specialist materials for the laser equipment	£2,500

How would you suggest each of these should be allocated or apportioned to each department?

Answer

The recommendations are:
1. Factory rates - apportioned on the basis of floor area, i.e. 40% to Department A, and 60% to Department B.
2. Foreman's wages - apportioned on the basis of time spent, i.e. one-third to Department A, and two-thirds to Department B. If the time spent was not known, a suitable basis would be the number of employees.
3. Factory heating and lighting - apportioned on the basis of floor area.
4. Depreciation of machinery - apportioned on the basis of machine value, ie four-fifths to Department A, and one-fifth to Department B.
5. Buildings insurance - apportioned on the basis of floor area.
6. Insurance of machinery - apportioned on the basis of machine value.
7. Specialist materials for the laser equipment - allocated to Department A, the cost centre which directly incurred the cost.

It is important to note that there are no fixed rules for the apportionment of overheads - the only proviso is that the basis used should be equitable, i.e that a fair proportion of the overhead is charged to the department.

The apportionment for Laser Engineering would take place as follows:

Cost	Basis of apportionment	Total £	Dept A £	Dept B £
Factory rates	Floor area	12,000	4,800	7,200
Wages of foreman	Time spent	15,000	5,000	10,000
Heating and lighting	Floor area	2,500	1,000	1,500
Dep'n of machinery	Machine value	10,000	8,000	2,000
Buildings insurance	Floor area	2,000	800	1,200
Machinery insurance	Machine value	1,500	1,200	300
Specialist materials	Allocation	2,500	2,500	-
		45,500	23,300	22,200

service departments

Many factories have service departments, such as stores, maintenance, transport, etc. Each service department is likely to be a cost centre, to which a proportion of overheads is charged. As service departments do not themselves have any cost units to which their overheads may be charged, the costs of each service department must be *re-apportioned* to the production departments (which do have cost units to which overheads can be charged). A suitable basis of re-apportionment must be used; for example, the overheads of a maintenance department might be reapportioned to production departments on the basis of value of machinery, or on the basis of time spent in each production department; the overheads of a stores department might be re-apportioned on the basis of value of stores issued to production departments.

Fig. 14.1 summarises the ways in which production overheads are allocated or apportioned to production cost centres, and the way the service department's costs are re-apportioned.

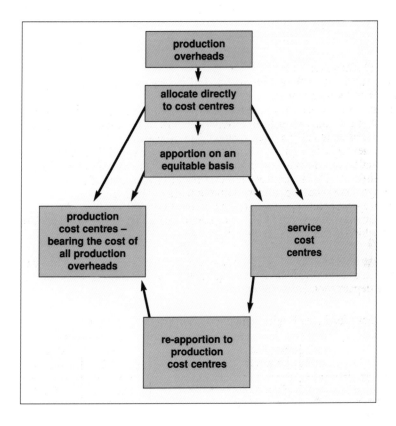

Fig. 14.1 Allocation and apportionment of production overheads

overhead absorption

Once overheads have been allocated or apportioned to production cost centres, the final step is to ensure that the overheads are changed to cost units. In the language of costing this is known as *absorption* ie the cost of overheads is charged to cost units which pass through that particular production department.

There are plenty of examples of overhead recovery in everyday life - it is not something used solely by large factories. For example, if you take a car to be repaired at a garage, the bill will be presented as follows:

Parts	£35.50
Labour: 3 hours at £30 per hour	£90.00
Total	£125.50

Within this example bill are the three main elements of cost: materials (parts), labour and overheads. The last two are combined as labour - the garage mechanic is not paid £30 per hour; instead the labour rate might be £10 per hour, with the rest, ie £20 per hour, being a contribution towards the overheads of the garage. Other examples are accountants, solicitors, etc who charge a 'rate per hour', part of which is used to contribute to the cost of overheads.

In order to absorb the overheads of a department, there are two steps to be followed:

1.   Calculation of the overhead absorption rate.
2.   Application of this rate to cost units.

Although there is a variety of methods available to a business, three commonly used overhead absorption methods are:

- units of output
- direct labour hour
- machine hour

units of output

Using this method overhead is absorbed on the basis of each unit of output.

1.   Calculation of the overhead absorption rate:

$$\frac{total\ cost\ centre\ overheads}{total\ cost\ units}$$

2.   Application of the rate:

cost units x overhead absorption rate

Example
Department A   total cost centre overheads for year   £50,000 expected
                          total output for year   20,000 units
                          output in March   1,500 units

1. Overhead absorption rate:
   $\frac{£50,000}{20,000}$ = £2.50 per unit

2. Application of the rate:
   1,500 x £2.50 = £3,750 of overhead absorbed in March

direct labour hour

With this method, overhead is absorbed on the basis of the number of direct labour hours worked.

1.   Calculation of the overhead absorption rate:

$$\frac{total\ cost\ centre\ overheads}{total\ direct\ labour\ hours\ (in\ cost\ centre)}$$

2.   Application of the rate:

direct labour hours worked x overhead absorption rate

Example

Department B	total cost centre overheads for year	£20,000
	expected direct labour for year	5,000
	actual direct labour hours in March	450

1. Overhead absorption rate:

$$\frac{£20,000}{5,000} = £4 \text{ per direct labour hour}$$

2. Application of the rate:

    450 hours x £4 = £1,800 of overhead absorbed in March

machine hour

Here the overhead is absorbed on the basis of machine hours.

1. **Calculation of the overhead absorption rate:**

    $$\frac{total\ cost\ centre\ overheads}{total\ machine\ hours\ (in\ cost\ centre)}$$

2. **Application of the Rate:**

    cost units x overhead absorption rate

Example

Department C	total cost centre overheads for year	£108,000
	expected machine hours for year	36,000
	actual machine hours in March	3,500

1. Overhead absorption rate:

$$\frac{£108,000}{36,000} = £3 \text{ per machine hour}$$

2. Application of the rate:

    3,500 hours x £3 = £10,500 of overhead absorbed in March

which method to use?

Only one overhead absorption rate will be used in a particular department and management must choose the method that suits their particular business.

Where units of production are identical, e.g. in mass production factories, the units of output method is appropriate. However, it would be entirely unsuitable where different types and sizes of products pass through the same department, because each unit would be charged the same rate.

The direct labour hour method is a very popular method (e.g. the garage mentioned earlier) because overheads are absorbed on a time basis. Thus the cost unit that requires twice the direct labour of another cost unit will be charged twice the overhead. However this method will be inappropriate where some units are worked on by hand while others quickly pass through a machinery process and require little direct labour time.

A machine hour rate is very appropriate where expensive machinery is used in the department. However, it would not be a suitable method where not all products pass through the machine but some are worked on by hand: in this case, no overheads would be charged to the cost units.

pre-determined overhead rates

Overhead absorption rates are *set in advance* by making forecasts of production and costs. The making of forecasts is known as *budgeting,* and this topic is discussed fully in Chapter 18. It is quite likely that actual overhead absorbed will be different from the estimates made at the beginning of the year. Thus overhead will either be *under-absorbed,* or *over-absorbed;* under-absorption means that less overhead has been recovered than has been incurred; over-absorption means that more overhead has been recovered than incurred.

Example

Department D	overhead absorption rate (based on units of output)	£3.00 per unit
	expected total output for year	6,000 units
	actual output in year	6,300 units

* Total overheads for the department are 6,000 units x £3.00 per unit = £18,000
* Actual overhead absorbed: 6,300 units x £3.00 per unit = £18,900
* Over-absorption of overhead: £18,900 - £18,000 = £900

The management of a business will constantly monitor actual production and will seek reasons for variances between this and budgeted production. While over-absorption of overheads, on first impressions, seems to be a 'bonus' for a business - profits will be higher - it should also be remembered that, perhaps, the overheads have been set too high. As a consequence, sales might have been lost because the selling price has been too high.

CHAPTER SUMMARY

❑ Cost units are units of production to which costs can be charged.

❑ Cost centres are sections of a business to which costs can be charged.

❑ Direct costs, such as materials and labour, are charged directly to cost units.

❑ Overheads are allocated to cost centres that have directly incurred the overhead.

❑ Overheads are apportioned between cost centres, using an equitable basis.

❑ Cost centre overheads are charged to cost units by methods which include units of output, direct labour hour and machine hour.

❑ The objective of overhead absorption is to ensure that overheads are recovered by the cost units which pass through the cost centre.

❑ With pre-determined overhead rates, there may be either under-absorption or over-absorption of overheads.

The next Chapter is concerned with the relationship between fixed and variable costs; it looks at how the nature of these costs can be used in break-even analysis, and in marginal costing, and in absorption costing.

✍ STUDENT ACTIVITIES

14.1 ABC Ltd. is a manufacturing business with three cost centres: Departments A, B and C. The following are the expected factory expenses for the forthcoming year:

Rent and rates	£7,210
Depreciation of machinery	£10,800
Supervisor's salary	£12,750
Insurance of machinery	£750

Departmental information is:

	Dept A	Dept B	Dept C
Floor area (sq. m)	300	150	250
Value of machinery	£25,000	£15,000	£10,000
Number of production-line employees	8	4	3

You are to:

(a) Apportion the expenses to the cost centres, stating the basis of apportionment.
(b) The factory works a 37 hour week for 48 weeks in a year. What is the overhead absorption rate (to two decimal places) of each department, based on direct labour hours?

14.2 Osborne Engineering Ltd. offers specialist engineering services to the car industry. It has two production departments - machinery and finishing - and a service department which maintains the machinery of both departments. Expected costs for the forthcoming year are:

	£
Rent and rates	2,760
Buildings insurance	660
Insurance of machinery	825
Lighting and heating	1,860
Depreciation of machinery	5,500
Supervisory salaries	15,000
Maintenance department salary	8,000
Factory cleaning	2,400

The following information is available:

	Machinery	Finishing	Maintenance
Floor area (square metres)	300	200	100
Number of employees	6	3	1
Value of machinery	£20,000	£7,500	-

The factory works a 40-hour week for 47 weeks each year.

You are to:

(a) Prepare an analysis of overheads showing the basis of apportionment and allocation to the three departments of the business.
(b) Re-allocate the service department overheads to production departments on the basis of value of machinery.
(c) Calculate an overhead absorption rate based on direct labour hours for each of the two production departments.

14.3 Messrs. Rossiter and Rossiter is a firm of chartered accountants, with two partners. Overhead costs for next year are estimated to be:

Office rent	£5,000
Secretarial salaries	£15,000
Rates	£2,400
Heating and lighting	£1,200
Stationery	£1,000
Postages and telephone	£2,550
Car expenses	£2,800

The two partners plan to work for 47 weeks next year. They will each be in the office for 40 hours per week, but will be working on behalf of their clients for 35 hours per week.

(a)   What is the overhead absorption rate per partner hour?

(b)   If each partner wishes to earn a salary of £20,000 per year, what is the combined rate, which includes overheads and their salaries?

(c)   If both partners actually work on their clients' behalf for 37 hours per week, what will be the total over-recovery of overheads for the year?

14.4 Steel Forgings (Worcester) Ltd. is a heavy engineering business making parts for the car industry. The factory works a 40 hour week and is divided into three manufacturing divisions, with each making a different type of forging. Details are as follows:

	Division 1	*Division 2*	*Division 3*
Cost of 1 tonne of raw materials	£65	£70	£75
Number of direct workers	5	4	6
Time rate (per hour)	£5.50	£6.00	£6.50
Labour hours required to output 1 tonne of finished goods	8 hours	10 hours	12 hours
Power costs per tonne of finished goods	£15	£18	£14

Factory overhead	£1,500 per week (to be apportioned between divisions on the basis of number of direct workers).
Administration overheads	£1,000 per week.
Selling costs	£750 per week.

Selling prices are established by marking up the factory cost by 50%.

You are to:

(a) Calculate the gross profit per week for each division.

(b) Calculate the net profit per week for the company as a whole.

14.5   A friend of yours is about to start in business making garden seats. She plans to make two different qualities - 'standard' and 'de luxe'. Costs per unit for raw materials and direct labour are expected to be:

	'Standard'	'De Luxe'
Direct materials	£12.50	£20.00
Direct labour:		
6 hours at £4.00 per hour	£24.00	-
7 hours at £5.00 per hour	-	£35.00
	£36.50	£55.00
Machine hours	2	5

Factory overheads are expected to be £1,000 per month.

Production (per month) is expected to be 80 'standard' seats and 40 'de luxe' seats.

You are to:

(a)   Suggest three different methods in which overheads can be absorbed.

(b)   Calculate the factory cost of each of the two qualities of garden seats using the three different methods of overhead absorption.

(c)   Compare the results of your calculations and suggest to your friend the most appropriate method of overhead absorption for this business.

15 BREAK-EVEN; MARGINAL AND ABSORPTION COSTING

This chapter looks at the relationship between *fixed costs* and *variable costs*. The nature of these costs is important in the determination of break-even analysis, and in two techniques known as *marginal costing* and *absorption costing*. These last two costing techniques are beneficial in helping a business to determine its pricing policy.

fixed and variable costs

We have seen in earlier chapters that the main costs for a manufacturing business are:

- raw materials
- labour
- overhead

In costing there is the division between *fixed costs* and *variable costs*. Fixed costs remain constant despite other changes; variable costs alter with changed circumstances, such as increases in production or sales. However, these 'rules' are only true within certain, restricted limits. For example, rent is usually regarded as a fixed cost; however a rapidly expanding business will soon reach the point at which more premises are needed and then rent, and other costs will increase. In the short-term, though, it is correct to classify costs between those that are fixed and those that are variable. In manufacturing, raw materials and direct labour are usually considered to be variable costs, while indirect labour is a fixed cost; overheads can be partly fixed, and partly variable.

break-even point

The point at which a firm makes neither a profit nor a loss is known as the break-even point (b.e.p.).

The break-even point of a business can be found:

- either by calculation,
- or by graph.

By calculation

$$\frac{\textit{Total fixed costs (£)}}{\textit{Contribution per unit (£)}} = \textit{Break-even point (number of units)}$$

Note: contribution per unit = selling price minus variable costs per unit

By graph

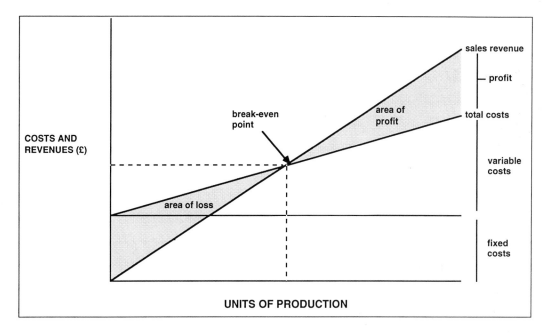

Note the following points:

- the vertical axis (the 'y' axis) shows money amounts; the horizontal axis ('x') shows the number of units produced.
- the fixed costs are unchanged at all levels of production.
- the variable costs commence, on the 'y' axis, *from the fixed costs amount.*
- the fixed costs and the variable costs form a *total costs line.*
- the point at which the total costs and sales revenue lines cross is the *break-even point.*
- at production below the break-even point the business makes a loss, as measured by the area of loss; above break-even point, the amount of profit can be found by measuring the area of profit at a given production level.

Case Problem: break-even

A business manufactures soft toys, and is able to sell all that can be produced. The selling price of each toy is £25, while the variable costs (raw materials and direct labour) are £10. The fixed costs of running the business are £4,500 *each month.* How many toys need to be produced and sold each month for the business to break-even?
Current production is 400 toys each month; what is the profit?

Answer:

By calculation

Selling price per toy	£25
Less variable costs per unit	£10
Contribution per unit	£15

Each toy gives a contribution of £15; this contributes towards the fixed costs and, in order to break-even, the business must have sufficient £15 'lots' to meet the fixed costs. Thus:

$$\frac{£4\,500}{£15} = 300 \text{ toys to break-even.}$$

By graph

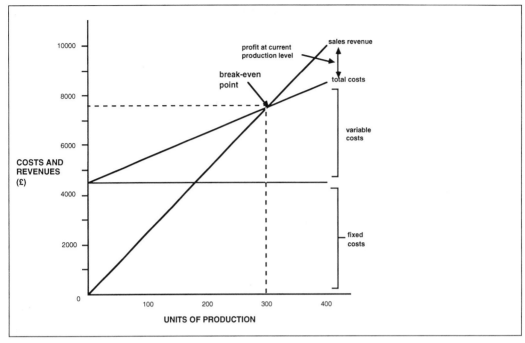

Current Production is 400 units each month. Thus 100 units are being made and sold beyond the break-even point. Profits are, therefore:

100 units x £15 contribution = <u>*£1,500 profit*</u>

This amount can also be read off the graph, as above.

limitations of a break-even graph

The problem of break-even analysis is that it assumes that the relationship between sales revenues, variable costs and fixed costs, remains the same at all levels of production. This is a rather simplistic view because, for example, in order to increase sales, a business will often need to offer bulk discounts, so reducing the sales revenue per unit at higher levels. The limitations of a break-even graph (and also break-even calculations) can be summarized as follows:

(a)   All costs and revenues are expressed in terms of straight lines. However, this is relationship is not always so. As indicated above selling prices may vary at different quantities sold; in a similar way, variable costs alter at different levels as a business takes advantage of lower prices to be gained from bulk buying, and/or more efficient production methods.

(b)   Fixed costs do not remain fixed at all levels of production: for example, a decision to double production is likely to increase the fixed costs.

(c)   It is not possible to *extrapolate* the graph; by extrapolation is meant extending the lines on the graph beyond the limits of the activity on which the graph is based. For example, in the Case Problem just considered, the graph cannot be extended to, say, 800 units of production and the profit read off at this point. The relationship between sales revenues and costs will be different at much higher levels of production.

(d)   The profit or loss shown by the graph or calculations is probably only true for figures close to current production levels - the further away from current figures, the less accurate will be the profit or loss shown.

(e)   A further disadvantage of break-even analysis is that it concentrates too much attention on the break-even point. While this aspect is important to a business, other considerations such as ensuring that production is as efficient as possible, and that costs are kept under review, are just as important.

break-even: margin of safety

The margin of safety is the amount by which sales exceed the break-even point. For example, in the Case Problem, current production was 400 units, while the break-even point was found to be 300 units. Thus the margin of safety is 100 units, or expressed as a percentage:

$$\frac{\textit{Production beyond b.e.p.}}{\textit{Units to break-even}} = \frac{100}{300} = 33.33\%$$

marginal costing and absorption costing

We have already seen in Chapter 14 that one of the objectives of a costing system is to ensure that all the costs of a business are recovered by being charged to production. Two different techniques are used in cost accounting as an aid to management decision-making:

1.   *Marginal costing*

     This technique recognizes that fixed costs vary with time rather than activity, and attempts to identify the cost of producing one extra unit. For example, the rent of a factory relates to a certain time period, e.g. one month, and remains unchanged whether 100 units are made or whether 500 units are made (always assuming that the capacity of the factory is at least 500 units); by contrast, the production of one extra unit will incur an increase in variable costs, i.e. direct materials and direct labour - this increase is the *marginal cost.*

2.   *Absorption costing*

     This technique absorbs all costs - both direct and indirect - into each unit of production. Thus each unit produced in the factory making 100 units will bear a greater proportion of the factory rent than will each unit when 500 units are made in the same time period.

Case Problem: Wyvern Bicycle Co.

The following monthly figures have been extracted by the cost accountant of the Wyvern Bicycle Co.:

Monthly manufacturing costs for producing 100 bicycles

	£
Direct materials (£20 per bicycle)	2,000
Direct labour (£25 per bicycle)	2,500
	4,500
Factory overheads	3,500
Total factory cost of producing 100 bicycles	8,000

The selling price is £100 per bicycle.

(a) What is the factory cost of producing one bicycle?
(b) A major retail store offers to buy
     either   50 bicycles each month at a price of £60,
     or   100 bicycles each month at a price of £40.

How would you advise the management? (It is to be assumed that these sales will be produced in addition to existing production, with no increase in fixed costs.)

Answer:

(a) The factory cost is:

    Absorption cost basis: £8,000 ÷ 100 units = £80 per bicycle

    Marginal cost basis: £20 (direct materials) + £25 (direct labour) = £45 per bicycle

(b) • Although below absorption cost, the offer is above marginal cost and increases profits by the extra contribution brought in, i.e. (£60 - £45) x 50 bicycles = £750 extra profit.

    • This is below absorption cost and below marginal cost; therefore, there will be a fall in profit if this order is undertaken of (£45 - £40) x 100 bicycles = £500 less profit.

Summary profit statements are as follows:

	Existing production	Existing production + 50 units @ £60 each	Existing production + 100 units @ £40each
	£	£	£
Sales revenue (per month):			
100 bicycles at £100 each	10,000	10,000	10,000
50 bicycles at £60 each	-	3,000	-
100 bicycles at £40 each	-	-	4,000
	10,000	13,000	14,000
Less production costs:			
Direct materials (£20 per unit)	2,000	3,000	4,000
Direct labour (£25 per unit)	2,500	3,750	5,000
Fixed factory overheads	3,500	3,500	3,500
GROSS PROFIT	2,000	2,750	1,500

The conclusion is that the first special order should be undertaken, and the second declined.

The general rule is that, once the fixed costs have been recovered, provided additional units can be sold at a price above marginal cost, then profits will increase.

marginal costing and absorption costing: profit comparisons

Because of the different ways in which marginal costing and absorption costing treat fixed costs, the two techniques produce different levels of profit when a business has a closing stock figure. This is because, under marginal cost, the closing stock is valued at variable cost (i.e. £45 per unit in the Case Problem above); by contrast, absorption cost includes a share of fixed costs in the closing stock valuation (i.e. £80 per unit).

We will now consider the effect of using marginal costing and absorption costing on the profit statement of a manufacturing business.

Case Problem: Chairs Ltd.

The company commenced business on 1 January 20-1; it manufactures a special type of chair designed to alleviate back pain. Information on the first year's trading is as follows:

Number of chairs manufactured	5,000
Number of chairs sold	4,500
Selling price	£50 per chair
Direct materials	£15 per chair
Direct labour	£20 per chair
Fixed manufacturing costs	£50,000

The directors enlist your help to produce profit statements using the marginal costing and absorption costing techniques. They say that they will use 'the one that shows the higher profit' to the company's bank manager.

Answer

CHAIRS LTD.
Profit statement for the year-ended 31 December 20-1

	MARGINAL COSTING		ABSORPTION COSTING	
	£	£	£	£
Sales		225,000		225,000
Variable costs				
Direct materials	75,000		75,000	
Direct labour	100,000		100,000	
	175,000			
Less closing stock (marginal cost)				
500 chairs at £35 each	17,500			
	157,500			
Fixed manufacturing costs	50,000		50,000	
			225,000	
Less closing stock (absorption cost)				
500 chairs at £45			22,500	
Less cost of goods sold		207,500		202,500
GROSS PROFIT		17,500		22,500

Notes:

- Closing stock is always calculated on the basis of this year's costs:
  marginal costing, variable costs only
  absorption costing, variable and fixed costs
  Thus, if closing stock is one-tenth of the units manufactured during the year (as in this Case Problem), then closing stock will be valued at one-tenth of the appropriate cost.

- Only fixed *manufacturing* costs are dealt with differently using the techniques of marginal and absorption costing - both methods charge general/administration expenses *in full* to the profit and loss account in the year to which they relate.

The reason for the difference in the profit figures is that, under marginal costing, the full amount of the fixed manufacturing costs has been charged in this year's profit statement; by contrast, under absorption costing, one-tenth of the fixed manufacturing cost (ie £5,000) has been carried forward in the stock valuation. However, with regard to the directors' statement that they will use 'the one that shows the higher profit', two points should be borne in mind:

- A higher profit does *not* mean more money in the bank.
- The two techniques simply allocate fixed manufacturing costs differently and, in a year when there is no closing stock, you will find that total profits *to date* are exactly the same - but they are allocated differently over the years.

pricing policy

We have already seen, earlier in this Chapter, the usefulness of identifying fixed and variable costs in order to make decisions on the price which is to be charged for the product. In particular, the pricing of 'special orders' at below absorption cost will increase profits provided the price quoted is above marginal cost, and that other 'full price' sales continue to be made.

In general terms there are three considerations that a business must bear in mind when establishing a pricing policy:

- establishing an acceptable return on capital
- understanding the relationship between fixed and variable costs
- knowing the price that the market will bear

Each of these cannot be considered independently, but needs to be taken into account.

Acceptable return on capital

It should be remembered that most businesses have the objective of giving a suitable return to the providers of capital. Investors will soon withdraw their funds if better investment opportunities appear elsewhere. Therefore, in pricing policy, a sufficiently high selling price should be established which provides an adequate return to investors. (In Chapter 19 we shall be looking at budgeted or forecast accounts, which show the estimated profit for a budgeted year's trading.)

Relationship between fixed and variable costs

We have already seen how 'special orders' can be priced at less than absorption cost (but always above marginal cost). Such special orders might be necessary in order to gain business but, in order to break-even, a business has to meet its fixed costs. To make a profit, the selling price needs to be set so that fixed costs are more than covered by the contribution from sales: any surplus contribution after fixed costs have been met, is profit.

We must also consider the different balances between fixed costs and variable costs. For example, it may be possible to carry out a manufacturing process in one of two different ways: the first might be labour intensive, but requiring a few inexpensive machines; the second might need costly machines, but few operators. Thus, with the first method, variable costs are high, but fixed costs are low; with the second method, variable costs are low, but fixed costs are high. The method that is chosen will depend on the costs involved and the likely demand and selling price of the product.

The price the market will bear

Unless a business manufactures a unique product for which there is considerable demand and on which it has sole manufacturing rights, it must set its prices in comparison with other manufacturers of the same or similar product. In a free economy buyers will purchase from the supplier than can produce the product at least cost. Thus, in an ideal world, inefficient producers will be forced out of the market and, in order to re-establish themselves, will have to look carefully at their costings and/or production techniques.

CHAPTER SUMMARY

❏   In break-even analysis it is essential to distinguish between fixed costs and variable costs.

❏   The relationship between fixed costs and variable costs can be used to calculate, or show by means of a graph, the break-even point.

❏   Break-even point is when a business makes neither a profit nor a loss.

❏   Marginal cost is the cost of producing one extra unit and, generally, comprises thE variable costs of production.

❏   Absorption cost is the total cost divided by the number of units produced.

❏   Marginal costing and absorption costing help a business with decision-making when faced with orders at 'special prices'.

❏   A firm's pricing policy depends on a number of factors, which include:
  • obtaining an acceptable return on capital
  • the relationship between fixed and variable costs
  • the price that the market will bear

The next Chapter continues the theme of costing by looking at two specialist techniques of cost collection: job costing and process costing.

STUDENT ACTIVITIES

15.1   Cuddly Toys Ltd. manufactures a popular children's teddy bear. At present production is limited by the capacity of the factory to 50 bears each week. The following information is available:

Wholesale price per teddy bear	£20
Raw materials per teddy bear	£4
Direct labour per teddy bear	£5
Weekly expenses	
• factory rent and rates	£100
• fuel and power	£20
• other costs	£34

You are to find the weekly break-even point by the graphical method, and check your answer by calculation.

15.2   Peter Parkinson is a central heating engineer who has designed a special type of thermostatic valve for use in heating systems. He has decided to set up in business to manufacture the product and he has carried out market research which suggests that demand for the product will be between 9,000 units and 20,000 units per annum. Accordingly he has produced the following estimated costs at different levels of production:

Budgeted sales (units)	9,000	12,000	15,000	20,000
Direct materials (£)	27,000	36,000	45,000	60,000
Direct labour (£)	9,000	12,000	15,000	20,000
Production overheads (£)	48,000	54,000	60,000	70,000
Administration, selling and distribution expenses (£)	18,000	18,000	18,000	18,000

Each thermostatic valve will sell for £10.

Peter asks you to help him interpret the results, and in particular he wishes to know:

(a)   The profit or loss he will make at each level of production
(b)   The break-even point
(c)   The fixed amount of production overheads

One market-research survey suggested that a level of sales of 25,000 units per annum might be achieved. Peter asks you to rework the budget at this level of production and to calculate the net profit or loss which will be achieved. He asks you to let him know of any limitations to the usefulness of your figures at this level.

15.3   The research department of Castlemayne Ltd., a design and engineering business, has recently developed a new type of electronic dispenser for serving exact quantities of beers and lagers. The company has taken the decision to manufacture the product but has not yet decided which one of two methods of manufacture should be used. Method 1 would involve the purchase of expensive computer-controlled machinery; method 2 would use more traditional machinery but would require more materials and direct labour. Details are as follows:

Method 1:   an investment of £240,000 would be required, made up of:

*   £200,000 of machinery with an estimated life of five years and a nil scrap value
*   £40,000 of working capital requirements

Fixed expenses (excluding depreciation) would amount to £60,000 per annum, and variable costs per unit would be £35.

Method 2:   an investment of £120,000 would be needed made up of

*   £80,000 of machinery with an estimated life of five years and a nil scrap value
*   £40,000 of working capital requirements

Fixed expenses (excluding depreciation) would amount to £29,000 per annum, and variable costs per unit would be £45.

The product is to be marketed at £60 per unit, and the maximum feasible production capacity under either method is 10,000 units per annum. The company depreciates plant on the straight-line basis. A target rate of return on capital invested of 20% is applied to all projects by the company.

As a cost clerk working for Castlemayne Ltd. you are to produce a report for the use of the management which shows:

(a)   Calculations of the number of units which must be produced and sold under either method each year in order to achieve a return of 20 per cent on the capital invested.

(b)   A discussion of the two alternative production methods, advising the particular circumstances under which one is preferable to the other.

Note: ignore taxation.

15.4 Radios Ltd. commenced business on 1 January 20-3. In the years 20-3 and 20-4 the company's production and sales were:

	20-3	20-4
Number of radios manufactured	11,000	10,000
Number of radios sold	9,000	11,000

In both years all sales were made at a constant price of £10 per radio. The company's manufacturing costs in the years 20-3 and 20-4 were:

	20-3	20-4
	£	£
Raw materials	14,300	13,000
Other variable costs	18,700	17,000
Fixed manufacturing costs	68,200	68,200

There were no stocks of raw materials of work-in-progress at the end of each year.

You are to:

(a) Calculate the gross profit or loss of Radios Ltd. for 20-3 and 20-4 using:
  * marginal costing
  * absorption costing

(b) Comment on the difference in the profit of the company using the two different costing techniques.

15.5 At the beginning of 20-1 Deer Ltd. was formed and manufactures a single product. At the end of the first year's operations the company's accountant prepared a draft profit and loss account which contained the following financial information.

Profit and Loss Account of Deer Ltd. for 20-1		
	£	£
Sales (200,000 units)		600,000
Less: Prime cost of units manufactured		
during 20-1 (500,000 units)	800,000	
Deduct closing stock	480,000	
Prime cost of goods sold	320,000	
Fixed costs:		
Factory expenses	200,000	
General expenses	100,000	620,000
Net loss		(20,000)

Additional finance is required, and the directors are worried that the company's bank manager is unlikely to regard the financial facts shown above as a satisfactory basis for a further advance. The company's accountant made the following observation and suggestion:

> *'The cause of the poor result for 20-1 was the decision to value closing stock on the marginal cost basis. An acceptable alternative practice would involve charging factory expenses to the total number of units produced and carrying forward an appropriate proportion of those expenses as part of the closing stock value.'*

You are to:

(a)   Prepare a revised profit and loss account, for presentation to the company's bank, valuing closing stock on the absorption cost basis suggested by the company's accountant.

(b)   Assuming that, in 20-2, the company again produces 500,000 units but sells 700,000 units, calculate the expected profit using each of the two stock valuation bases. Assume also that, in 20-2, sales price per unit and costs incurred will be the same as for 20-1.

(c)   Comment briefly on the accountant's suggestion and its likely effect on the bank manager's response to the request for additional finance.

15.6   The Last Co. Ltd. is famous for its 'Snowdon' range of hill-walking boots. The management of the company are considering the production for next year and have asked you, as cost clerk, to help with certain financial decisions.

The following information is available:

Wholesale selling price (per pair)	£30.00
Raw materials (per pair)	£7.50
Direct labour (per pair)	£5.50
Fixed costs	£150,000.00 p.a.

The company is planning to manufacture 12,500 pairs of boots next year.

(a)   You are asked to calculate:
  • the marginal cost per pair
  • the absorption cost per pair
  • the break-even point (in pairs of boots)
  • the profit or loss if 12,500 pairs of boots are sold

(b)   A mail order company, Salesbypost Ltd., has approached The Last Co. Ltd. with a view to selling the 'Snowdon' boot through its catalogue. Salesbypost Ltd. is prepared to guarantee to sell 2,500 pairs of boots each year but, in view of the large quantity, offers a price of £20 per pair. As The Last Co. Ltd. usually sells through specialist shops, it is not expected that 'normal' sales will be affected. This 'special order' is within the capacity of the factory, and fixed costs will remain unchanged. You are to advise the management as to whether this offer should be accepted.

(c)   A manufacturer in the Far East has offered to make the 'Snowdon' boot under licence at a price of £20 per pair up to 10,000 pairs, and then £15 per pair above this level. Quality is guaranteed and, if this option is taken, The Last Co. Ltd. would cease manufacturing and would act as distributors: as a result fixed costs would fall to £50,000 pa. You are to advise the company, in financial terms, if this offer should be taken up. Are there any other points, besides financial, that The Last Co. Ltd. should consider before making its decision?

16 JOB COSTING AND PROCESS COSTING

In Chapter 14 we have seen how overheads are apportioned or absorbed by units produced in the factory. In the previous Chapter we have seen that, when all the costs (materials, labour and overheads) are spread evenly over all the units produced, the result is an *absorption cost*. In this Chapter and the next we shall look at three absorption costing techniques that are commonly used by businesses to recover their overheads:

1. job costing,
2. process costing,
3. standard costing.

The first two are dealt with in this Chapter while standard costing is examined in Chapter 17.

The important point to remember in costing is that businesses must recover their overheads in the total price charged to their customers - this applies not only to manufacturing industry, but also to service industries, such as shops, banks, etc. Only when the full cost of overheads has been recovered can the business give thought to marginal costing techniques for the pricing of special orders.

job costing

Job costing is used where:

- each job can be separately identified from other jobs
- costs are charged to the job

Thus the job becomes the *cost unit* to which costs are charged. Examples of job costing include engineering firms that produce 'one-offs' to the customer's specifications, printing businesses, vehicle repairs, jobbing builders, etc.

the main steps in job costing

Fig 16.1 shows the main steps involved in job costing. The important points are:

- a separate *job cost sheet* is prepared for each job, listing the estimates of direct materials, direct labour, and overhead.

- the actual costs incurred are compared with the estimated costs, and variances between the two are analysed (there is more on *variance analysis* in Chapter 17). Action can then be taken to correct the variances, which will help when preparing future estimates

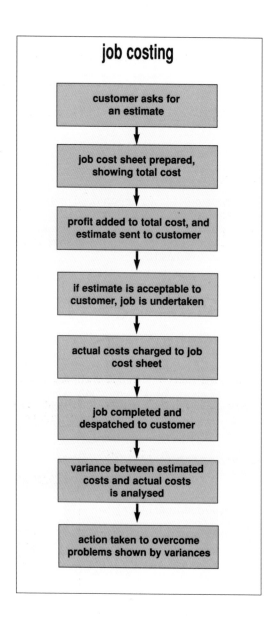

Fig. 16.1 Main steps in Job Costing

Case Problem: 'FASHIONAID' - a charity programme

Students at the local college have decided to organize an evening fashion show, to be called *'FashionAid'*. The objective of the show is to raise money to send to a children's charity working in Africa. The committee has asked you to arrange printing of a programme for the evening's events. You approach Pearshore Printers for an estimate of the cost of printing 750 copies of a 16 page programme.

From their point of view, Pearshore Printers will allocate a number to the job. They prepare the costs of the job as follows:

JOB NO. 6789
'FashionAid' Programme: 750 copies

	£
Direct Materials	
Paper - text: white glossart paper 135g. per square metre	82.00
Paper - cover: coated board 200g. per square metre	55.00
Printing plates	15.00
Direct Labour	
Printing: 10 hours at £5.00 per hour	50.00
Finishing: 4 hours at £4.50 per hour	18.00
Overheads (based on direct labour hour)	
14 hours at £10.00 per hour	140.00
Total Cost	360.00
Profit	54.00
Total price	414.00

Assuming that the price is acceptable, the job will go ahead and Pearshore Printers will charge the actual costs to the job, and will calculate any variances, as follows:

JOB NO. 6789

	ESTIMATE £	ACTUAL £	VARIANCE * £	
Direct materials				
Paper: text	82.00	90.00	8	ADV
Paper: cover	55.00	50.00	5	FAV
Printing plates	15.00	15.00	-	
Direct labour				
Printing: actual 12 hours at £5.00 per hour	50.00	60.00	10	ADV
Finishing: actual 4 hours at £4.50 per hour	18.00	18.00	-	
Overheads				
16 hours at £10.00 per hour	140.00	160.00	20	ADV
Total cost	360.00	393.00	33	ADV
Profit	54.00	21.00	33	ADV
Total price	414.00	414.00	-	

* The variances are either *adverse* or *favourable* (see also Chapter 17).

Pearshore Printers would need to analyse the reason for the variances (see Chapter 17), and to take corrective steps to overcome the problems caused by them.

process costing

While job costing is suitable for specific orders, process costing is used where a factory or a production line makes a particular product using a continuous process.

The objective of process costing is the find the cost per unit produced.

There are many examples of process costing in manufacturing industry, for example, the cost of making a bar of soap, or a car, or a gallon of petrol, or a packet of cereal. The concept of unit costs can also be extended to service industries, for example the cost per passenger-mile of a bus service, the cost of clearing a cheque, the cost per student hour of a college, etc.

Where a product passes through a number of separate operations, before it is completed, the costs of each process can be calculated. For example, the costs of producing 2,000 identical units of a product are:

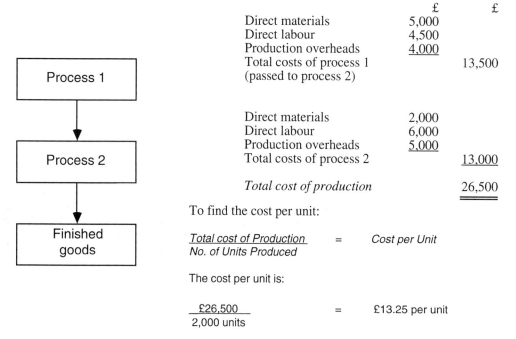

	£	£
Direct materials	5,000	
Direct labour	4,500	
Production overheads	4,000	
Total costs of process 1		13,500
(passed to process 2)		
Direct materials	2,000	
Direct labour	6,000	
Production overheads	5,000	
Total costs of process 2		13,000
Total cost of production		26,500

To find the cost per unit:

$$\frac{\text{Total cost of Production}}{\text{No. of Units Produced}} \quad = \quad \text{Cost per Unit}$$

The cost per unit is:

$$\frac{£26,500}{2,000 \text{ units}} \quad = \quad £13.25 \text{ per unit}$$

work-in-progress

With most manufacturing processes it is likely that, at any one time, there will be some units which are partly completed. For example, the production line at a car factory will always have cars which vary from being only just started, to those nearing the end of the line which are almost complete.

In calculating the cost per unit, it is necessary to take into account the degree of completeness of the work-in-progress. This is done by making *equivalent-unit* calculations:

Number of units in progress x *percentage of completeness* = *equivalent units.*

Thus, 100 units which are exactly 40% complete are equal to 40 completed units.

The formula for calculating the cost per unit now becomes:

$$\frac{Total\ cost\ of\ production}{No.\ of\ units\ produced\ +\ equivalent\ units\text{-}in\text{-}progress} = cost\ per\ unit$$

Case Problem: *Cradley Cider Company*

This company brews a popular local cider at its cider house in rural Herefordshire. The figures for the first month of the new season's production of its award-winning 'Five Crowns' variety are:

Total cost of production	£8,500
Units completed	800 barrels
Units in progress	100 barrels

The units in progress are exactly half-finished. What is the equivalent units-in-progress, and the cost per barrel, for the month?

Answer:

Completed units	= 800 barrels
Equivalent units 100 x 50%	= 50 barrels
Cost per unit $\dfrac{£8,500}{800 + 50}$	= £10 per barrel

work-in-progress: different cost elements

Although in the Case Problem above, it was assumed that the work-in-progress was exactly half-finished, this may well not be the case for all the elements of cost. For example, while direct materials might be 100% complete, direct labour, and overheads might be 50% complete. Allowance has to be made for these differences in the calculation of the valuation of work-in-progress, and the layout used in Case Problem below is one way in which the calculations can be made.

Case Problem: *Toy Manufacturing Company*

The Toy Manufacturing Company makes a plastic toy called a 'Humber-Wumber'. The toy is in great demand and the figures for the first month's production are:

Direct materials	£6,600
Direct labour	£3,500
Production overheads	£4,000
Units completed	900
Units in progress	200

The units in progress are complete as regards materials, but are 50% complete for direct labour and overheads.

What is the cost per unit of the first month's production, and the month-end valuation figure for work-in-progress?

Answer

Cost element	Month's Costs	Completed Units	Work-in-progress			Total Equivalent Units	Cost per Unit	WIP valuation
			Units	% complete	Equivalent Units			
	£						£	£
Direct materials	6,600	900	200	100	200	1,100	6.00	1,200
Direct labour	3,500	900	200	50	100	1,000	3.50	350
Production overheads	4,000	900	200	50	100	1,000	4.00	400
Total	14,100						13.50	1,950

900 completed units at £13.50 each	=	£12,150
Work-in-progress valuation	=	£ 1,950
Total costs for month	=	£14,100

opening work-in-progress

When there is opening work-in-progress, the values of the different cost elements should be added to the input costs of the period. For example, if in the month which follows Case Problem 3, direct labour costs are £4,000, the figure shown in the column *Month's costs* will be:

Work-in-progress at start	=	£350
Input costs (month's costs)	=	£4,000
Total costs for the month	=	£4,350

The calculation of costs per unit and work-in-progress valuation at the month-end can then be made as before, i.e.

$$\frac{Opening\ work\text{-}in\text{-}progress\ +\ input\ costs\ for\ period}{No.\ of\ units\ produced\ +\ equivalent\ units\text{-}in\text{-}progress} \quad = \quad cost\ per\ unit$$

CHAPTER SUMMARY

❑   Job costing is used by firms that carry out 'one-off' or special orders for customers; the job becomes the cost unit, to which costs are charged.

❑   Process costing is used where mass production of identical units is carried out.

❑   The cost per unit is calculated for the process by dividing the number of units produced (including equivalent units) into the total costs for the period.

❑   In process costing the valuation of closing stock is the number of equivalent units multiplied by the cost per unit.

❑   Job costing and process costing are both examples of *absorption costing*, ie the cost includes direct materials, direct labour and overheads.

The next Chapter looks in detail at ways in which costs can be established at the beginning of a manufacturing process by means of *standard costs*. It then goes on to analyse the variances that might occur between the standard cost and the actual cost.

STUDENT ACTIVITIES

16.1 A clothing manufacturer has been asked to give a quotation for the supply of a batch of uniforms for a band. Materials for the uniforms will be:

100 metres of cloth at £7.50 per metre
75 metres of braiding at £4 per metre.

It is estimated that the job will take the machinists a total of 35 hours. They are paid at the rate of £4.00 per hour. The overhead absorption rate is £8.50 per direct labour hour.

You are to:
(a) Calculate the cost of the job.
(b) Calculate the selling price if the company is to make a profit of 20% on the cost price.

16.2 Rowcester Engineering Co. Ltd. is asked to quote for the supply of a replacement cylinder head for a large stationary engine installed in a local factory. The item will need to be cast in the foundry and then passed to the finishing shop for machining to specification.

Materials needed will be a 100 kg. ingot of high strength steel, which costs £10 per kg.

Direct labour will be 10 hours in the foundry, and 15 hours in the finishing shop, of which 12 hours will be machine hours. Foundry workers are paid £5 per hour, while machine operators in the finishing shop are paid £6 per hour.

Overheads are charged on the basis of 80% of direct labour cost in the foundry, and on the basis of £10 per machine hour in the finishing shop.

Profit is to be 25% of cost price.

(a) Calculate the estimated cost of the job, and the selling price.

(b) Prepare an *actual cost statement* on the basis of the following:
   • the cost of materials was £11 per kg.
   • the job took 12 hours in the foundry
   • the job took 14 hours in the finishing shop
   • machine operators are now paid £6.50 per hour
   • machine time in the finishing shop was 11 hours.

(c) Prepare a variance statement, and show the actual profit (or loss) made on this job.

16.3 OB Printers has been asked by John Dun, a local poet, to quote for the cost of printing a small book of poetry. John Dun is not sure how many copies to order, and has asked for quotations for 500, 1,000 and 2,000 copies.

The estimates by OB Printers are as follows:

Setting up the printing machine: 6 hours at £10.00 per hour.
Artwork: 7 hours at £12.00 per hour.
Typesetting: 20 hours at £15.00 per hour.
Paper (for 500 copies): £100.00.
Other printing consumables (for 500 copies): £50.00.
Direct labour (for 500 copies): 10 hours at £6.50 per hour.
Overheads: 80% of direct labour costs.
Profit: 25% on cost price.

You are to:

(a)   Prepare quotations for 500, 1,000 and 2,000 copies.

(b)   Calculate the cost per book at each of the three different production levels.

(c)   Reply to John Dun who, on seeing your quotations, says:
"Why is your price per copy so high for 500 copies? I am a starving poet, and I can't afford to have a large quantity printed. If the book sells well I shall regret not having had 2,000 copies printed."

16.4   Which costing method - job or process - would be used to price each of the following?

(a)   printing an advertising brochure
(b)   making pocket calculators
(c)   installing a new bathroom
(d)   making bathroom taps
(e)   production of cars
(f)   canning baked beans
(g)   building work

Give reasons for your choice.

16.5   Agchem Ltd. is a manufacturer of specialist chemicals for the agricultural industry. One of its products is called 'Oxytone' and passes through three manufacturing processes: 1, 2 and 3. The following information covers a week's production during which 25 000 litres were completed:

	Process 1	**Process 2**	**Process 3**
	£	£	£
Direct materials	3,350	1,170	825
Direct labour	1,200	800	1,000
Direct expenses	750	-	220

Production overheads for the week were £1,860 and are apportioned to each process on the basis of direct labour costs.

There was no loss during processing; nor was there any opening or closing work-in-progress.

You are to calculate:

(a)   the cost per litre for each process.
(b)   the total cost of one litre of 'Oxytone'.

16.6   A manufacturer of plastic toys has the following information concerning the first month of production:

Direct materials	£11,500
Direct labour	£9,000
Production overheads	£18,000
Toys completed	20,000
Toys in process	5,000

The work-in-progress is complete as regards materials, but is 50% complete as regards direct labour, and production overhead.

You are to:

(a) Calculate the cost per toy of the first month's production.
(b) Calculate the month-end valuation for work-in-progress.

16.7   At the beginning of January, Processing (Rowcester) Ltd. had 5,000 units in process. The costs of this work-in-progress were made up as follows:

	£
Direct materials	18,200
Direct labour	7,350
Production overheads	8,500

During January a further 20,000 units were put into the process, with additional costs of:

	£
Direct materials	79,100
Direct labour	36,300
Production overheads	42,200

At the end of January, 18,000 units had been fully processed, and 7,000 units remained in process. The closing work-in-progress was complete as regards direct materials, and 50% complete as regards direct labour and overheads.

You are to:

(a) Tabulate the month's production and cost figures.
(b) Calculate the cost per unit for completed output in January.
(c) Calculate the value of work-in-progress at the end of January.

6 Newtown Printers: Overhead Absorption and Job Costing

> **covering**
> the need for financial information for planning, control and decision-making;
> absorption and marginal costing

SITUATION

Newtown Printers is run by Ed Shaw and operates from modern premises on an industrial estate. Ed originally set up the business some ten years ago and, until recently, it was like many other printers, with heavy machinery and traditional ways of doing things. However, he realised that technology had made great advances in recent years and he has invested heavily in computer-controlled equipment and new methods of typesetting. The business is divided into two departments:

Department A
This department comprises the older, more traditional, printing machinery: it is a labour-intensive department with six employees.

Department B
This contains a new computerised machine; this requires only two employees, but is much more capital intensive.

In addition there is a stores section which issues paper, card, and other items to both departments.

Ed Shaw has asked you to help him to devise a costing system suitable for the type of organization he runs. In particular, he is anxious to ensure that the firm's overheads are "correctly charged to output". He has given you the following information:

1. Floor area, Dept A: 400 sq metres, Dept B: 250 sq metres, stores: 100 sq metres

2. Number of direct labour employees, Dept A: 6, Dept B: 3.

3. Direct labour employees are paid on a time-rate basis: those in Dept A earn £5 per hour, while those in Dept B earn £6.50 per hour.

4. A storekeeper is employed and he earns £7,580 per year.

5. A foreman supervises the day-to-day running of the two departments, together with the stores. He is paid £12,000 per year, and estimates that he spends 50% of his time in Department A, 40% in Department B, and 10% in the stores.

6. The valuation of machinery and equipment is Dept A: £15,000, Dept B: £40,000.

7. The following are the overheads of the factory for this year, and Ed tells you that next year's costs will be almost exactly the same:

Rates	£4,500
Rent	£6,000
Heating and lighting	£2,400
Depreciation of machinery	£11,000
Machinery insurance	£825

8. The business works a thirty-five hour week for 47 weeks a year.

9. The stores department spends two-thirds of its time dealing with Department A, and one-third with Department B.

10. The business uses the FIFO system of stock control.

TASKS

1. Ed Shaw asks you to calculate an *overhead recovery rate* for each of his two departments, using a suitable basis. He mentions that the basis is likely to be different for each department, and asks you to justify the basis you choose.

2. He now asks you to apply your calculations to two jobs which have just come in (on 20 December).

Job No 1.
This is a simple printing job from the customer's 'camera-ready' copy. It will be handled entirely by Department A. The job will take six hours of direct labour, and the materials needed are 10 reams of A4 paper with a weight of 80 grams per square metre.

The stock record card for this paper is as follows:

	A4 Paper			
1 Dec.	Brought forward	100 reams	@	£2.00 per ream
3 Dec.	Issued	20 reams		
5 Dec.	Issued	30 reams		
8 Dec.	Received	200 reams	@	£2.10 per ream
12 Dec.	Issued	25 reams		
14 Dec.	Issued	20 reams		

Job No 2.
This job will pass through both departments. It will start in Department B, where there will be five direct labour hours and four machine hours spent on it. Then it will be passed to Department A where it will be printed on A3 paper, folded and then bound in card covers. Five reams of A3 paper and one ream of card will be needed for the job which will take eight direct labour hours in this department. Stock records cards are:

	A3 Paper			
1 Dec.	Brought forward	10 reams	@	£3.50 per ream
3 Dec.	Issued	8 reams		
4 Dec.	Received	20 reams	@	£3.75 per ream
7 Dec.	Issued	6 reams		
12 Dec.	Issued	5 reams		
15 Dec.	Received	20 reams	@	£3.80 per ream
17 Dec.	Issued	8 reams		

White card: 200 gsm				
1 Dec.	Brought forward	2 reams	@	£15.00 per ream
3 Dec.	Issued	1 ream		
4 Dec.	Received	5 reams	@	£14.75 per ream
12 Dec.	Issued	2 reams		
15 Dec.	Received	6 reams	@	£15.50 per ream

You are to calculate the factory cost for each job, and then to add 30% to cover administration overheads and profit. This will then give the price to be quoted to the customer for each job.

3. No further jobs are carried out before the end of his financial year, and Ed asks you to prepare a stock valuation for each of these three stock items.

17 STANDARD COSTING AND VARIANCE ANALYSIS

All businesses need methods of controlling the costs of materials, labour and overheads that go to make up the finished product. Imagine a car factory where the cost and amount of the materials to make the car is not known; where the hours of work and the rates of pay are not known; where the cost of the overheads is not known. Under such circumstances, the costs could not be controlled, and it would also be impossible to quote a price for the product to a customer. Manufacturing firms usually establish a *standard cost* for their 'production line' products.

standard cost

A standard cost is a pre-determined cost, based on expected effective working conditions, in the period ahead, of materials, labour and overhead costs. It can be used as a method of cost control through variance analysis, and also for establishing selling prices.

* **Materials** The quantity of each material to be used in production, and the price of such materials is pre-determined. *Standard materials cost* is the expected quantity multiplied by expected material price.

* **Labour** The labour hours required to manufacture a quantity of goods, and the cost of the labour is pre-determined. *Standard labour cost* is the expected labour hours multiplied by expected wage rates.

* **Overheads** The expected quantity of goods produced divided into the expected overheads will determine the *standard overhead cost.*

setting standards

In standard costing, it is important that care should be taken over the setting of standards. Poorly set standards will be worse than useless to the management of a business when they come to use the figures in an analysis.

The main people within a business who can provide information to enable standards to be set are:

* **Buyer** The buying department of a business will be able to determine prices, and their future trends, of materials used.
* **Personnel** This department will have current wage rates, together with bonus and overtime details, of the various grades of worker; forecasts of changes can also be ascertained.
* **Management Services** Often called *work study,* this department will determine the standard amount of time that each work-task in the manufacturing process should take.

• **Production** This department has overall responsibility for production and will know the quantities of raw materials required for each unit of production and is likely to have knowledge of overhead costs.

Case Problem: DMS Engineering Limited

This company manufactures car bumpers. It has been asked by its major customer, Okassa (Japan) Ltd. to prepare a quotation for bumpers for a new car, which is code-named 'OK10'. The elements of cost for 100 bumpers have been calculated by DMS Engineering as:

Materials:	Steel (of specified quality), 200 kilos at £1.10 per kilo
	Matt black finishing material, 10 litres at £5.40 per litre
Labour:	10 hours at £5.75 per hour
	3 hours at £8.50 per hour
Overheads:	13 hours at £20 per hour

Calculations required

• The standard cost of producing 100 bumpers.
• If DMS Engineering Ltd. add 20% profit on to their total cost, what will be the cost of one bumper to Okasa (Japan) Ltd?

Answer

	£	£
Materials		
Steel: 200 kilos at £1.10 per kilo		220.00
Finishing material: 10 litres at £5.40 per litre		54.00
		274.00
Labour		
10 hours at £5.75	57.50	
3 hours at £8.50	25.50	
		83.00
		357.00
Overheads		
13 hours at £20 per hour		260.00
Total cost		617.00
Profit (20% of total cost)		123.40
Total selling price		740.40

Therefore one bumper costs £7.40

variance analysis

Having established standard costs, the management of a business needs to put these to use by comparing the standards set with the costs that actually occurred. The outline of the procedure is as follows:

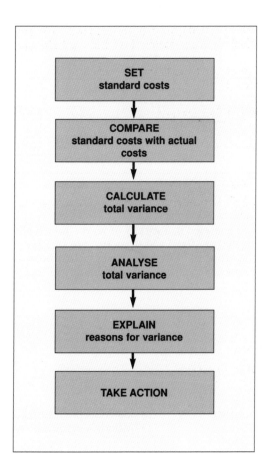

A variance can be either *favourable* or *adverse:*

- a *favourable* variance occurs when actual costs are lower than standard costs.
- an *adverse* variance is when actual costs are higher than standard costs.

The total variance can be analysed into a number of subsidiary variances, principally concerned with the three main elements of cost: materials, labour and overheads. These are illustrated in the diagram on the next page.

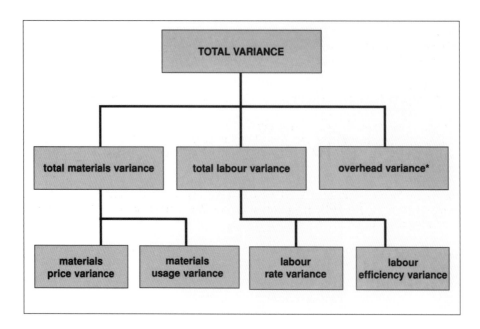

* The overhead variance can be analysed in a variety of ways - principally the distinction can be made between those overheads that are fixed and those that are variable. However, the analysis of such variances is outside the scope of a general accounting textbook such as this, and it may be that your further studies of cost and management accounting will lead you to this topic.

materials variances

The variances for materials costs are:

variance	*sub-variances*
• total materials variance	• materials price variance
	• materials usage variance

The money amounts of each variance are calculated from the areas indicated in the following diagram:

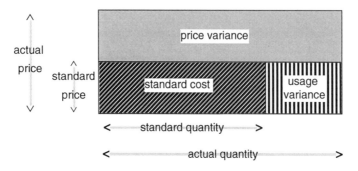

Materials price variance
     (standard price – actual price) x   actual quantity

Materials usage variance
     (standard quantity – actual quantity) x standard price

Materials variance
     (standard quantity x standard price) – (actual quantity x actual price)

Notes from the diagram on the previous page:
- The change in the price of materials, based on the quantity actually used, forms the materials price variance – shaded ▭ in the diagram. This variance is the responsibility of the buying department.

- The change in the actual quantity used, based on the standard price, forms the materials usage variance – shaded ▐▌▌▌▌▌ in the diagram. This variance is the responsibility of the production department.

- For clarity of presentation, the diagram shows adverse price and usage variances; these variances can also be favourable, ie less than the standard cost.

example
A manufacturer of clay garden gnomes has prepared the following information:
- the standard price of clay used to make the gnomes is 50p per kilo
- the standard usage is 2 kilos per gnome

The results achieved for last month's production are:
- the actual price of clay used was 60p per kilo
- the actual usage was 1.5 kilos per gnome

Here both the price and usage have differed from the standard to give the following *materials variance*:

(2 kgs x 50p per kg)	–	(1.5 kgs x 60p per kg)	=	
£1	–	90p	=	£0.10 FAVOURABLE

Note: A favourable variance is a positive figure, eg £1.00 – 90p = £0.10; ie the actual cost is *less* than standard, so increasing profit. By contrast, an adverse variance is a negative figure, ie the actual cost is *more* than the standard cost, so reducing profit.

While the overall materials variance is favourable by £0.10, as both price *and* usage differ from standard, the sub-variances must be calculated:

Materials price variance

(standard price	–	actual price)	x	actual quantity	
(50p	–	60p)	x	1.5 kgs	= £0.15 ADVERSE

Materials usage variance

(standard quantity	–	actual quantity)	x	standard price	
(2 kgs	–	1.5 kgs)	x	50p	= £0.25 FAVOURABLE

MATERIALS VARIANCE   £0.10 FAVOURABLE

labour variances

The variances for labour costs are:

      variance   *sub-variances*
       • total labour variance   • labour rate variance
                                   • labour efficiency variance

The money amounts of each variance are calculated from the areas indicated in the following diagram:

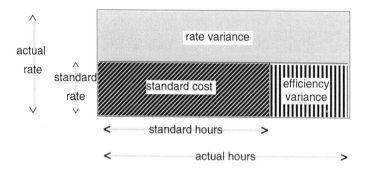

Labour rate variance
       (standard rate   –   actual rate)   x   actual hours

Labour efficiency variance
       (standard hours   –   actual hours)   x   standard rate

Labour variance
       (standard hours   x   standard rate)   –   (actual hours   x   actual rate)

Notes from the above diagram:
• The change in the labour rate, based on the actual hours, forms the labour rate variance – shaded ▭ in the diagram. This variance is the responsibility of the personnel department.

• The change in the actual hours, based on the standard hours, forms the labour efficiency variance – shaded ▨ in the diagram. This variance is the responsibility of the production department.

• For clarity of presentation, the diagram shows adverse rate and efficiency variances; these variances can also be favourable, ie less than the standard cost.

example
A manufacturer of clay garden gnomes has prepared the following information:
• the standard cost of direct labour is £6.00 per hour
• the standard efficiency is production of one gnome every 20 minutes (0.333 of an hour)

The results achieved for last month's production are:
• the actual cost of direct labour was £8.00 per hour
• the actual production was one gnome every 30 minutes (0.5 of an hour)

Here both the rate and efficiency have differed from the standard to give the following *labour variance*:

$$(0.333 \text{ hours} \times £6.00 \text{ per hour}) \quad - \quad (0.5 \text{ hours} \times £8.00 \text{ per hour}) \quad =$$
$$£2.00 \qquad\qquad - \qquad\qquad £4.00 \qquad\qquad = £2.00 \text{ ADVERSE}$$

Note: The calculation gives a negative figure of £2.00; this means that the actual cost is *more* than the standard cost, ie it is adverse. By contrast, a favourable variance is a positive figure, ie the actual cost is *less* than the standard cost.

While the overall labour variance is adverse by £2.00, as both rate *and* efficiency differ from standard, the sub-variances must be calculated:

Labour rate variance

| (standard rate | – | actual rate) | x | actual hours | |
| (£6.00 | – | £8.00) | x | 0.5 hours | = £1.00 ADVERSE |

Labour efficiency variance

| (standard hours | – | actual hours) | x | standard rate | |
| (0.333 hours | – | 0.5 hours) | x | £6.00 | = £1.00 ADVERSE |

LABOUR VARIANCE £2.00 ADVERSE

conclusion

Standard costs are set in order to give the individual departmental managers, responsible for aspects of the organisation's output, suitable targets to aim for. When actual costs are compared with standard costs, an analysis can be carried out to see why the variances have occurred, and to see what can be done about them for the future.

CHAPTER SUMMARY

❑ Standard costs are established for the main elements of cost: materials, labour and overheads.

❑ Actual costs incurred are recorded.

❑ A comparison is made between standard costs and actual costs, and variances are calculated.

❑ Total materials variance is analysed into:
  • price variance: (standard price - actual price) x actual quantity
  • usage variance: (standard quantity - actual quantity) x standard price

❑ Total labour variance is analysed into:
  • rate variance: (standard rate - actual rate) x actual hours
  • efficiency variance: (standard hours - actual hours) x standard rate

❑ Investigation should be made in order to find out why the variances have occurred and corrective action taken.

The next chapter looks at how standard costs can be incorporated into the budget of an organisation, the preparation of budgets, and their uses in the control of a business.

✍ STUDENT ACTIVITIES

17.1 (a)   What is meant by the term 'standard costing'?
　　　　 (b)   What are the advantages to a business in using such a costing scheme?

17.2 Calculate the materials variance for each of the following, and analyse the variance between a price variance and a usage variance. (Indicate whether each variance is *adverse* or *favourable*.)

> *Material: sheet steel*
> | | |
> |---|---|
> | Standard usage | 0.5 sq. metres |
> | Standard price | £5 per sq. metre |
> | Actual usage | 0.5 sq. metres |
> | Actual price | £6 per sq. metre |
>
> *Material: alloy*
> | | |
> |---|---|
> | Standard usage | 2 kgs |
> | Standard price | £1.50 per kg |
> | Actual usage | 2.5 kgs |
> | Actual price | £1.50 per kg |
>
> *Material: flour*
> | | |
> |---|---|
> | Standard usage | 0.5 kgs |
> | Standard price | 50p per kg |
> | Actual usage | 0.6 kgs |
> | Actual price | 40p per kg |
>
> *Material: gelling fluid*
> | | |
> |---|---|
> | Standard usage | 3 litres |
> | Standard price | £1.50 per litre |
> | Actual usage | 2.5 litres |
> | Actual price | £2 per litre |

17.3 Calculate the labour variance for each of the following, and analyse the variance between a rate variance and an efficiency variance. (Indicate whether each variance is *adverse* or *favourable*.)

> *Casting*
> | | |
> |---|---|
> | Standard hours | 5 hours |
> | Standard wage rate | £6 per hour |
> | Actual hours | 6 hours |
> | Actual wage rate | £6 per hour |
>
> *Machining*
> | | |
> |---|---|
> | Standard hours | 2 hours |
> | Standard wage rate | £6.50 per hour |
> | Actual hours | 2 hours |
> | Actual wage rate | £7.50 per hour |
>
> *Finishing*
> | | |
> |---|---|
> | Standard hours | 1 hour |
> | Standard wage rate | £6 per hour |
> | Actual hours | 1.25 hours |
> | Actual wage rate | £6.40 per hour |

Packing

Standard hours	1 hour
Standard wage rate	£4 per hour
Actual hours	0.75 hours
Actual wage rate	£3.60 per hour

17.4 From the following data you are to calculate:

    (a) materials price variance
    (b) materials usage variance
    (c) total materials variance

(Indicate whether each variance is *adverse* or *favourable*.)

	Standard Price	Standard Usage	Actual Price	Actual Usage
Material A	£5 per kg	10 kgs	£4 per kg	12 kgs
Material B	£20 per unit	12 units	£22 per unit	10 units
Material C	£10 per litre	6 litres	£9 per litre	5 litres
Material D	£2 per metre	3 metres	£3 per metre	2.5 metres

17.5 From the following data you are to calculate:

    (a) labour rate variance
    (b) labour efficiency variance
    (c) total labour variance

(Indicate whether each variance is *adverse* or *favourable*.)

	Standard Hours	Standard Wage Rate	Actual Hours	Actual Wage Rate
Job No. 1	8	£5.00	7	£5.50
Job No. 2	3	£4.50	4	£5.00
Job No. 3	24	£6.00	30	£5.75
Job No. 4	12	£8.00	15	£8.50

17.6 The cost accountant of Rowcester (Engineering) Ltd. estimates that a particular job – to produce 10 identical castings for a customer – will require the following:

Job No. 12345: 10 castings
Materials:
       55 kgs of ordinary steel at £3.50 per kg.
       20 kgs of high-tensile steel at £10.00 per kg.

Labour:
       10 hours foundry-workers' wages at £6.00 per hour
       25 hours in the machine shop at £7.50 per hour

Overheads:
       £225.00

When the job is finished, it is found that actual results were:

Materials:
    60 kgs of ordinary steel at £3.00 per kg.
    22 kgs of high-tensile steel at £12.00 per kg.

Labour:
    12 hours foundry-workers' wages at £6.50 per hour.
    22 hours in the machine shop at £7.25 per hour.

Overheads:
    £225.00

Tasks

(a)   You are to prepare a statement which shows:
    1.   the standard cost of the job
    2.   the actual cost of the job
    3.   the variances from standard, analysed between the sub-variances

(b)   1.   Based on the standard cost, a price was quoted to the customer which gave Rowcester (Engineering) Ltd a profit of £255. What will be the actual profit earned?

    2.   To what use will the cost accountant put the actual cost of the job calculated in (a) above?

17.7   Eveshore Packaging Ltd. make cartons for the food industry. A job that has just come in is to make 10,000 cartons for fruit juices. The cost accountant estimates that the materials and labour required will be:

Materials:
    2,000 sq. metres of card at £15 per 100 sq. metres
    50 litres of wax coating at £4.50 per litre

Labour:
    Cutting   30 hours at £3.50 per hour
    Waxing   20 hours at £4.50 per hour
    Finishing   16 hours at £5.00 per hour

The actual costs of the job are:

Materials:
    1,950 sq. metres of card at £15.60 per 100 sq. metres
    45 litres of wax coating at £4.75 per litre

Labour:
    Cutting   35 hours at £3.25 per hour
    Waxing   19 hours at £5.00 per hour
    Finishing   15 hours at £5.50 per hour

You are to prepare a statement which shows:

    (a) the standard cost of the job
    (b) the actual cost of the job
    (c) the variances from standard, analysed between the sub-variances

18 BUDGETS AND BUDGETARY CONTROL

All businesses need to plan for the future. In large businesses such planning, usually known as *corporate planning,* is very formal while, for smaller businesses, it will be less formal. Planning for the future falls into three time scales:

- *long-term:* from about three years up to, sometimes, as far as twenty years ahead.
- *medium-term:* one to three years ahead.
- *short-term:* for next year.

Clearly, planning for these different time scales needs different approaches: the further on in time, the less detailed can be the plans. In the medium and longer term, a business will establish broad *corporate objectives.* Such corporate objectives do not have to be formally written down, although in a large organization they are likely to be; for smaller businesses, corporate objectives will certainly be thought about by the owners or managers. This is very similar to each one of us having personal objectives, which we are likely to think about, rather than write down.

In this Chapter we are concerned with planning for the more immediate future, i.e. the next financial year. Such planning takes the broader corporate objectives and sets out how these are to be achieved in the form of detailed plans known as *budgets.*

what is a budget?

A budget can be defined as a planning and control tool relevant to the management of a business.

The main purposes of budgeting are:

- to assist in the assessment and evaluation of different courses of possible action;
- to create motivation by expressing a proposed plan of action in terms of targets;
- to monitor the effectiveness of performance being accomplished against the budget, and to report variances.

Most budgets are prepared for the forthcoming financial year, and are usually broken down into shorter time periods, commonly monthly. This enables control to be exercised over the budget: as time passes by, so the business' actual results can be compared to the budget; discrepancies between the two can be investigated.

what budgets are prepared?

The end result of the budgeting process is the production of a *master budget* which takes the form of estimated operating statements (manufacturing account, trading account, and profit and loss account) together with an estimated balance sheet at the end of the budgetary period. However, before the master budget can be produced, a number of subsidiary budgets covering all aspects of the business need to be prepared, e.g. sales, production, capital expenditure, administration, selling and distribution, cash (see Fig. 18.1). The cash budget and master budget are discussed more fully in Chapter 19.

limiting factors

From Fig. 18.1, it can be seen that sales is, for most businesses, the starting point for the budget; this is because sales is often the limiting factor. A limiting factor is some aspect of the business which prevents further expansion. Other limiting factors include shortages of:

- raw materials
- skilled labour
- factory space
- capital
- expenditure on research and development

Whatever the limiting factor, the budget needs to be designed to incorporate any restrictions imposed by the factor.

Case Problem: Fitta Fabricators Ltd. - Production Budget

Jim Lewis is the production manager of Fitta Fabricators Ltd., manufacturers of the Fitta De Luxe Exercise Cycle. The sales manager has just presented Jim with the budgeted sales for the forthcoming twelve months, as follows:

January	150 units
February	150 "
March	200 "
April	400 "
May	400 "
June	400 "
July	500 "
August	300 "
September	200 "
October	200 "
November	700 "
December	425 "

Stock in the warehouse on 1 January at the start of the year is budgeted to be 100 units. Jim's problem is that the factory, working at normal capacity, can produce 350 units each month. More units can be made if overtime is paid, but the directors are not keen to see this happen, just as they do not like to see too much under-utilisation of the factory. Jim has to work out an even production budget which will keep the factory working at near or full capacity, but without incurring too much overtime. He has three other constraints:

- month-end stock must never fall below 100 units;
- the warehouse is fairly small and cannot hold more than 600 units;
- the factory is closed for half of August.

Jim asks you to help him plan the production budget.

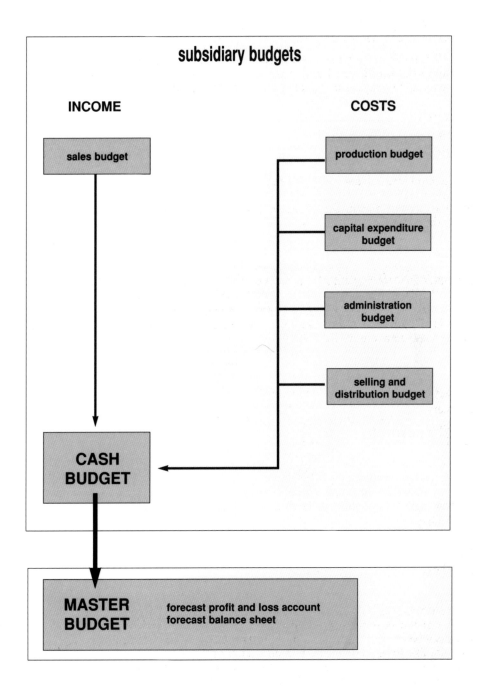

Fig. 18.1 Subsidiary Budgets and the Master Budget

Answer:

FITTA FABRICATORS LTD
Production Budget (units) for the year-ended 31 December

	JAN	FEB	MAR	APR	MAY	JUN	JUL	AUG	SEP	OCT	NOV	DEC
UNITS												
Opening stock	100	275	450	600	550	500	450	300	175	325	475	125
Add Units produced	325	325	350	350	350	350	350	175	350	350	350	400
Less Sales	150	150	200	400	400	400	500	300	200	200	700	425
Closing stock	275	450	600	550	500	450	300	175	325	475	125	100

Notes:
• January and February: under-production by 25 units each month.
• December: overtime payments in respect of 50 units.

budgetary planning

The planning of a budget is co-ordinated by a member of the accounts department. However, managers of individual departments are made responsible for preparing budgets for their own departments. Many larger organizations take a highly formal view of planning the budget and form a *budget committee*. Fig. 18.2 shows a diagrammatic approach to budgetary planning.

An important aspect of budgetary planning is to test for feasibility before submitting the master budget for the approval of the owner or board of directors. The test of feasibility would check, for example, that the sales budget and the production budget linked together (so that stock-piling or stock shortages do not occur), that the production budget is within the capacity of the facilities available, that the cash budget does not show excessive short-term borrowing which could be avoided by rescheduling major purchases.

budgetary control

Once a budget has been approved by the owner or, in the case of a limited company, by the board of directors it becomes the official plan of the business for the period of the budget. There is no point in a business spending a lot of time and effort in preparing a budget if it is not used as a control mechanism throughout the period: this aspect is known as *budgetary control*.

The main aspect with which budgetary control is concerned is in comparing actual results with what was planned to happen in the budget. Fig. 18.3 shows how budgetary control should be used to provide information both to those who are responsible for managing budgets and to the owner or board of directors.

advantages of budgets

Performance targets are established
The process of budgeting establishes targets:
• for the business as a whole - in the form of a master budget
• for section managers - in the form of subsidiary budgets

Comparisons can be made of budget and actual performance
By comparing the budget with what happens in reality allows:
• management to know that a variance has occurred
• an investigation to take place into the causes of the variance
• action to take place to correct the reason for the variance

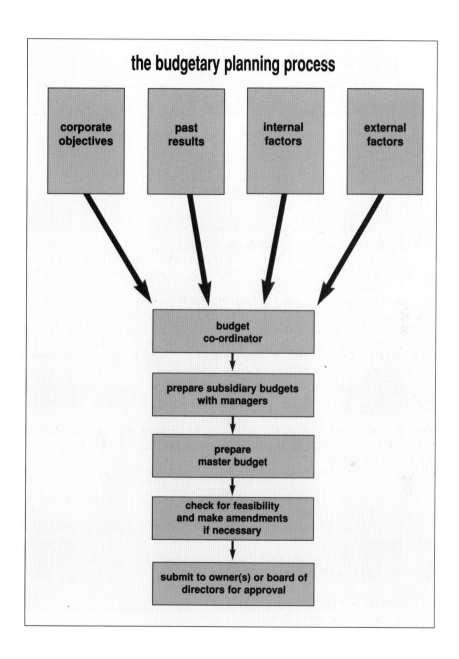

Fig. 18.2 Budgetary Planning

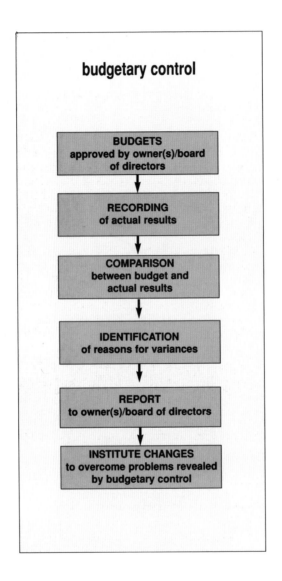

Fig. 18.3 Budgetary Control

Planning is beneficial

It is too easy for a business to meander along from day-to-day and week-to-week without any real idea of where it is going. A budget forces the management to think ahead and this, in turn, leads to better use of the resources of the business.

For a budget to be useful to business, it must be a realistic forecast of what can be achieved. If it is not, then the people who have to work to the budget will simply 'give up' and will not try to achieve the targets set. At the same time, the senior management of the business, starting at the top with the owner or board of directors, must be convinced of the usefulness of the budget. If budgeting is seen as a necessary chore to be undertaken without much enthusiasm, then this attitude will soon permeate down through the organization.

fixed and flexible budgets

Fixed budgets

A fixed budget is one that is set at the start of the budgetary period and remains unchanged whatever the level of activity. For example, a budget is set for production of 10,000 units each month; actual production is 9,000 units per month. A fixed budget will compare the budgeted costs of producing 10,000 units with the actual costs of 9,000. Therefore the total variable costs, ie the *actual* figures, will be different from those budgeted for.

Flexible budgets

A way of overcoming the difficulty caused by a fixed budget is to use a *flexible budget*. This recognizes the different behaviour patterns of fixed costs and variable costs, depending on the level of output. Thus, an amended budget is produced on the basis of costs expected to be incurred at different production levels. For instance, in the example given above, a flexible budget would be produced for a production level of 9,000 units per month - the variable costs, eg materials, labour, and parts of the overhead, would be altered or 'flexed' to a level of 9,000 units. Then the actual costs can be directly compared with those of the flexible budget.

Case Problem: fixed and flexible budgets

John Brown (Manufacturing) Ltd. makes barbecue sets for garden use. The monthly budget has been prepared as follows:

Sales per month 1,000 barbecues at £20 each.	
Production costs:	
materials	£5 each
labour	£4 each
variable overheads	£1 each
fixed overheads	£7,500 per month

Because of poor weather, sales are down to 700 units each month and you have been asked to help in the preparation of revised budgets. Accordingly you should prepare a statement to show:

- the original monthly budget, showing the budgeted profit;
- the flexed budget for production levels of 700 units each month.

Answer:

JOHN BROWN (MANUFACTURING) LTD.
Monthly Budget

	FIXED BUDGET	FLEXIBLE BUDGET
Sales volume	1,000 units	700 units
Production volume	1,000 units	700 units
	£	£
Sales revenue (£20 each)	20,000	14,000
less : materials (£5 per unit)	(5,000)	(3,500)
labour (£4 per unit)	(4,000)	(2,800)
variable overheads (£1 per unit)	(1,000)	(700)
Contribution to fixed costs	10,000	7,000
less: fixed costs	(7,500)	(7,500)
Budgeted profit/(loss)	2 500	(500)

---

zero-based budgeting

The starting point for most budgets is to commence with last year's budget and then to 'add a few per cent to allow for inflation'. Such a policy, which is particularly prevalent in local and public authorities, has the major disadvantage that inefficiencies, provided they take place within the terms of the budget, remain 'in the system'.

One way to avoid this is to use *zero-based budgeting*. With this system, the budget starts from zero, and each item going into the budget has to be justified on the basis of business activity. For example, a stationery budget for an office, instead of starting with last year's figure and 'adding a bit', will start at zero and the manager of the office must justify each item which goes into the budget. The advantage of such a system is that managers have to justify their own budget.

CHAPTER SUMMARY

❑ A budget is a planning and control tool relevant to the management of a business.

❑ Subsidiary budgets are prepared for each main activity of the business; these come together in the master budget which takes the form of budgeted operating statements and balance sheet.

❑ Budgetary planning establishes the targets and, when approved by the owners/board of directors, the budget becomes the official plan of the business for the budget period.

❑ Budgetary control uses the budget to make comparisons between actual results and budgeted results. Investigation of variances can be carried out and corrective action can be taken.

In the next Chapter we shall look in more detail at one particular subsidiary budget - the cash budget. We shall also see how the master budget is prepared in the form of forecast final accounts.

✍ STUDENT ACTIVITIES

18.1 Radionics Ltd. is a manufacturer of radios. Most parts for the radios are bought in and assembled at the company's factory, which is situated on a modern industrial estate near Slough. The directors are currently planning the company's progress over the next twelve months.

You are a trainee in the accounts department of Radionics Ltd. You have been asked by your boss, the Finance Director, Mr. R. Perrin, to prepare a short paper for him to present at the next board meeting of the company which is to be held next week. The paper is to cover the following points:

- the different budgets that the company should prepare for the forthcoming year,
- any limiting factors that the directors must bear in mind when considering budget proposals, and how such factors are likely to affect the company.

18.2 Shades Ltd. manufactures good quality sunglasses at its 'hi-tech' factory unit near Cambridge. Although there is some all-year round demand for sunglasses, highest demand is in late spring, and in summer. Because of the quality of the product, and the high skills needed from the workforce, there is little possibility of increasing production to meet peak demand; instead the company adopts a policy of keeping the factory working at full or near-full capacity throughout the year. The disadvantage of this policy is that completed stock needs to be warehoused until demand increases. Overtime can be worked to increase production by a maximum of 10%.

The sales director has been preparing a sales budget (in numbers of units of sunglasses) expected to be sold in the forthcoming year. Here is her budget:

January 5,500, February 4,500, March 3,500, April 4,000, May 7,000, June 12,500, July 15,000, August 10,000, September 2,000, October 3,000, November 5,000, December 5,000.

The production director now has to work out a production budget, taking into account the following:

- Stock at 1 January is 8,500 units
- Maximum monthly output without working overtime: 7,500 units. However, the factory is closed for one week in April (Easter), for two weeks in August (annual holiday), and for one week at Christmas. Each week of holiday loses one-quarter of that month's production.
- At the end of each month there must always be in stock two-thirds of the next month's budgeted sales.
- Overtime can be worked to produce a maximum increase in output of 10%.

You are to:
(a) Prepare a month-by-month production budget for Shades Ltd. which:
   - shows when and how much overtime working will be necessary
   - shows closing stock (in units) at each month-end.

(b) What are the limiting factors suffered by Shades Ltd., from the point of view of both production and sales?

18.3 A friend of yours has recently started work as a book-keeper with a major car manufacturer. Explain to him the difference between budgetary planning and budgetary control.

Outline the steps that would be undertaken in each, relating as far as possible, to motor vehicle manufacture.

18.4   (a) Explain what is meant by:
- fixed budgets, and
- flexible budgets.

What is the main objective of preparing flexible budgets?

(b) Seats Ltd. manufactures chairs which sell to schools and colleges throughout Britain. The company is currently producing budgets for the next year. The sales director is budgeting for sales of 90,000 chairs; the selling price is £10 each. Production costs are budgeted as being:

materials	£2.50 per chair
labour	£2.75 per chair
variable overheads	£0.50 per chair
fixed overheads	£242,000 per year

However, a general election was announced a few days ago, and conversation at today's board meeting of the company's directors goes as follows:

"The outcome of the election looks unpredictable".

"If the government is re-elected, they are committed to a 10% cut in education spending."

"On the other hand, if the opposition party win, they have pledged to increase education spending by 25%."

"Until we get further information we had better assume that our sales will be affected by the same percentages."

As an accounts assistant, you are to:

(a) Prepare the fixed budget for the year based on sales of 90,000 chairs, to show budgeted profit.

(b) Prepare two flexible budgets based on the changes in educational spending proposed by each of the main political parties.

(c) Write a memorandum to the directors explaining the reason for the different budgeted profit figures.

18.5   Greenlawn Ltd. manufactures a combined lawn weedkiller and fertiliser at its recently completed chemical works in Birmingham. Output last year was 1,000,000 litres which sold for £5 per litre. However, this is well below the production capacity of the works and it is planned to increase production, and reduce the selling price.

The company wishes to prepare flexible budgets for output of 1,500,000 litres, 2,000,000 litres, and 2,500,000 litres (which is the maximum capacity of the works).

The selling price is to be reduced by 50p per litre for each increase in output. Variable costs are £2,000,000 at an output level of 1,000,000 litres; fixed costs are £1,500,000; semi-variable costs are £750,000 at the present capacity, and are expected to increase by equal increments to £150,000 at the maximum production level.

You are to:

(a) Prepare a budget based on last year's level of output.

(b) Prepare flexible budgets at the different production levels, showing budgeted profit.

(c) Advise the management of Greenlawn Ltd. of the production level which they should set for next year.

19 CASH BUDGETS AND FORECAST FINAL ACCOUNTS

We saw in the previous Chapter that the cash budget is the subsidiary budget that brings together all the other individual budgets. From a cash budget (which is often known as a *cash flow forecast*) can be produced the *master budget*. This takes the form of forecast financial statements, i.e. projected trading and profit and loss account, and balance sheet. In this Chapter we shall look, in some detail, at the cash budget and the master budget.

cash budget: purpose

The purpose of a cash budget is to detail the expected cash/bank receipts and payments, usually on a month-by-month basis, for the next three, six or twelve months (or even longer), in order to show the estimated bank balance at the end of each month throughout the period.

From the cash budget, the managers of a business can decide what action to take when a surplus of cash is shown to be available or, as is more likely, when a bank overdraft needs to be arranged.

cash budget: format

A cash budget is set out in the following form, with example figures:

Cash budget for the .... months ending ....

	Jan £000	Feb £000	Mar £000	etc £000
Receipts				
eg cash sales	150	150	161	170
from debtors	70	80	75	80
Total receipts for month	220	230	236	250
Payments				
eg to creditors	160	165	170	170
expenses	50	50	50	60
fixed assets		50		
Total payments for month	210	265	220	230
Bank balance (overdraft) at start of month	10	20	(15)	1
Add Receipts for month	220	230	236	250
Less Payments for month	(210)	(265)	(220)	(230)
Bank balance (overdraft) at end of month	20	(15)	1	21

As you can see, a cash budget consists of three main sections:

- receipts for the month,
- payments for the month,
- summary of bank account.

The receipts are analysed to show the amount that is expected to be received from cash sales, debtors, sale of assets, issue of shares, etc. Payments will show how much is expected to be paid for cash purchases, to creditors, expenses, purchases of assets, repayment of shares and loans. The summary bank account shows estimated opening bank balance at the beginning of the month, to which estimated receipts for the month are added, and payments deducted, resulting in the estimated closing bank balance at the end of the month. Where the bank balance is overdrawn, it should be indicated by brackets.

Important Note: The main difficulty in the preparation of cash budgets lies in the *timing* of receipts and payments - for example, debtors may pay two months after date of sale, or creditors may be paid one month after date of purchase: the information given in the question should be studied carefully to ensure that such receipts and payments are correctly recorded. Note too that the cash budget, as its name suggests, deals only in cash; thus non-cash items, such as depreciation, and provision for bad debts, should never be shown in a cash budget. Similarly, where cash discounts are allowed or received, only the actual amount of cash expected to be received or paid should be entered.

Case Problem: John Wilson trading as 'Online Software'

A friend of yours, John Wilson, who is interested in computers, has decided to establish a small mail-order business selling computer software. The software, which is mainly computer games and small business software, is to be bought in bulk from the manufacturer and then to be sold by means of advertisements in computer magazines.

John, with your assistance, has produced estimates for his new business for the next six months, as follows:

- He will commence trading in January 20-1, with a capital of £1,250.

- At the beginning of January he will purchase a 'base' stock of software which will cost him £1,000. As he is not yet established in business, he will have to pay for this straight away.

- He has estimated his sales to be:

January	£500
February	£800
March	£900
April	£1,000
May	£2,000
June	£1,200

    The reason for the higher sales figure estimated for May is because John plans to have a stand at a major computer exhibition.

- Most sales will be for cash, but he does expect a quarter of each month's sales will be made to computer shops; he plans to allow those customers one month's credit.

- His software purchases will be at cost price, being 50 per cent of his selling prices. He will replenish his stocks during the month in which the sale is made so that his month-end closing stock is always £1,000. For example, in January he will commence trading with a 'base' stock valued at £1,000; during January, he will sell software with a selling price of £500 and a cost price of £250; software with a cost to him of £250 will therefore be purchased in order to give a month-end closing stock of £1,000.

- Apart from the purchase of initial stock, all purchases will be made from suppliers who will allow him one months' credit.

- He will spend £250 each month on advertising; this must be paid for straightaway. The stand at the computer exhibition in May will cost £400, and must be paid for in April.

- Various sundry expenses, including post and packing, are expected to cost £100 each month for January, February and March, and £150 per month for April, May and June.

- As John plans initially to operate his business from his parents' house, there will be no office rental costs. He will, however, need to buy office equipment in January at a cost of £500; this will be paid for straightaway. John expects this equipment to last for five years before it will need replacement.

- For the first six months, John will take £100 per month as drawings; once the business is established, he hopes he will be able to draw out more.

John, who knows very little about accounting, is aware that he may need a small bank overdraft in the early stages. Being an accountant and wishing to help him, you decide that a cash budget needs to be prepared for the first six months of operations. Your calculations produce the following:

JOHN WILSON T/A 'ONLINE SOFTWARE' Cash Budget for the six months ending 30 June 20-1						
	Jan £	Feb £	Mar £	Apr £	May £	Jun £
Receipts						
Capital introduced	1,250					
Cash sales	375	600	675	750	1,500	900
From debtors	-	125	200	225	250	500
Total receipts for month	1,625	725	875	975	1,750	1,400
Payments						
Stock purchase	1,000					
To creditors	-	250	400	450	500	1,000
Advertising	250	250	250	250	250	250
Stand rental at computer exhibition				400		
Sundry expenses	100	100	100	150	150	150
Office equipment	500					
Drawings	100	100	100	100	100	100
Total payments for month	1,950	700	850	1,350	1,000	1,500
Bank balance, start of month	-	(325)	(300)	(275)	(650)	100
Add Receipts for month	1,625	725	875	975	1,750	1,400
Less Payments for month	(1,950)	(700)	(850)	(1,350)	(1,000)	(1,500)
Bank balance, end of month	(325)	(300)	(275)	(650)	100	Nil

This cash budget shows that there is a need, in the first six months at least, for some bank finance, and an early approach to the bank needs to be made.

cash budgets: limitations

While a cash budget is a very useful guide, it is only as good as the estimates on which it is based. A cash budget which is based on optimistic sales for the next six or twelve months will show an equally optimistic picture of the bank balance; a budget that looks too far into the future will probably prove to be inaccurate in later months. Like all budgets, as we have seen in the previous Chapter, it is necessary to make comparisons between actual and budget figures: variances need to be investigated. Indeed, many cash budget and cash flow forms have columns for both *projected* and *actual* figures.

A cash budget does not indicate the profits, or losses, being made by a business. It does not follow that a cash budget which reveals an increasing bank balance necessarily indicates a profitable business. To supplement the cash budget, it is quite usual to prepare a *master budget,* in the form of forecast final accounts, and this aspect is considered later in this Chapter.

cash budgets and 'what if?' questions

As we have seen just now, a cash budget is prepared on the basis of certain assumptions, for example:

- debtors pay, in full, in the month following sale
- purchases from suppliers are paid for two months after the month of purchase

Often the managers of a business will wish to change the assumptions on which the cash budget is based by saying 'what if?' For example:

- *What if* half our debtors take two months to pay?
- *What if* we buy a new machine three months earlier than planned?
- *What if* we take advantage of cash discounts offered by our creditors and pay within, say, 14 days of purchase?

Each of these examples will change the cash budget substantially, and any two of the three, or all three together, is likely to have a considerable effect on a previously calculated budget, and may lead to an increased bank overdraft requirement.

To answer *'what if?'* questions, the whole cash budget has to be reworked on the basis of the new assumptions. The reason for this is that, as the estimates of receipts and payments change each month, so the estimated closing month-end bank balance changes. This is where a computer spreadsheet is ideal for the preparation of cash budgets: each change can be put in, and the computer can be used to rework all the calculations. A printout can be taken of each assumption and then passed to the managers for their consideration.

cash: a limiting factor

It might be that the cash budget shows, for certain months, a potential bank overdraft which is beyond the limits of the business. It might be unacceptably high for the business because of the interest cost, or the bank may not be prepared to allow such overdraft facilities. Thus a shortage of cash may be the *limiting factor* for a business, and it may have to rethink the other budgets in order to change its plans so as to work within its cash resources. After all, it is a shortage of cash that forces most companies into liquidation, even if they provide a good product or service: thus the efficient use of cash resources is one of the most important control aspects for the management of a business.

the master budget

As already mentioned earlier in this Chapter, a *master budget* is the next logical step once all other budgets, including the cash budget, have been prepared.

A *master budget takes the form of forecast financial statements, i.e. forecast trading and profit and loss accounts, and balance sheet.*

Case Problem (continued): 'Online Software'

Following a first visit to the bank with his cash budget, John Wilson has been asked by the bank manager to produce forecast final accounts. You help John to prepare the following:

JOHN WILSON T/A 'ONLINE SOFTWARE'

Forecast Trading and Profit and Loss Accounts for the six months ending 30 June 20-1

	£	£
Sales		6,400
Opening stocks (initial purchase)	1,000	
Add Purchases	3,200	
	4,200	
Less Closing stocks	1,000	
Cost of goods sold		3,200
Gross Profit		3,200
Less expenses		
Advertising	1,500	
Stand rental at computer exhibition	400	
Sundry expenses	750	
Depreciation on office equipment	50	
		2,700
Net Profit		500

Forecast Balance Sheet as at 30 June 20-1

	£	£
Fixed assets		
Office equipment		500
Less depreciation		50
		450
Current assets		
Stocks	1,000	
Debtors	300	
Bank	-	
	1,300	
Less current liabilities		
Creditors	600	
Working capital		700
NET ASSETS		1,150
FINANCED BY		
Opening Capital		1,250
Add Net profit		500
		1,750
Less Drawings		600
		1,150

Points to note when preparing forecast final accounts:

- The sales figure shown in the trading account is the total amount of goods sold, whether paid for or not (sales made, but not yet paid for, are recorded as debtors in the balance sheet).

- Likewise, the figure for purchases is the total of goods bought, with amounts not yet paid for recorded as creditors in the balance sheet.

- Depreciation, which *never* appears in the cash budget, is shown amongst the expenses in the profit and loss account, and deducted from the cost of the fixed asset in the balance sheet. (Note that, in the example above, depreciation is for a period of six months.)

comments on cash budgets and the master budget

Besides preparing the cash budget and master budget, you may need to comment on them, either to the owner of the business, or to a potential lender. It is therefore vitally important that the subsidiary budgets used in the preparation of the cash budget are accurate, as anything that follows will be 'thrown' by an inaccurate budget.

You may need to prepare answers to the following questions:

- Will bank finance be needed at any time during the period covered by the cash budget? If so, how long will it take to repay such borrowing?

- Is there a build-up of cash that needs to be invested on a short-term basis?

- Is the business profitable?

- Are the credit terms allowed to debtors similar to those received from creditors?

- How much is the owner taking out of the business in relation to the forecast net profit?

- If the purchase of fixed assets creates a large overdraft, could other forms of finance be considered, eg hire purchase, or leasing?

In addition to these points, ratio analysis (see Chapter 22) can be used to analyse the forecast final accounts, and comparisons can be made with what was achieved by the same business in the previous year or half-year (assuming it was then trading).

CHAPTER SUMMARY

❏   A cash budget (or cash flow forecast) records the expected cash receipts and payments, usually on a monthly basis, for a period ahead of up to one year.

❏   A bank summary section on a cash budget shows the expected month-end bank balance. From this it is possible to see if short-term overdraft facilities need to be arranged.

❏   The master budget consists of forecast trading and profit and loss accounts, and balance sheet.

In the next two Chapters we shall be paying particular attention to the working capital of a business. Although the cash/bank balance is important, it forms only one item in the working capital of a business.

STUDENT ACTIVITIES

19.1 Jim Smith has recently been made redundant; he has received a redundancy payment and this, together with his accumulated savings, amounts to £10,000. He has decided to set up his own business selling computer stationery and this will commence trading with an initial capital of £10,000 on 1 January. On this date he will buy a van for business use at a cost of £6,000. He has estimated his purchases, sales, and expenses for the next six months as follows:

	Purchases £	Sales £	Expenses £
January	4,500	1,250	750
February	4,500	3,000	600
March	3,500	4,000	600
April	3,500	4,000	650
May	3,500	4,500	650
June	4,000	6,000	700

He will pay for purchases in the month after purchase; likewise, he expects his customers to pay for sales in the month after sale. All expenses will be paid for in the month in which they are incurred.

Jim realizes that he may need bank overdraft facilities before his business becomes established. He asks you to help him with information for the bank and, in particular, he asks you to prepare:

(a)   a month-by-month cash budget for the first six months.
(b)   a budgeted trading and profit and loss account for the first six months. (For this he tells you that his closing stock at 30 June is expected to have a value of £3,250, and that he wishes to depreciate the van at 20% per annum.)
(c)   a budgeted balance sheet as at 30 June.

19.2 The accountant of Wilkinson Ltd. is preparing the company's cash budget for the first half of 20-7. The following budgeted figures are available:

	Sales £	Purchases £	Wages and salaries £	Other expenses £
January	65,000	26,500	17,500	15,500
February	70,000	45,000	18,000	20,500
March	72,500	50,000	18,250	19,000
April	85,000	34,500	18,500	18,500
May	65,000	35,500	16,500	20,500
June	107,500	40,500	20,000	22,000

The following additional information is available:

- Sales income is received in the month after sale, and sales for December 20-6 amounted to £57,500.
- 'Other expenses' each month includes an allocation of £1,000 for depreciation; all other expenses are paid for in the month in which they are incurred.
- Purchases, and wages and salaries are paid for in the month in which they are incurred.
- The bank balance at 1 January 20-7 is £2,250.
- Stock at 1 January 20-7 is valued at £15,500 and, at 30 June 20-7, is expected to have a value of £17,350.

You are to prepare:
(a)   a month-by-month cash budget for the first six months of 20-7.
(b)   a budgeted trading and profit and loss account for the six months ending 30 June 20-7.
(c)   a statement which reconciles the net profit for the six months with the bank balance at 30 June 20-7.

19.3   Mayday Ltd. was recently formed and plans to commence trading on 1 June 20-1. During May the company will issue 200,000 ordinary shares of £1 each at par and the cash will be subscribed at once. During the same month £130,000 will be spent on plant and £50,000 will be invested in stock, resulting in a cash balance on 1 June of £20,000.

Plans for the twelve months commencing 1 June 20-1 are as follows:

- Stock costing £40,000 will be sold each month at a mark-up of 25%. Customers are expected to pay in the second month following sale.

- Month-end stock levels will be maintained at £50,000 and purchases will be paid for in the month following delivery.

- Wages and other expenses will amount to £6,000 per month, payable in the month during which the costs are incurred.

- Plant will have a ten-year life and no scrap value. Depreciation is to be charged on the straight line basis.

You are to prepare:

(a)   a month-by-month cash budget for Mayday Ltd. for the year to 31 May 20-2.

(b)   the company's budgeted trading and profit and loss accounts for the year ending 31 May 20-2, together with a budgeted balance sheet at that date.

19.4   Peter Sanderson has worked for some years as a sales representative for an arts and craft company, but has recently been made redundant. He intends to start up in business in October on his own, using £15,000 which he currently has invested with a building society. He has a number of good business contacts, and is confident that his firm will do well, but thinks that additional finance will be required in the short term; he plans to approach his bank for the necessary finance. Peter, whom you have known for some time, asks you for advice. He provides the following information:

- Arrangements have been made to purchase fixed assets costing £8,000. These will be paid for at the end of September and are expected to have a five year life, at the end of which they will have a nil scrap value.

- Stocks costing £5,000 will be bought and paid for on 28 September, and subsequent monthly purchases will be at a level sufficient to replace forecast sales for the month.

- Forecast monthly sales are £3,000 for October, £6,000 for November and December, and £10,500 from January 20-4 onwards.

- Selling price is fixed at the cost of stock plus 50%.

- Two months' credit will be allowed to customers, but only one month's credit will be received from suppliers of stock (but the initial stock will be paid for immediately).

- Running expenses, including rent but excluding depreciation of fixed assets, are estimated at £1,600 per month.

- Peter intends to make monthly cash drawings of £1,000.

Required:

(a)   A month-by-month cash budget for the six months to 31 March 20-4.

(b)   A budgeted trading and profit and loss account for the six months to 31 March 20-4, and a budgeted balance sheet at 31 March 20-4.

(c)   An assessment of his forecasts and financial requirements from a lender's (ie bank's) viewpoint.

19.5 The balance sheet of Antonio's Speciality Food Shop at 31 August 20-1 was:

	£ Cost	£ Dep'n	£ Net
Fixed assets	15,000	3,000	12,000
Current assets			
Stocks		5,000	
Debtors		800	
		5,800	
Less current liabilities			
Creditors	3,000		
Bank overdraft	1,050		
		4,050	
Working capital			1,750
NET ASSETS			13,750
FINANCED BY			
Antonio's capital			13,750

On the basis of past performance, Antonio expects that his sales during the coming six months will be:

September	October	November	December	January	February
£8,000	£8,000	£10,000	£20,000	£6,000	£6,000

Antonio allows credit to some of his regular customers, and the proportions of cash and credit sales are usually:

	Cash sales	Credit sales
November	80%	20%
December	60%	40%
All other months	90%	10%

Customers who buy on credit normally pay in the following month. Antonio's gross profit margin is consistently 25 per cent of his selling price. He normally maintains his stocks at a constant level by purchasing goods in the month in which they are sold: the only exception to this is that in November he purchases in advance 50 per cent of the goods he expects to sell in December.

Half of the purchases each month are made from suppliers who give a 2 per cent cash discount for immediate payment and he takes advantage of the discount. He pays for the remainder (without discount) in the month after purchase.

Expenditure on wages, rent and other running expenses of the shop are consistently £2,000 per month paid in the month in which they are incurred.

Fixed assets are depreciated at 10 per cent per annum on cost price.

You are to:

(a) Prepare:
- a cash budget showing Antonio's bank balance or overdraft for each month in the half year ending 29 February 20-2;

- Antonio's balance sheet at 29 February 20-2.

(b) If Antonio's bank manager considered it necessary to fix the overdraft limit at £3,500, explain what Antonio should do in order to observe the limit.

7 Health 'n Burger Park:
feasibility study for a new shop

> **covering**
> final accounts, incomplete records, costing, budgeting, cash and credit control, evaluation of problems, social/human implications of financial decision making

SITUATION

Franchising is a business technique which enables those with relatively limited capital to run their own business under the 'flag' of a national, or even international, name. Franchise operations in Britain include names such as Kentucky Fried Chicken, MacDonalds, Tandy, Benetton and Dyno-Rod.

Health 'n Burger Park Limited is a franchisor of whole-food service and take-away businesses. A number of franchises and some company-owned outlets have been established in the south-east of England.

You are invited to assess the possibilities of establishing a franchise in a selected town or city in your area. The franchisor has options on suitable premises (details given): the franchisee will rent the premises from the franchisor, but will be responsible for all the refurbishment costs.

Under the terms of the franchise agreement you would have sole rights to sell Health 'n Burger Park products in the selected town or city: all purchases of food, etc must be made from the company, and *national selling prices must be adhered to*. A licence fee is payable to the franchisor based on sales turnover. Further details are as follows:

Town/City	Annual Rental (payable quarterly in advance)	*Equipment and Refurbishment Costs (to be paid by the franchisee at the start of trading)
	£	£
Redgrove	18,000	65,000
Evelode	10,000	50,000
Mereford	30,000	85,000
Carpminster	20,000	60,000
Malwich	15,000	60,000
Newtown	35,000	90,000
Rowcester	32,500	75,000

AVAILABLE PREMISES

* The franchise agreement requires the outlet to be completely refurbished every five years.

FURTHER DETAILS OF EACH TOWN/CITY

Redgrove is an industrial town some twenty miles to the south of a large city. The population is about 35,000 and many people commute daily to the large city. There is a college of further education, and the population is 'younger' than the average town. Redgrove was, at one time, reliant on heavy engineering, but this has now largely gone causing many redundancies. However, some light engineering companies have recently moved into the area; nevertheless, unemployment in the town is higher than average.

Evelode is an agricultural market town with a population of around 15,000. The town acts as a 'draw' for the surrounding rural area; many school children are 'bussed in' and the town has a smaller college of further education.

Mereford is a small cathedral city with a population of 50,000. It is the centre of a farming community, and has a further education college. There is a good tourist trade, and regular cattle markets are held every Monday and Wednesday.

Carpminster is a nineteenth century working town which formerly relied on one industry. Nowadays this industry has contracted and the town has suffered high unemployment amongst its 45,000 population. The town has started to recover, although it cannot be said to be prosperous. There is a college of further education.

Malwich is a spa town with a population of 20,000. It is popular with visitors, and has a large number of private schools, although there is no further education college. The town has also attracted many retired people.

Newtown is a large 'new town' with a young population of 75,000. There are many light engineering factories; the town centre has a number of major shops and is a considerable 'draw' for some 20 miles around. The town has many schools and a large further education college.

Rowcester is a medium-sized cathedral city and county town. It has a fine cricket team. The population is about 85,000 and is slightly older than average. The city has an unemployment rate close to the national average. There is a large college of further education, together with a new university.

FRANCHISOR'S PRICE LIST

		£
Nut Rissoles	per 100	94.00
Bean Burgers	per 100	64.00
Chips	5 kg	15.00
Whole Wheat Rolls	per 50	14.00
Soup	100 servings	42.00
Coleslaw	100 servings	34.00
Dandelion Coffee	100 sachets	28.00
Herbal Tea	100 sachets	22.00
Frying Medium	5 litres	18.00
Packaging (subject to VAT)	per 1000	100.00

SAMPLE MENU

HEALTH 'N BURGER PARK

MENU OF DELICACIES

A WHOLE LOT BETTER for very little more!

	£
Nutritious Nut Rissole in a Tasty Whole Wheat Roll	2.80
Green Bean Burger in a Tasty Whole Wheat Roll	1.60
Nut Rissole and Chips	3.60
Bean Burger and Chips	2.20
Organic Coleslaw Salad	1.00
Hot Bean Soup	1.20
Tasty Whole Wheat Roll	0.60
Dandelion Coffee	0.90
Herbal Tea	0.60

OUR GUARANTEE

All delicacies are made from organically grown natural produce.
All frying in natural poly-unsaturated frying medium.
All food is served in hygienic bio-degradable disposable containers.
All prices include VAT.

SAMPLE ANNUAL OPERATING STATEMENT

Operating Statement for 20-4	£	£
Sales turnover (excluding VAT)		780,000
Costs		
Food and packaging	335,400	
Licence fee (paid to franchisor)	7,800	
Wages	171,600	
Advertising: national	8,000	
local	16,500	
Rent and rates	90,000	
Other overheads (excluding bank interest charges)	77,480	
		706,780
Operating profit (before bank interest charges and taxation)		73,220

Note:
National advertising is arranged by the franchisor and charged to franchisees.
Local advertising/promotions are the sole responsibility of individual franchisees.

TASKS

In working groups of three or four:

1. Identify the potential types of customers who might patronise a 'Health 'n Burger Park' outlet. One method of doing this would be to observe the customers at burger and health food establishments, noting age groups and social groups. You should then select one of the towns/cities described on page 205 as the location for your group's 'Health 'n Burger Park' outlet. Relate the population of the town in which you live to the population of the chosen town/city, and estimate the number of customers per week who are likely to patronise your outlet.

2. Estimate the annual sales in the chosen town/city at three levels: high, low, and most probable. (One possible way of estimating the annual sales would be to find out what the average person spends on each visit - a questionnaire might be appropriate).

3. Examine the ways in which you can advertise locally, e.g. radio, newspapers, leaflet distribution, etc. Find out the costs and choose what method you consider to be the most cost effective. Design appropriate advertising material, or write the script for a radio advertisement.

4. Prepare a month-by-month cash budget (incorporating your proposed advertising costs) for the first year of business. Attach a sheet to explain the assumptions and reasoning you have made, including reference to sources of finance.

5. Prepare an estimated operating statement for the first year, together with an estimated year-end balance sheet. (Base the operating statement on the sample statement given, but make allowances for different levels of wages, rent and rates, etc.)

6. Draw up a break-even analysis on the basis of your high, low, and most probable sales projections.

7. Submit to the representatives of the franchisor a proposal for your group to take up the franchise in your selected town/city. The proposal should include an outline of your market research, giving your conclusions with any justifications you consider necessary. (You should make use of the cash budget and estimated operating statements, balance sheet and break-even analyses which you have already prepared.)

20 WORKING CAPITAL MANAGEMENT

In the previous Chapter we looked at how a business can budget (or forecast) its cash position. Cash - in the form of cash itself and money at the bank - is an important ingredient in the *working capital* of a business. As we have seen, without cash a business cannot pay its debts as they fall due. We shall now look at working capital and will see that, without sufficient working capital, a business cannot survive for long.

what is working capital?

Working capital is the surplus of current assets over current liabilities. For example:

	£	£
Current assets		
Stocks	20,000	
Debtors	29,000	
Bank/cash	1,000	
		50,000
Less current liabilities		
Creditors	22,000	
Bank overdraft	3,000	
		25,000
Working capital		25,000

Therefore the calculation is:

WORKING CAPITAL = CURRENT ASSETS − CURRENT LIABILITIES

All businesses need a certain minimum amount of working capital, but there is no legal requirement, nor is there any amount that is considered acceptable by the accountancy profession. The reason for this is that the amount required will vary from business to business, depending on the *nature of the business* (for example, a shop is likely to need less working capital than an engineering business), and on the *size of the business* (for example, a small corner shop will need less working capital than a large departmental store). If we cannot decide on the *amount* of working capital required, we can at least agree on the *ratio* between current assets and current liabilities. This ratio is called the *current ratio* or *working capital ratio*.

current ratio

This expresses the balance between current assets and current liabilities in the form of a ratio:

$$\underline{\text{CURRENT ASSETS}} \quad = \quad \text{CURRENT (or WORKING CAPITAL) RATIO}$$
$$\text{CURRENT LIABILITIES}$$

For example, a business with current assets of £50,000 and current liabilities of £25,000 has a current ratio of:

$$\underline{\text{£50,000}} \quad = \quad 2{:}1$$
$$\text{£25,000}$$

This shows that there are £2 of current assets to each £1 of current liabilities.

As a 'rule of thumb', it is often considered that a 2:1 current ratio is 'about right', but it will depend very much on the nature of the business. A shop, for example, will be able to work to a lower current ratio (ie less than 2:1), because it should have fewer debtors than an engineering business. Therefore, a ratio of 1.5:1 might be acceptable for some businesses.

A working capital ratio can be too high: if it is above 3:1 an investigation of the make-up of the current assets and current liabilities should reveal that the business has either too much stock, too many debtors, too much money in the bank, or even too few creditors.

liquid capital and liquid ratio

It is also appropriate to calculate the *liquid capital* of a business, as follows:

$$\text{(CURRENT ASSETS - STOCK)} \quad - \quad \text{CURRENT LIABILITIES} \quad = \quad \text{LIQUID CAPITAL}$$

Liquid capital differs from working capital in that stock is deducted from current assets.

An appropriate ratio can also be calculated. This is known as the *liquid ratio,* the *quick ratio,* or the *acid-test ratio:*

$$\underline{\text{(CURRENT ASSETS - STOCK)}} \quad = \quad \text{LIQUID (or QUICK or ACID-TEST) RATIO}$$
$$\text{CURRENT LIABILITIES}$$

The reason that stock is omitted from this ratio is because it is the most illiquid current asset: in most cases it has to be sold, turned into debtors, and then the cash has to be collected from debtors; although, for a shop making a cash sale, stock is immediately turned into cash. Also, some of the stock held by a business may be unsaleable or obsolete.

The 'ideal' liquid ratio is thought to be about 1:1, i.e. £1 of liquid assets (debtors and bank) to each £1 of current liabilities. At this ratio, a business should be able to pay its current liabilities from its liquid assets. A figure below 1:1, e.g. 0.75:1, indicates that the business would have difficulty in meeting pressing demands from creditors. However, as with the current ratio, certain types of business are able to operate with a lower liquid ratio than others.

With both current and liquid capital ratios (and indeed with any ratios) it is important to note trends in the ratio for the same business, or to make comparisons with similar types of business. As both of these calculations are expressed as a ratio, it is possible to compare different sizes of organization in the same line of business.

Case Problem: 'Mrs Smith's' – a small shop

Mrs. Smith, with the help of her husband, runs a small 'ever-open' corner shop in your town. The shop is located in an area of terraced Victorian properties, many of which have been converted into bed-sits. She does well with the shop, particularly in the evenings when there is demand for frozen meals, pies and pasties, all suitably washed down with a bottle or two from the off-licence section of the shop.

As a regular customer of the shop, and knowing that you have some knowledge of accounting, she asks you to help her interpret the balance sheet which has just been prepared by her accountant - in particular, she mentions her concern at never seeming to have much cash to take out for drawings. As a first analysis, you decide to look at the working capital position and the figures you extract are:

	Last year	This year
	£	£
Stocks	3,550	4,210
Debtors	1,425	2,320
Bank/cash	overdraft 890	overdraft 1,650
Creditors	1,765	2,835

From the above, calculate working capital, liquid capital, current ratio and liquid ratio. Comment on the figures, so far as you have information.

Answer:

	Last year	This year
Working capital	£2,320	£2,045
Liquid capital	(£1,230)	(£2,165)
Current ratio	1.87:1	1.46:1
Liquid ratio	0.54:1	0.52:1

Working capital has decreased, and the liquid capital position has also worsened; both current and liquid ratios have declined. While the overall position is reasonably acceptable for a shop, it would be more worrying for a manufacturing business. The reason for this is that, in a shop, stock is sold and turned into cash immediately without having to allow debtors time to pay. However, Mrs. Smith does seem to be allowing her regular customers time to pay - debtors are at rather too high a level for this type of business and this should be pointed out to her. Creditors show a considerable increase, as does the bank balance; stocks have increased.

Overall, Mrs. Smith needs to exercise considerable control over the working capital items: over the two years all figures have gone the 'wrong way' and it is no wonder than she never seems to have any cash for personal drawings.

control of working capital items

The major working capital items are:

• stock
• debtors
• cash/bank
• creditors

We will now consider each in turn to see how they can best be managed by a business.

stock control

Stock, for manufacturing businesses, consists of up to three categories, ie raw materials, work-in-progress, and finished goods. For a wholesale or retail business, it will consist only of goods that have been bought in for resale. The methods of keeping stock records in order to assist with cost accounting have already been dealt with in Chapter 13.

For most businesses, the problem is in maintaining a balance between the disadvantage of holding *too much* stock and the disadvantage of holding *too little* stock.

Disadvantages of holding too much stock

- Cash has been paid out early to finance extra stock - the cash could have been put to better use in the business.
- Some of the stock may deteriorate or become obsolete, and so have to be written off.
- A large stock may need a larger warehouse or premises than is necessary, and stockholding costs will be higher.

Disadvantages of holding too little stock

- The main disadvantage to a retail business is that sales will usually be lost because the customer will go elsewhere.
- In a manufacturing business, to be out of stock of a small component could bring the factory to a halt.

The middle course

A balance needs to be maintained between holding too much stock, and too little stock. This is usually achieved by:

- setting maximum and minimum stockholding quantities for each item of stock
- establishing appropriate re-order quantities.

Much routine stock control work can be carried out by a computer accounting system using a stock control program.

stock turnover

Stock turnover is a measure of the number of the number of days' stock held on average. It is calculated as follows:

$$\frac{\text{AVERAGE STOCK *}}{\text{COST OF GOODS SOLD}} = \text{STOCK TURNOVER (IN DAYS)}$$

> * *Note:* average stock is usually found by taking the average of the opening and closing stocks, ie (opening stock + closing stock) ÷ 2.

Comparisons of stock turnover need to be made for a business over a number of accounting periods, and also with similar businesses. Clearly different types of businesses will have different stock turnover figures. For example, a market trader selling fresh flowers who finishes each day when sold out will have a stock turnover of one day. By contrast, a jewellery shop – because it may hold large stocks of jewellery – will have a much slower stock turnover, perhaps ninety days or more.

An organization which is improving in efficiency will have a faster stock turnover when you compare recent figures with those for earlier years, or compare stock turnover of similar organizations.

control of debtors

The control of debtors is the routine administrative task of ensuring that:

- credit references are obtained for all new customers
- credit limits are established for each debtor
- sales invoices and month-end statements are processed and sent out promptly
- action is taken swiftly to chase overdue debts and, where necessary, legal action is pursued
- goods are not sold to debtors who are likely to 'go bad' – eg if their cheques are 'bouncing'

A measure of the efficiency of debtor collection is to calculate the debtors' turnover, as follows:

$$\frac{\text{DEBTORS}}{\text{CREDIT SALES FOR YEAR}} \quad \text{x} \quad 365 \text{ days*} \quad = \quad \text{DEBTOR COLLECTION TIME (in days)}$$

Note: The calculation can, of course, be expressed in weeks, or months.

The debtor collection time can be compared with that for the previous year, or for a similar organization. In Britain, most debtors make payment between 30 to 60 days from date of invoice or statement, although some organisations are slower in paying and have to be chased.

One way to encourage debtors to pay faster is to offer a *cash discount* for quick settlement, eg

2.5% cash discount for settlement within seven days; normal terms 30 days

Assuming that such terms encourage debtors to pay in one week, instead of 30 days, this means that, on a debt of £100, it is costing £2.50 to have the use of £97.50 for three weeks. This is a very high rate of interest - somewhere around 45% per annum! It follows that a firm's cash discount policy needs to be looked at carefully - it may be costing more than it is worth. Also, many debtors are likely to deduct the 2.5% cash discount and continue to settle at their usual time!

control of cash and bank

Estimates of future inflows and outflows of funds are made, as we have seen in the previous chapter, by means of a cash budget. In this way, overdrafts can be anticipated and arranged in advance, while surplus funds can be invested. It is also appropriate to check the actual bank balance against the budget and to investigate major variances - perhaps debtors are not paying as quickly as expected, or new fixed assets have had to be purchased earlier than originally planned.

using credit from suppliers (creditors)

Creditors are the 'other side of the coin' from debtors, and here we can measure the speed it takes to pay 'our' suppliers/creditors as follows:

$$\frac{\text{CREDITORS}}{\text{CREDIT PURCHASES}} \quad \text{x} \quad 365 \text{ days} \quad = \quad \text{CREDITORS' PAYMENT TIME (in days)}$$

While creditors can be a useful source of short-term finance, delaying payment for too long may cause problems, eg suppliers may refuse to deliver goods or services until the current amount due has been paid. In short, pay bills at the latest possible time, but do pay them!

CHAPTER SUMMARY

❑ Working capital is *current assets minus current liabilities.*

❑ Liquid capital is *(current assets - stock) minus current liabilities.*

❑ A current ratio of about 2:1 is often considered to be ideal, although many businesses, particularly those in the retail trade, can operate on lower ratios, eg 1.5:1, or even less.

❑ A liquid capital ratio of about 1:1 is the ideal.

❑ Both current and liquid ratios can be too high, indicating too many current assets or too few current liabilities.

❑ The turnover figure for stock, debtor collection time, and creditors' payment time are all used as measures of the efficiency of working capital management in a business.

The next Chapter continues the theme of working capital by looking at the effect of changes in the make-up of the working capital items.

STUDENT ACTIVITIES

20.1 The following information has been extracted from the balance sheets of Harry Riley's engineering business:

	31 Dec. 20-1	31 Dec. 20-2
	£	£
Debtors	7,220	9,355
Creditors	5,785	6,175
Stocks	3,210	3,890
Bank balance/overdraft	760	1,650 (overdraft)
Accruals	220	110
Prepayments	385	275

Harry Riley asks you to calculate:

* the amount of working capital
* the amount of liquid capital
* current ratio
* liquid ratio

As his accountant, write him a letter (address: H Riley & Co Ltd, Unit 27, Argos Industrial Estate, Newtown, NT2 8BT) explaining to him what each term means, and the significance of each of the figures to his business. Comment in your letter on any trend shown by your calculations.

20.2   At 31 December 20-4, George Harvey's business, a newsagents shop, had the following **assets**:

	£
Premises	35,500
Fixtures and fittings	3,500
Stocks	6,850
Debtors	1,685
Cash	395

Capital and **liabilities** were:

	£
Capital account	12,250
Loan: mortgage on premises	25,450
Creditors	8,650
Bank	1,580

(a)   State the amount of his:
- current assets
- current liabilities
- working capital
- liquid capital

(b)   Calculate the:
- current ratio
- liquid ratio

(c)   During the first week of 20-5, he sells 10% of his stock for £1,100, receiving cheques for £880 and cash of £220 in payment; he also receives cheques totalling £725 from his debtors. All cheques are banked as soon as they are received. He pays creditors of £2,050 by cheque.

Calculate the amount of his working capital and liquid capital at the end of the week, together with the current ratio and liquid ratio. Comment on any changes that have taken place.

20.3   You work in the accounts department of Jet Stationery Co. Ltd., which is a wholesaler of stationery supplies. The office manager is concerned that goods are being supplied to customers on credit by the dispatch department without any reference to the amount they owe. Also, from time to time goods have been supplied to new customers without an account being formally opened for them.

The office manager asks you to prepare a flow chart which will establish procedures to be followed by the stores department before:

- supplying goods to existing customers

- supplying goods to new customers

The flow chart should also include procedures to be followed by the accounts department in order to ensure speedy collection of amounts due from debtors and to minimise the risk of bad debts.

21 FURTHER ASPECTS OF WORKING CAPITAL

In the previous Chapter we looked at the calculation of working capital and liquid capital, current ratio, and liquid ratio. We also examined the particular qualities of the main working capital items of stock, debtors, cash/bank and creditors, together with the ways in which these items can be analysed from year to year.

This Chapter will look at the flow of working capital, and the effect of changes in the make-up of the main working capital items.

the flow of working capital

Working capital is the life-blood of any business, and the following diagram will help you to appreciate the flow of working capital:

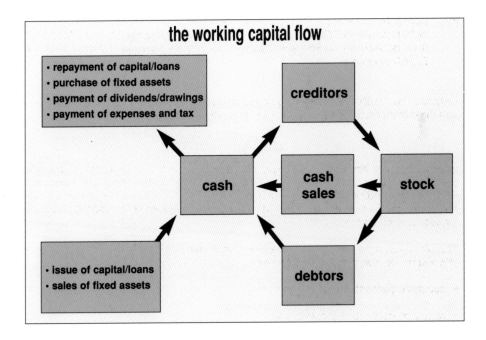

From the diagram you should note that, while a business has a certain amount of working capital, external funds may flow *into* working capital items and increase the amount of working capital. For example, new capital, and the sale of fixed assets, will increase the cash/bank balance and, consequently, the amount of working capital. An outflow of working capital items, to fund the purchase of fixed assets, or repayment of capital, will reduce the cash/bank balance and, consequently, the amount of working capital. Note that a change *entirely within* the working capital items will not affect the *amount* of working capital. For example, the purchase on credit of a stock of goods for resale will increase stocks (a current asset), and increase creditors (a current liability) by the same amount - the working capital amount is unaltered. The only changes may be in the current and liquid ratios.

Case Problem: James Brown – working capital

James Brown operates a wholesale health-food business. He buys from manufacturers and producers, and sells to health-food shops. James has prepared budgets for the next twelve months, and asks you to help him with certain aspects of these. He provides you with the following budgeted information:

- sales for the year will be £240,000
- purchases for the year will be £180,000
- net profit for the year will be £20,000

Note: both sales and purchases take place at an even rate throughout the year.

A summary of his forecast balance sheet at the end of the year is:

	£	£	£
JAMES BROWN			
Forecast Balance Sheet as at 31 December			
Fixed assets			30,000
Current assets			
Stock		20,000	
Debtors		20,000	
		40,000	
Less Current liabilities			
Creditors	15,000		
Bank overdraft	5,000		
		20,000	
Working capital			20,000
NET ASSETS			50,000
FINANCED BY			
Capital			45,000
Add Net profit			20,000
			65,000
Less Drawings			15,000
			50,000

First, James asks you to calculate and comment on:

- current ratio
- liquid ratio
- debtor collection time
- creditors' payment time

He then asks you what the effect will be:
- on his forecast net profit
- on his bank balance/overdraft
- on the current ratio
- on the liquid ratio

if certain proposals are implemented. These proposals, which are to be considered separately, are:

(a)   James wishes to increase depreciation by an *extra* £5,000 this year.
(b)   A number of his customers have asked if they can have two months in which to pay, instead of the current terms.
(c)   He has wondered if he could take 1.5 months' credit from his suppliers.
(d)   He would like to purchase new fixed assets at a cost of £30,000 (no depreciation on these fixed assets will be charged in 20-4).

Answer – initial comments on performance ratios

- Current ratio   2:1   • Liquid ratio   1:1
  Both of these ratios are 'about right'.

- Debtor collection time: 1 month • Creditor payment time: 1 month
  Very good figures for any business.

Answer – effects of new proposals

Proposal	Net Profit	Bank/ (Overdraft)	Current Ratio	Liquid Ratio
(a)	£15,000	(£5,000)*	2:1*	1:1*
(b)	£20,000*	(£25,000)	1.5:1	1:1*
(c)	£20,000*	£2,500	1.9:1	1:1*
(d)	£20,000*	(£35,000)	0.8:1	0.4:1

*   indicates figures unchanged from original forecasts

COMMENTS

Proposal (a):   Net profit is reduced by £5,000 because of extra charge for depreciation. The bank overdraft remains unchanged, because depreciation is a non-cash expense. Both current and liquid ratio are unchanged because depreciation forms no part of working capital.

Proposal (b):   Net profit is unchanged because total sales are not affected, only the timing of the receipt of those sales. The bank balance is an extra £20,000 overdrawn because an additional £20,000 of debtors has to be financed.
The current ratio is £60,000 (£20,000 + £40,000) ÷ £40,000 (£15,000 + £25,000) = 1.5:1.
The liquid ratio is £40,000 ÷ £40,000 = 1:1.

Proposal (c):   Net profit is unchanged because only the timing of the payment for the purchases is altered, not the total. Creditors now become £22,500 and the bank balance benefits from the extra credit received to become £2,500.
The current ratio is £42,500 (£20,000 + £20,000 + £2,500 bank) ÷ £22,500 (creditors) = 1.9:1.
The liquid ratio is £22,500 ÷ £22,500 = 1:1.

Proposal (d):   Net profit is unaffected. The bank overdraft is £35,000.
Current ratio is £40,000 (£20,000 + £20,000) ÷ £50,000 (£15,000 + £35,000) = 0.8:1. Liquid ratio is £20,000 ÷ £50,000 = 0.4:1.

Conclusion

Changes in the pattern of trading, for example allowing longer credit to debtors, or taking longer to pay creditors, have an effect on the bank balance and the current ratio. Transactions such as the purchase of fixed assets reduce the working capital of a business (unless the fixed assets are financed in another way) and have a significant effect on current and liquid ratios. The general conclusion is that the working capital of a business is not a fixed amount but changes according to the nature of business transactions.

working capital cycle

A further use of ratios covering the working capital items, ie the turnover of debtors, creditors and stocks is to calculate the *working capital cycle* (sometimes known as the cash operating cycle). This aspect of working capital management calculates the period of time between the payment for goods received into stock and the collection of cash from customers in respect of their sale. The shorter the length of time between the initial outlay and the ultimate collection of cash, the lesser the value of working capital to be financed by the business. The length of the working capital cycle is calculated in three stages, by calculating:

1   the time that goods are in stock
2   the time that debtors take to pay
3   deduct from 1 + 2 the period of credit received from suppliers

All time periods are best expressed in days, and the cash operating cycle calculations can take the following format (with example figures):

WORKING CAPITAL CYCLE	DAYS
Time period that goods are in stock	
Stock turnover: (average stock ÷ cost of goods sold) x 365	37
Time period that debtors take to pay	
Debtor collection time: (debtors ÷ sales) x 365	40
	77
Less: Period of credit received from suppliers	
Creditors payment time: (creditors ÷ purchases) x 365	30
WORKING CAPITAL CYCLE	47

Like all accounting ratios and statistics, a comparison needs to be made - either with the figure for the previous year, or with a similar firm. The working capital cycle is likely to show either an overall position that is better, ie the cycle has been reduced, or one that is worse, where the total time has been increased. There are three ways in which the cycle can be reduced:

• reducing stocks (which will lower the number of days that stock is held)
• speeding up the rate of debtor collection (i.e. less time is allowed to debtors to pay)
• slowing down the rate of creditor payment (i.e. taking longer to pay the creditors)

It should be noted that it may not always be possible to put these three policies into practice; also they may have unexpected consequences for a particular business. For example:

• reducing stocks might mean that a poorer service is offered to customers, who may take their business elsewhere
• giving debtors less time to pay may cause customers to seek alternative suppliers who are offering better terms
• taking extra credit from suppliers may be difficult, and they might decline to supply goods unless immediate payment is forthcoming

overtrading - a danger

We have just looked at the working capital cycle and seen how this can be timed, and steps taken to reduce its timing. Profits are made each time stock is sold to debtors, so the faster the cycle can be made to operate, the faster profits will accumulate. But a business that has too little working capital is likely to get into difficulties. The working capital may become depleted, perhaps because of losses, or excessive dividends/drawings. A rapidly expanding business which experiences a rising demand for its products may have to build a new factory, or buy new machinery in order to satisfy the demand. Unless the business has adequate reserves of working capital, it may find that little is left after all the additional fixed assets have been bought. The only recourse may be heavy borrowing with resultant interest charges, or reliance on extended trade credit in order to purchase stocks of raw materials and goods. If creditors start to demand repayment, the only way to repay the debts may be to sell some of the fixed assets. The next step is usually bankruptcy or liquidation, as no business can continue to operate without a full complement of fixed assets. A business trying to manage with too little working capital is said to be *overtrading*.

These are often symptoms of overtrading:

- a rapid increase in sales
- a considerably increased bank overdraft
- a rapid increase in creditors

Let us now look at an example of overtrading.

Case Problem: Joyce Banner – overtrading

Joyce Banner has recently opened a fashion shop in the centre of a university town. After twelve months of trading, and sales of £50,000, she has made satisfactory profits. Her balance sheet appears as:

JOYCE BANNER
Balance Sheet as at 30 June

	£	£
Fixed assets		5,000
Current assets		
Stocks	12,000	
Debtors	3,000	
Bank	1,000	
	16,000	
Less Current liabilities		
Creditors	4,000	
Working capital		12,000
NET ASSETS		17,000
FINANCED BY		
Capital		15,000
Add Net profit		7,500
		22,500
Less Drawings		5,500
		17,000

On Joyce Banner's balance sheet, working capital is £12,000, with the current ratio at 4:1. The liquid ratio is 1:1.

Joyce tells you that she is keen to expand the business and wishes to open a new shop in the college area of town. She has already seen suitable premises to rent and has estimated the cost of fitting them out at £10,000. To stock the new shop she will need to buy stocks at a cost of £12,000: half of these will have to be paid for in cash, the other half can be bought on one month's credit.

To help her make a final decision she asks you to draft her balance sheet as it will appear immediately after these transactions have taken place.

Answer:

JOYCE BANNER			
Balance Sheet			
	£	£	£
Fixed assets £5,000 + £10,000			15,000
Current assets			
Stocks		24,000	
Debtors		3,000	
		27,000	
Less Current liabilities			
Creditors £4 000 + £6 000	10,000		
Bank £1 000 - £10 000 - £6 000	15,000		
		25,000	
Working capital			2,000
NET ASSETS			17,000
FINANCED BY			
Capital			17,000

Working capital is now only £2,000, with a current ratio of 1.1:1 and a liquid ratio of only 0.1:1. This is a very different position from that illustrated before the expansion. Joyce and her business now face a number of problems:

- creditors will soon be pressing for payment and it is unlikely that the bank will wish to see a further increase in the overdraft;

- the working capital that has been used to purchase fixed assets, £10,000, will only be replaced gradually as profits are made and, in addition, some of this profit must be used to pay interest on the bank overdraft;

- if stock is not turned over quickly there will be no money with which to pay the creditor (there is now little working capital to fall back on) and an unpaid creditor could force the business into liquidation.

Expansion on such a scale would be better financed by an increase in permanent capital: perhaps Joyce could go into partnership. Of course it does not follow that every business will come to an end if it tries to expand: if the fall in working capital is quickly replaced by extra profits coming in from increased trade, then all will be well. Steady expansion of a business is not usually a hazard; the danger comes when the expansion is too rapid and the working capital is inadequate.

CHAPTER SUMMARY

❑   Working capital is the life-blood of any business.

❑   The working capital cycle can be 'timed' to measure the effectiveness of the management of working capital.

❑   A business that tries to expand too fast with too little working capital is said to be *overtrading*.

❑   A change in each of the main working capital components of stock, debtors, creditors will have a direct effect on the bank balance.

STUDENT ACTIVITIES

21.1   The following statement shows the working capital of OS Ltd., a wholesaler of office stationery and other supplies:

	£
Stock	69,000
Debtors	55,000
Bank	4,000
	128,000
Less creditors	40,000
Working capital	88,000

The directors are considering the following separate proposals:

(a)   buying a further £10,000 of stock on credit
(b)   selling goods in stock which had cost £3,000, for £5,000 on credit
(c)   issuing a further 20,000 shares at £1.50 each
(d)   paying a dividend of £8,000
(e)   selling fixed assets for £5,000

You are to:
•   Alter the working capital statement for each proposal (treat each proposal separately).
•   Calculate for each proposal:
   (a)   the current ratio
   (b)   the liquid ratio

21.2   The following forecasts for 20-1 have been prepared for Jameson Ltd., a company which trades in a single product:

	£000
Sales	2,700
Purchases	1,800
Cost of goods sold	1,830
Average debtors	300
Average creditors	160
Average stocks	305

All purchases and sales are made on credit, and transactions are expected to occur at an even rate throughout the year.

You are to:

(a)   Calculate stock turnover in days, debtor collection time in days, creditors payment time in days.

(b)   Calculate the expected working capital cycle for the year.

(c)   Explain to the directors of Jameson Ltd three ways in which they might achieve a reduction of £20,000 in the company's bank overdraft requirement.

Note: assume a 360-day year for the purpose of your calculations.

21.3   The budgets of the Cymru Craft Co. Ltd., a wholesaler of giftware and souvenirs, show that the company's balance sheet at 31 December 20-8 is expected to be as follows:

	£	£	£
Fixed assets			
Freehold property			100,000
Vehicles		40,000	
Less depreciation to date		20,000	
			20,000
			120,000
Current assets			
Stocks		80,000	
Debtors		70,000	
		150,000	
Less Current liabilities			
Creditors	40,000		
Bank overdraft	10,000		
		50,000	
Working capital			100,000
NET ASSETS			220,000
FINANCED BY			
Share capital			150,000
General reserve			50,000
Profit and loss account			20,000
			220,000

The following figures have been extracted from the budgeted trading and profit and loss accounts:

	£
Sales	640,000
Purchases	300,000
Depreciation	10,000
Profit	20,000

The directors are discussing a number of amendments to the budgeted accounts and are considering the following:

(a)   Depreciation for the year 20-8 to be amended to £8,000.

(b)   A new vehicle is to be purchased on 31 December 20-8 at an estimated cost of £10,000.

(c)   The terms of payment allowed to debtors are to be altered so that, in the balance sheet at the end of the year, debtors will be equal to one-and-a-half months' sales.

(d)   The period of credit received from the creditors is to be altered to two months.

(e)   £10,000 is to be transferred to general reserve from profit and loss account.

(f)   The freehold property has recently been professionally revalued at £150,000 and this amount is to be incorporated into the accounts.

You are asked to assist the directors in their discussions by providing information on the effect of each change on certain aspects of the company's finances. You are to provide them with a statement showing the net profit, bank balance/overdraft, current ratio, and liquid ratio which would result from making each individual amendment. Where an item is unchanged, the appropriate figure derived from the original estimates is to be shown.

Consider each amendment independently and present your statement as follows:

Amendment	Net profit for 20-8	Bank balance/ (overdraft)	Current ratio	Liquid ratio
(a)				
(b)				
(c)				
(d)				
(e)				
(f)				

Note: ignore taxation

21.4 The following figures have been extracted from the account of Builders Merchants Ltd.:

	20-1 £	20-2 £
Sales	685,400	722,300
Purchases	372,700	450,500
Cost of goods sold	360,750	342,400
Average debtors	45,500	70,350
Average creditors	37,250	63,050
Average stocks	62,750	75,400

All purchases and sales are made on credit, and transactions occur at an even rate throughout the year.

You are to:
(a) For each year, calculate stock turnover in days, debtor collection time in days, creditors payment time in days.
(b) Calculate the working capital cycle for each year.
(c) Write a memorandum to your boss Jim Anderson, the finance director, explaining your findings. Suggest possible ways in which the situation might be improved.

Note: assume a 365-day year, and take each of your calculations to the nearest day.

21.5 Just over a year ago Jeff Judge bought a small bookshop called 'Spa Books' in Walvern, a spa town in the 'shire' counties. The previous owner of the bookshop had been ill for some time and business had remained at a fairly low level.

During the first year of business Jeff has been 'learning the ropes' and getting to know the area. His balance sheet at the end of the first year is as follows:

Balance Sheet as at 30 June 20-1

	£	£	£
Fixed assets			
Premises at cost			50,000
Fixtures and fittings		2,000	
Less depreciation to date		400	
			1,600
			51,600
Current assets			
Stocks		3,500	
Debtors		550	
Bank		600	
		4,650	
Less Current liabilities			
Creditors		1,650	
Working capital			3,000
			54,600
Less Long-term Liabilities			
Building society loan			45,000
NET ASSETS			9,600
FINANCED BY			
Capital			9,000
Add net profit			5,400
			14,400
Less drawings			4,800
			9,600

Jeff is now actively trying to build up the business. Walvern has a number of private schools and he has obtained contracts to supply a number of them with books and stationery. In order to persuade these schools to leave their present supplier, Jeff has offered two months' credit on all purchases they make from him.

Knowing that you have bought a number of accounting books from him in the past, Jeff asks if you will look at his plan to increase sales in this way and to point out any 'snags' (if any). As he says, "I am going to make good profits on this deal because I always mark up my buying prices by 50%, and the schools haven't asked for any discount; I just can't lose."

July	He will buy the books and stationery on one month's credit at a cost of £20,000.
August	He will deliver the goods, with invoices to the schools.
September	He will pay his creditors.
October	Payment will be received from the schools.

To help him, you decide to:

(a) Prepare working capital summaries at the end of July, August, September and October. (For the purpose of this, you can ignore transactions from his 'normal' trading).

(b) Calculate appropriate working capital ratios at the end of June, July, August, September and October.

(c) Advise him of any practical points he should do before entering into this transaction. Also, point out any dangers in the transaction itself.

4

presentation and analysis of accounting information

22 ACCOUNTING RATIOS

The final accounts of businesses frequently need to be interpreted for decision making. The interpretation will not necessarily be made by an accountant; interested parties might include:

- the *general management of the business,* who need to make financial decisions affecting the future development of the business

- the *bank manager,* who is being asked to lend money to finance the business operations

- the *shareholder* of a public limited company who wishes to be reassured that the investment is a sound one

- the *prospective investor* in quoted companies who wishes to compare comparative strengths and performances

In all of these cases the interested party will be able to calculate key ratios, percentages and performance indicators, and, like a doctor examining a patient, will assess the various strengths and weaknesses, before making an appropriate diagnosis. In order to obtain a clean bill of health a business will need to be seen to be at least satisfactory in the areas of profitability, liquidity and working capital management. In this Chapter we will examine each area in turn, illustrate the major ratios and performance indicators, and see how they apply in different situations.

types of accounting ratios and performance indicators

The term *ratio* is in fact partly misleading, because the performance indicators known as "ratios" include percentages and time periods as well as ratios in the strict sense. The term *performance indicators* may be a more apt description.

Most performance indicators and ratios are applicable to sole traders, partnerships, and limited companies alike, although, as we will see, there are a number which refer specifically to the share capital of limited companies. The main areas covered are:

- *profitability:* the relationship of profit to assets and sales turnover

- *liquidity:* the ability of the business to meet current obligations

- *working capital management:* as seen in the last two Chapters, the way in which the business manages its stock, debtors (credit control) and payment to creditors

- *investment appraisal:* specific ratios which examine the return on shares of limited companies

the proper use of accounting ratios

It is tempting as an academic exercise to examine a set of final accounts and calculate a large number of accounting ratios. This might look impressive on paper, but will prove useless in itself because, in order to be relevant, the ratios must be placed *in context,* and related to some form of reference point or standard. These points of reference might include:

- *ratios from past years* to provide a standard of comparison
- *comparison with budgets* to show whether business performance is up to expectation
- comparison with other businesses *in the same industry*
- comparison with *standards assumed by the interested organization* (e.g. a bank) to be satisfactory

Later in this Chapter we will see precisely how different ratios are used by different organizations, and how they are presented. First we will examine the accounting ratios themselves.

profitability indicators

Gross Profit Percentage

$$\frac{\text{GROSS PROFIT FOR THE YEAR}}{\text{SALES FOR THE YEAR}} \times \frac{100}{1} = \text{GROSS PROFIT PERCENTAGE}$$

This percentage relates the trading profit to sales. Generally speaking this percentage should remain steady from year to year, and any wide variation from one year to the next will need to be investigated. There is no *norm* for this percentage: a business working on a high mark-up will obviously show a higher gross profit percentage.

Net Profit Percentage

$$\frac{\text{NET PROFIT FOR THE YEAR}}{\text{SALES FOR THE YEAR}} \times \frac{100}{1} = \text{NET PROFIT PERCENTAGE}$$

This percentage shows the net profit of the business in relation to its sales. Press releases of company profits are often the net pre-tax profits. The owner(s) of a business will want to see a steady increase in this figure over the years, and any fall should be critically investigated to see which item (e.g. fall in sales, increase in particular costs) is the cause of the problem.

Return on Capital Employed (ROCE)

$$\frac{\text{NET PROFIT FOR THE YEAR}}{\text{CAPITAL EMPLOYED AT THE START OF THE YEAR}} \times \frac{100}{1} = \% \text{ RETURN ON CAPITAL EMPLOYED}$$

This indicator relates the profitability of the business to the size of the capital, and show the owner(s) how much profit is being made on the investment. The owner(s) would hope that this percentage will at least equal the return on, say, a building society account. Capital employed normally includes long term loans and, in the case of a limited company, share capital, reserves and long term loans.

Return on Assets

$$\frac{\text{NET PROFIT}}{\text{NET ASSETS}} \times \frac{100}{1} = \text{PERCENTAGE RETURN ON NET ASSETS}$$

This is an important ratio as it relates the profitability of the business to the value of the net assets held. It is probably more easily understood by the non-financial manager who may find difficulty in understanding the concept of *capital employed.*

liquidity ratios and working capital management

These indicators have been discussed in full in Chapters 20 and 21, and readers should study those two Chapters to gain a full understanding of this critical area of the analysis of business performance. For revision purposes we list here the principal ratios together with brief notes on their significance.

Liquidity Ratios

Current Ratio

CURRENT ASSETS : CURRENT LIABILITIES
This working capital ratio should ideally be 2 : 1, but will obviously vary with different types of business

Liquid Ratio

CURRENT ASSETS *less* STOCK : CURRENT LIABILITIES
This critical ratio measures the ability of the business to repay its immediate liabilities. A ratio of less than 1 : 1 for most businesses is a sign of a shortage of liquidity.

Working Capital Management Ratios

Stock Turnover

$$\frac{\text{AVERAGE STOCK}}{\text{COST OF GOODS SOLD}} \times 365$$

Stock turnover is the average number of days in the financial year that the stock is held by the business. *Average stock* is usually taken as the average of the opening and the closing stock. The rule for assessment is to look at the *type* of business: compare a fish merchant and a furniture shop.

Debtor Collection Period

$$\frac{\text{DEBTORS}}{\text{CREDIT SALES FOR YEAR}} \times 365$$

This calculation gives the number of *days* it takes on average for the debtors of a business to settle their accounts. A figure much over the standard 30 days' credit period should be investigated.

Creditor Payment Period

$$\frac{\text{CREDITORS}}{\text{PURCHASES}} \times 365$$

This calculation gives the number of *days* it takes on average for the business to pay its creditors. Again, an over-long period should be investigated.

investment ratios: limited companies

Enterpreneurs and investors who intend either to buy a whole business or holdings of shares in limited companies, will need to examine very closely the value of the shares and the performance of the company in which they wish to invest. The following ratios are commonly used in making such decisions:

Gearing

$$\frac{\text{TOTAL EXTERNAL DEBT}}{\text{OWNERS EQUITY or SHAREHOLDERS' FUNDS}} \times \frac{100}{1} = \text{GEARING \%}$$

Any investor (or lender) will want to know how much of the business is financed by debt. Clearly, the higher the gearing, the less secure the equity capital of the business, partly because debt is costly in terms of repayments and interest, and partly because it can, strictly speaking be recalled at any time. It is difficult to set a standard for acceptable gearing: in general terms most investors (or lenders) would not want to see debt exceeding equity (share capital and reserves): in short a gearing in excess of 100% might be undesirable.

Dividend Yield

$$\frac{\text{DIVIDEND}}{\text{MARKET PRICE OF SHARE}} \times \frac{100}{1} = \text{DIVIDEND YIELD}$$

Investors in quoted companies can obtain this information from the share price pages of the financial press. The dividend yield gives the investor the annual percentage return on a quoted share. If you examine the financial press you will be surprised at how *low* some yields are compared with comparable after-tax yields from banks and building society investments; this is because investors often buy shares to obtain capital growth rather than income.

Dividend Cover

$$\frac{\text{NET PROFIT BEFORE TAX PER SHARE}}{\text{DIVIDEND PER SHARE}} = \text{DIVIDEND COVER}$$

This figure shows the safety margin between the amount of profit a company makes and the amount paid out in dividends. The figure must obviously be higher than 1; a figure of 5 means that profit exceeds dividend by five times, a healthy sign. The share price pages in the financial press quote this figure as "cover" or simply "cvr."

use of accounting ratios

We stated earlier that a study of accounting does not require the extraction of a long list of ratios from a given set of accounts. Accounting involves the analysis of the relationships between the figures in the accounts and the presentation of those figures in a meaningful way to interested parties. In the Case Problem which follows we will take two years' figures from Premiere Patisserie Limited, a manufacturer of quality cakes, and interpret them for the benefit of the bank that is being asked to lend further money.

Case Problem: Premiere Patisserie

Premiere Patisserie Limited is planning to raise an extra £50,000 from the bank by way of a further long term loan and an overdraft to finance the expansion of its premises and the purchase of freezers for its perishable products. The management have called in an accountant to help them draft a business plan. This document will set out by means of forward projections including a cash flow forecast:

- how much money the company will need to borrow from the bank
- how the money will be spent
- how it will be repaid

The management will also need to convince the bank that their business is flourishing, and they will achieve this by presenting their final accounts from previous years and extracting key accounting ratios to support their case.

The following extracts from the business plan set out:

- two years' final accounts set side by side for comparison
- key accounting ratios together with positive comments about the company's performance.

Note: for the sake of simplicity, tax and dividends have not been included on the balance sheet.

**EXTRACTS FROM THE ACCOUNTS OF PREMIERE PATISSERIE LIMITED
FOR THE YEARS TO 31 DECEMBER 20-1 AND 20-2**

TRADING AND PROFIT AND LOSS ACCOUNT

	£	£
	Year 20-1	*Year 20-2*
Purchases (all on credit)	72,000	95,000
Sales (all on credit)	225,000	278,000
Cost of Sales	70,000	93,000
Gross Profit	155,000	185,000
Net Profit	45,000	68,000

BALANCE SHEET

	£	£
	31 Dec 20-1	*31 Dec 20-2*
Fixed Assets	205,500	265,700
Current Assets		
Stock	3,500	5,500
Debtors	30,000	31,300
	33,500	36,800
Current Liabilities		
Creditors	10,000	12,000
Bank Overdraft	14,000	10,000
	24,000	22,000
Working Capital	9,500	14,800
	215,000	280,500
Less Long-term Liabilities		
Long-term loan	35,000	32,500
NET ASSETS	180,000	248,000

FINANCED BY

Authorised and Issued Share Capital		
100,000 shares £1 each fully paid	100,000	100,000
Reserves	80,000	148,000
Shareholders' Funds	180,000	248,000

Premiere Patisserie Limited
key accounting ratios for the years 20-1 and 20-2

profitability

	20-1	20-2
Sales Turnover	£225,000	£278,000
Gross Profit Percentage	68.89%	66.55%
Net Profit Percentage	20.00%	24.46%
Return on Capital Employed	20.93%	24.24%

Comments
- *sales* have increased by 24% over the year, which compares well with annual inflation at 5%
- *gross profit percentage* remains steady, the slight drop of 2% representing a rise in raw material costs, notably dairy products
- *net profit percentage* increased by 4% to 24%, reflecting increased efficiency and trimming of overhead expenses
- *return on capital employed* rose from 21% to 24%, showing a healthy return on capital invested

liquidity

	20-1	20-2
Current Ratio	1.40 : 1	1.67 : 1
Liquid Ratio	1.25 : 1	1.42 : 1

Comments
This business, which deals with perishable goods, keeps a low stock level, which reduces the liquidity ratios of the company. The *current ratio* increased from 1.40 : 1 to 1.67 : 1, indicating a rise in working capital to a very acceptable level, taking into consideration the low stock holding, and the guideline 2 : 1 ratio.

The *liquid ratio*, which excludes stock, is therefore of less significance for this company. It has increased over the year from 1.25 : 1 to a comfortable 1.42 : 1. Both figures are better than the guideline of 1 : 1.

working capital management

	20-1	20-2
Debtor Collection Period	49 days	41 days
Creditor Payment Period	51 days	46 days
Stock Turnover Period	*18 days	17 days

*closing stock for 20-1 assumed to be average stock

Comments
- *debtor collection period* has shortened from 49 to 41 days, improving the cash flow of the company
- *creditor payment period* has shortened form 51 to 46 days, which remains longer than the debtor collection period, which is to the advantage of the company's cash position
- *stock turnover period* has changed from 18 to 17 days, a high figure for both years, as would be expected with a company dealing with perishable goods. If the company did not have the freezers in which it keeps some of its stock, the figure would be even higher.

the reaction of the bank: the decision to lend

Premiere Patisserie has reason to be pleased with its financial bill of health, and it would be hoped that the bank or any prospective lender would be impressed with the figures as they are presented. After the receipt of the figures, a further ratio would be calculated by the lender: the *gearing ratio,* which relates shareholders' funds to external borrowing. In the case of Premiere Patisserie on the basis of the figures for the year ending 31 December 20-2, the gearing would be:

- *before* the £50,000 new borrowing:

$$\frac{£42,500 \text{ (long term loan and bank overdraft)}}{£248,000 \text{ (shareholders' funds)}} \quad x \quad \frac{100}{1} \quad = \quad 17\%$$

- *after* the £50,000 new borrowing:

$$\frac{£92,500 \text{ (long term loan, overdraft and new £50,000 loan)}}{£248,000 \text{ (shareholders' funds)}} \quad x \quad \frac{100}{1} \quad = \quad 37\%$$

Both ratios are entirely acceptable, being well below the 100% guideline.

Another important document in the business plan, the cash flow forecast (the format of which is discussed in Chapter 19) would also be examined by the bank in detail to ensure that the company had sufficient cash coming in to repay the further borrowing. If the bank is satisfied on this point and with the company and its security position (a mortgage over the fixed assets), there will be no reason why the bank should not lend the £50,000 requested.

shortcomings of accounting ratios

Although accounting ratios set out in the business plan can usefully highlight strengths and weaknesses, they do have a number of shortcomings, and these should always be borne in mind:

1. **Retrospective nature of accounting ratios**
    Accounting ratios are usually *retrospective,* based on previous performance and conditions prevailing in the past. They may not necessarily be valid for making forward projections.

2. **Differences in accounting policies**
    When the accounts of a business are compared, either with previous years' figures, or with figures from a similar business, there is a danger that the comparative accounts are not drawn up on the same basis as those in question. Different accounting policies, in respect of depreciation and stock valuation for instance, may well result in distortion and invalid comparisons.

3. **Inflation**
    Inflation may prove a problem, as most financial statements are prepared on an historic cost basis, that is, assets and liabilities are recorded at their original cost. As a result, comparison of figures from one year to the next may be difficult. In countries where inflation is running at high levels any form of comparison becomes practically meaningless.

4. **Reliance on Standards**
    We have already mentioned guideline standards for some accounting ratios, for instance 2 : 1 for the current ratio. There is a danger of relying too heavily on such *suggested* standards, and ignoring other factors in the balance sheet. An example of this would be to criticise a business for having a low current ratio when the business sells the majority of its goods for cash and consequently has a very low debtors figure. This would in fact be the case with many large and successful retail companies.

CHAPTER SUMMARY

❏ Accounting ratios and performance indicators are useful as methods of highlighting the strengths and weaknesses of a set of financial statements.

❏ Accounting ratios and performance indicators are useful for a number of interested parties: managers of the business, potential lenders, shareholders and investors.

❏ The areas which accounting ratios highlight include
  • profitability
  • liquidity
  • working capital management
  • return on capital for investors

❏ Accounting ratios have shortcomings: they should be used with caution and can be misleading if used indiscriminately and inexpertly

❏ Accounting ratios should be used with one other important ingredient: common sense.

STUDENT ACTIVITIES

You are a clerk at the Greenham branch of the National Bank plc. Your present job involves assessing lending applications from your customers and writing analytical notes for your manager, Lionel Stirling. This process of credit analysis requires you to examine sets of final accounts and to extract relevant accounting ratios and performance indicators. During the course of a day's work you are requested to undertake a number of tasks.

Task One: Becker Packaging Limited

Becker Packaging Limited is the holding company of a group of companies whose account you hold at the bank. It has two principal subsidiaries, Cardbox Limited and Easywrap Limited. You have recently received the audited accounts of these two subsidiaries at the branch.

You are to extract relevant accounting ratios for both companies and set them out in a table for comparison purposes. Write analytical notes covering profitability, liquidity, working capital management and gearing for the guidance of Mr Stirling. You are given the following extracts from trading and profit and loss accounts for the year ended 31 March 20-4 and the balance sheets as at that date:

	Cardbox Ltd £	Easywrap Ltd £
Sales	175,000	200,000
Cost of sales	120,000	150,000
Gross profit	55,000	50,000
Net profit	25,000	35,000
Fixed assets	100,000	120,000
Stock	45,000	50,000
Debtors	17,500	25,000
Creditors	15,000	21,500
Bank overdraft	9,200	8,500
Share capital and reserves	118,300	130,000
Long term loan	20,000	35,000

Assume for your calculations that all sales are credit sales, the closing stock figure is an average for the year, and that cost of sales equals purchases.

Task Two: Connors Sportsware Limited

Connors Sportsware Limited is a good customer of your bank and has recently negotiated a long term loan of £20,000 to refit and expand the business premises. The directors have recently approached your bank with a request for an overdraft of £10,000 for new stock. The cash flow forecast shows that the company can repay this amount over six months, after which time the situation can be reviewed. Mr Stirling hands you the audited accounts for the last two years and asks you to work out ratios to show if the company is as sound as he thinks it is.

You are to work out relevant ratios for the two years and then write notes comparing the two years in respect of profitability, liquidity, working capital mangement and gearing.

Extracts from trading and profit and loss accounts for the years ended 30 June 20-3 and 20-4, and the balance sheets at that date:

	20-3	20-4
	£	£
Sales	240,000	400,000
Cost of sales	160,000	300,000
Purchases	160,000	318,000
Gross profit	80,000	100,000
Net profit	60,000	70,000
Fixed assets	70,000	75,000
Stock	14,000	32,000
Debtors	24,000	40,000
Bank	2,000	3,000
Creditors	20,000	40,000
Share capital and reserves	70,000	90,000
Long term loan	20,000	20,000

Assume for your calculations that all sales are credit sales, and average stock for 20-3 is closing stock.

Task Three: MacInrays Mints Limited

MacInrays Mints Limited manufactures confectionery. The company does not bank with the National Bank, but the Financial Director, John MacInray has recently approached Mr Stirling to ask for a overdraft of £25,000 for trading purposes. Mr Stirling is a little wary of this request and suspects that the company has been refused an overdraft by its own bankers. John MacInray has brought in the latest set of audited accounts for the year ended 30 June 20-4, and Mr Stirling has asked you to analyse them.

You are to extract the relevant accounting ratios and write comments for Mr Stirling on the financial strength or otherwise of the company.

	£
Sales	175,000
Cost of sales	145,000
Gross profit	30,000
Net profit	1,500
Fixed assets	25,000
Stock	70,000
Debtors	10,000
Creditors	65,000
Bank overdraft	12,000
Share capital andreserves	13,000
Medium term loan	15,000

Assume for your calculations that all sales are credit sales, the closing stock figure is an average for the year, and that cost of sales equals purchases.

ASSIGNMENT

8 *Interpreting the accounts*

covering
final accounts, cash flow statements, analysis of performance indicators

SITUATION

A friend of yours works in the office of the Deansway Trading Co Ltd. The company imports cotton shirts from Taiwan and Malaysia, and sells to a large number of small retail outlets throughout Britain.

Your friend asks for your assistance in analysing the accounts of the company. She is keen to know more about the financial results of the business, and the office manager has provided her with the last two years' balance sheets, and with some figures extracted from the trading and profit and loss accounts (see separate memorandum).

The balance sheets are as follows:

DEANSWAY TRADING CO LTD

Balance Sheet as at 31 December

	20-5			20-6		
	£000	*£000*	*£000*	*£000*	*£000*	*£000*
Fixed assets						
Land and buildings at cost			180			250
Vehicles, machinery, etc.						
(see note)			106			130
			286			380
Current assets						
Stocks	44			86		
Debtors	42			56		
Bank	2			-		
		88			142	
Less Current liabilities						
Creditors	34			52		
Bank overdraft	-			38		
Proposed dividend	16			14		
Corporation tax	6			8		
		56			112	
Working capital			32			30
NET ASSETS			318			410

FINANCED BY

	£000	20-5 £000	£000	£000	20-6 £000	£000
£1 ordinary shares			200			300
Profit and loss account			58			60
			258			360
10% Debentures			60			50
			318			410

Note: During 20-6 movements on the vehicles and machinery account were:

	£
Balance at 1 January 20-6	106,000
Additions during year	40,000
	146,000
Less depreciation for year	16,000
	130,000

Copy of the memorandum sent by the office manager to your friend:

MEMORANDUM

TO: Sam Day
FROM: Gabrielle Smith,   Office Manager
DATE: 3 March 20-7

ANNUAL ACCOUNTS

I recently sent you a copy of the last two years' balance sheets.
To help you with your analysis, I give below details of sales and
purchases for each year (all sales and purchases were made on
credit):

	20-5	20-6
Credit sales	£440,000	£655,000
Credit purchases	£266,000	£348,000

Also, the net profit before tax for 20-5 was £16,500.

GS.

GABRIELLE SMITH
Office Manager

TASKS

1. Your friend says: "How do I work out the profit before tax for 20-6, so that I have a comparable figure to that given in the memorandum?" Show the calculations you would make.

2. She then comments that the balance sheets show the bank balance going heavily into overdraft. As she says: "This must indicate that the business is making large losses." Prepare a statement for her that either proves or disproves her remark.

3. As a start towards analysing the accounts, she has seen the following accounting ratios in a textbook:

    - Current (working capital) ratio
    - Liquid (acid-test) ratio
    - Debtors' turnover (credit allowed)
    - Creditors' turnover (credit taken)
    - Return on capital employed
    - Net profit/sales percentage

    She asks you to work out these ratios for both years.

4. As a final comment, she says: "What does all this mean? Has the company done well over the last two years? Is the business expanding or contracting?"

    Using the information, present your reply.

23 STATISTICAL TECHNIQUES AND ACCOUNTING DATA

There are three kinds of lies: lies, damn lies, and statistics.

He uses statistics as a drunken man uses a lamp post - for support rather than illumination.

Statistics is a scientific method of collecting, organising, summarising, presenting and analysing data.

From these very different views of statistics three main points may be derived:

- statistics is a scientific way of dealing with data
- statistics can mislead
- statistics are often mistrusted

In this Chapter we will examine basic statistical techniques which may be used for organising, summarising, presenting and analysing accounting data in a reliable, scientific and illuminating way. Those of you familiar with graphs showing sales trends and pie or bar charts setting out the break-down of profits are seeing the end-product of the use of statistics in accounting. Statistical techniques are used in accounting

- for the analysis of *past events* and the *present situation.*
- for the forecasting of *future trends*

In this Chapter we will deal with the statistical analysis of past events and examine the type of presentation used to communicate that analysis. We will deal with the analysis of present trends and the use of forecasting in the next Chapter.

statistical analysis of past events

When a large public company announces its annual results, it will publish the details of the figures in a number of forms:

- the published annual report and accounts sent to shareholders
- press releases for the financial newspapers and journals
- employee reports distributed to the workforce and management of the company, and sometimes also to the shareholders (see pages 244 and 245 for the Employee Report of J Sainsbury plc)

In all these written reports the accounting data is usually presented in tabular and also in pictoral form, because it is generally recognised that the average individual can understand a picture - a graph or a chart - better than a paragraph of descriptive prose; and it must be remembered that it is the average person, not the accountant, who will read the reports.

There are two main types of statistical analysis used when presenting accounting data:

- *time series analysis,* which presents numeric data recorded at set intervals of time, for example: line graphs, bar charts, and indices
- *proportional analyses,* which break down a single figure into its constituent elements, for example, pie charts

time series analysis: Vector Cars plc

For the purpose of illustrating time series analysis we will take as an example the sales figures for Vector Cars plc, a major UK car manufacturer:

- for three years (the time series)
- broken down into home sales and overseas sales
- in comparison with the total sales projections for the three years

The starting point for any statistical presentation is a table of the constituent figures:

Vector Cars plc: Projected and Actual Sales

	Year 1 £M	Year 2 £M	Year 3 £M
UK Sales	3,102	3,593	4,239
Overseas Sales	3,815	3,692	2,470
Total Sales	6,917	7,285	6,709
Projected Sales	6,800	6,950	7,100

This data has been collected and summarised by the accounting process, but not yet analysed. In order to detect trends from looking at this table, it is necessary first to read each row of figures, relate them to the other figures, and then to interpret them. The process is slow and laborious because there is no pictorial assistance. Contrast this table with the line graph presentation of the Vector Cars plc sales figures illustrated below, or the bar charts illustrated on pages 240 and 241.

the line graph

A line graph is the joining up of points plotted on two axes either by straight lines or by a curve.

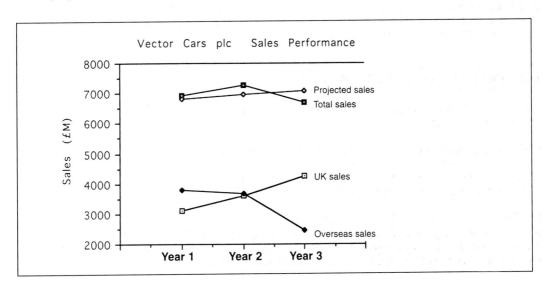

the simple bar chart

A bar chart is a series of bars drawn between two defined axes. The height of the bars represents the amount of the dependent variable.

The following bar chart shows the total sales for Vector Cars plc over the three years:

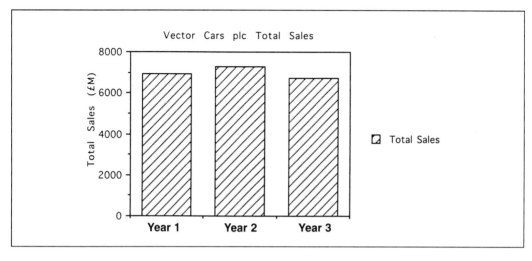

The simple bar chart is limited because it can only compare individual items from one set of data over the time series, in this case the total sales of Vector Cars plc. Its visual impact is strong, and it is consequently very popular. Note that it is the *height* of the bar that must be accurately charted. The width is of no statistical significance.

the compound bar chart

A compound bar chart is a bar chart which sets out more than one variable for each of the points in the time series.

The following compound bar chart sets out the total sales and projected total sales for Vector Cars plc. Note that the two separate bars should be clearly distinguished by a contrasting infill.

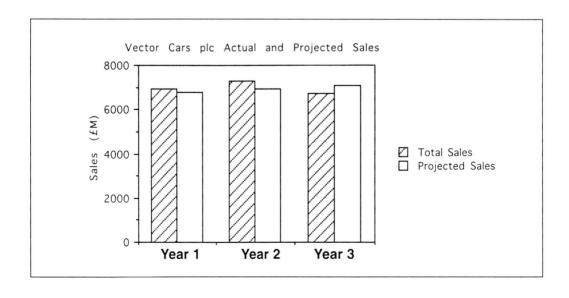

component bar chart

A component bar chart is a bar chart which subdivides each bar into its component elements.

This type of chart is useful in showing the make-up of variable figures over a time series. In the example below total sales for Vector Cars plc is subdivided into UK and overseas sales. It is very evident from this chart that the disappointing result for Year 3 is directly a result of the fall in overseas sales. Note the different shading of the components of the individual bars.

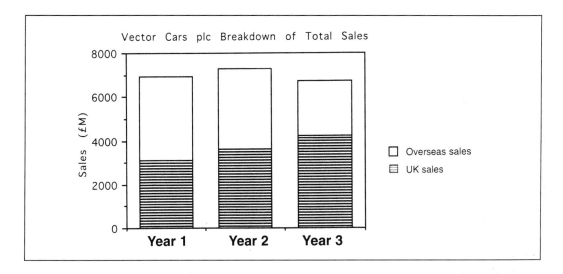

time series analysis: indexing

A further method of presenting a numeric trend over a time series, such as sales or profit over a period of years is converting the numbers in question into an *index number sequence.*

An index is a sequence of numbers where the first number is equated to 100 and the subsequent numbers are proportionally related to 100

The object of using an index system is to simplify comparison of complex values by replacing the complicated figures with simple ones, all related to a base of 100. Commonly quoted indices are the Retail Price Index (RPI) which measures the cost of living and the Financial Times All-Share Index which measures the value of shares quoted by Stock Exchange market makers.

The procedure for creating an index series is as follows:

1. Take a series of values, for example the total sales for Vector Cars Limited over the three years:

Year 1	£6,917M
Year 2	£7,285M
Year 3	£6,709M

2. Equate the first figure (the base year) with 100, i.e. assume £6,917M = 100

3. Convert each of the subsequent years' figures to index numbers by applying the formula:

    $$\frac{\textit{subsequent year's figure}}{\textit{base year figure}} \times 100 \quad = \quad \textit{index number of subsequent year}$$

4.   The calculation for the index for the sales of Vector Cars plc is therefore:

Year 1   6,917 (base year figure)   =   100

Year 2 $\frac{7,285}{6,917}$ x 100   =   105

Year 3 $\frac{6,709}{6,917}$ x 100   =   97

If Vector Cars plc uses Year 1 as its base year and equates total sales with 100, it then easy to see that there has been a rise to 105 in Year 2 and a fall to 97 in Year 3. In due course subsequent years' sales could similarly be given an index number and comparison be made with previous years.

Another advantage of using indices is that *like* can be compared meaningfully with *unlike*. Trends in variables such as share prices, inflation and exchange rates can be compared over time.

proportional analysis: the pie chart

Whereas *time series analysis* shows a trend derived from a series of figures over a period of time, *proportional analysis* examines a single figure divided into component elements at a single moment in time. It is commonly presented in the form of a pie chart.

A pie chart is a circle divided into sectors to represent proportionally the parts of a whole.

The word pie is derived from the Greek π (used in the calculation of circle dimensions and area) and also from the more homely baked variety. A pie chart is a visually impressive way of illustrating the parts of a whole, but it has a number of shortcomings, including the fact that it cannot show a trend, the calculations are laborious and the labelling can be complicated.

calculating the sectors of a pie chart

A pie chart might be used to show the breakdown by area of the sales of Vector Cars plc. The starting point is the accounting data:

Sales of cars by area by Vector Cars plc in Year 3

Area	£M
UK	4,239
Europe	1,040
North America	912
Japan	518
Total Sales	6,709

The total sales of £6,709M will become the whole circle of the pie divided into segments, each of which will proportionally represent a geographical sales figure. As the angle at the centre of a circle is 360° it is necessary to work out the angle for *each* segment individually. The formula is as follows:

Figure for the part of the whole x *360°* = *the angle at the centre for the segment* (°)
Figure for the whole

Applying the formula to the geographical sales figures for Vector Cars plc, the calculation is:

Area of Sales	Calculation		Angle of segment (°)
UK	$\frac{4\ 239}{6\ 709}$ x 360°	=	227
Europe	$\frac{1\ 040}{6\ 709}$ x 360°	=	56
North America	$\frac{912}{6\ 709}$ x 360°	=	49
Japan	$\frac{518}{6\ 709}$ x 360°	=	28

The pie chart is set out below. Note the labelling and shading, and the fact that the degrees are *not* indicated (they are of no interest to the reader).

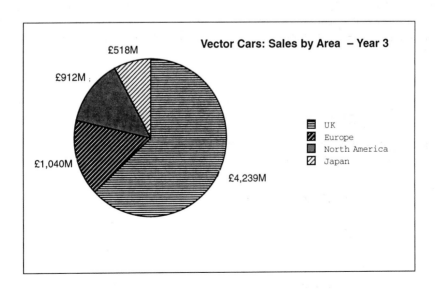

using the computer to present statistical data

The traditional way of constructing the charts illustrated in this chapter is to use the time-honoured materials of graph paper, pencil, ruler, protractor and compasses: these are convenient and accurate. It is likely, however, that you will have access to a computer which will produce these charts for you. Software packages which will do this include:

• specific "chart and graph" graphics packages
• graphics functions within a computer spreadsheet package

Whichever type of package you use, you will be asked to enter the numeric data in a grid, and will then be given a choice of the type of graph or chart required. The advantages of using a computer graphics package are:

• speed of processing and accuracy of presentation
• flexibility: you can choose whichever graph or chart that you want; if it is unsatisfactory, you can choose another
• high quality of output (given a suitable printer)

The charts and graphs illustrated in this chapter were all produced using a computer graphics package.

CHAPTER SUMMARY

❑   Statistics is a useful science with an unfortunate reputation.

❑   Statistics may be used for organising, presenting and analysing a wide variety of accounting data.

❑   Statistics can be used for the analysis of past events and present trends, and for making forecasts of future trends.

❑   Methods of statistical presentation include time series analysis and proportional analysis.

❑   Time series analysis is best presented in the form of line graphs, bar charts and indices.

❑   Proportional analysis is best presented by means of pie charts.

In the next Chapter we will look at the way statistics examine present trends by means of averaging, and then use those results to forecast future trends.

✎ STUDENT ACTIVITIES

You work in the public relations department of Hyzaku Limited, the UK subsidiary of the Japanese lawnmower manufacturer which has made substantial inroads into the UK market with its revolutionary "Trojan" battery powered rotary mower. You are given three sets of statistics and are asked to present them in the manner indicated and to make comments on the result.

23.1   Market Share: UK Market for Lawnmowers

	Year 1 £M	Year 2 £M	Year 3 £M
UK lawnmowers	295	280	275
Hyzaku lawnmowers	150	195	250
Others	140	130	115

(a)   present this data in the form of a line graph
(b)   comment on the trends exhibited

23.2   Actual and Projected Sales of Hyzaku Lawnmowers in the UK Market

	Year 1 £M	Year 2 £M	Year 3 £M
Actual Sales	150	195	250
Projected Sales	140	180	220

(a)   present this data in the form of a compound bar chart
(b)   comment on the trend exhibited

23.3   Breakdown of UK Sales by Area

	Year 1 £M	Year 2 £M	Year 3 £M
South East	100	125	175
Midlands	25	45	25
Other Areas	25	25	50
Total Sales	150	195	250

(a)   present this data in the form of a component bar chart
(b)   comment on the regional trends; what should be done about the Midlands?
(c)   one of your directors doesn't like your bar chart; present the data in another form that will show the trends clearly

23.4   Take the figures for the UK sales of Hyzaku lawnmowers in Year 3 and draw up a pie chart showing the breakdown of sales by area.

24 STATISTICAL FORECASTING TECHNIQUES

In the last Chapter we examined time series analysis and proportional analysis in relation to past activity within a business. There are also a number of statistical techniques which are useful to the management of a business in assessing *the present situation* and making decisions about *the future* as a result of that assessment. The use of *averages* is one such technique.

averages

It is important that the management of a business knows the answers to questions such as:

*   how much credit are we given by our suppliers?
*   what sales are we likely to achieve in December?
*   how long do we keep stock in the warehouse before it is sold?
*   how long a credit period do we give to our debtors?

Only by keeping firm control over areas such as these does the business increase efficiency and profitability. Control is only possible when the precise answer to these questions is known. It would be an easy option to reply " about . . ." or "approximately . . . " and give a rule of thumb answer. The scientific and statistical approach is to calculate an *average.*

There are three types of average, the *arithmetic mean,* the *median* and the *mode,* all of which we will illustrate in the following Case Problem.

Case Problem: the average drink

You are organising a reception for eleven sales representatives at the launch of a new product. You have been told by your Sales Director that because of economies in the budget you are restricted to offering only one type of drink at receptions. The questions is, what drink do you offer?

The following statistics are available:

Age of the 11 sales representatives attending: 20, 25, 35, 35, 35, 36, 37, 55, 60, 65, 65.

Preference for drinks (by age):

18 - 29	Beer
30 - 39	Bacardi and Coke
40 - 65	Whisky

The obvious answer is to serve the drink appropriate to the average age of your guests. But which average should you choose? We will now calculate the average age by using the arithmetic mean, the median and the mode.

The Arithmetic Mean

The arithmetic mean is the sum of all the figures divided by the number of figures

The sum of 20, 25, 35, 35, 35, 36, 37, 55, 60, 65, 65 = 468

The arithmetic mean   = $\dfrac{468}{11}$ =   42.5 years

The Median

The median is the middle figure in a series of figures

Note: if there is no middle figure, as in an even numbered series, the median is the arithmetic mean of the two figures nearest to the middle.

In this case the median is 20, 25, 35, 35, 35, **36**, 37, 55, 60, 65, 65   =   36 years

The Mode

The mode is the value that occurs most often in a series

In this case the most common age is 35 years (3 representatives), followed closely by 65 years (2 representatives). Note that these two ages are very widely dispersed.

Solution

The *arithmetic mean* tells you that the average age is 42.5 years (despite the fact that there is no guest present within five years of 42.5); this leads you to choose whisky. The median age is 36 (bacardi and coke) and the mode is 35 (bacardi and coke). The answer to the problem is that there is *no* definitive answer. In this case you will either give them all orange juice in the interests of health and safety, or you will choose the mode: "What do *most* people drink?"

averages in statistics

In general practice and also in statistics it is the *arithmetic mean* which is seen to be the most reliable and the most commonly used average. We will now examine statistical techniques used for forecasting, and as you will see, calculating averages plays an important role in establishing trends.

statistical techniques used in forecasting

Forecasts in accounting are based on information about the way in which trends have established themselves in the past and are exhibiting themselves in the present. It is then assumed that these trends will continue into the future, given that the economic and industrial conditions remain reasonably stable for the business in question. If one takes a sales trend, for example, established in the past, it is possible to predict a sales trend for the future using statistical techniques based on time series analysis.

Types of Trend
There are four basic types of trend:

- the long term trend
- cyclical fluctuations superimposed on the long term trend
- seasonal fluctuations superimposed on the long term trend
- irregular fluctuations caused by external events

For example, if a business selling toys in the UK examines the option of importing teddies from

Taiwan, there will be a *long term trend* for prices to rise, *cyclical fluctuations* caused by exchange rate changes, *seasonal rises* when supplies are short before Christmas, and the possibility of *irregular fluctuations* caused by the imposition of import tariffs.

Use of Time Series Analysis: Line Graphs

By using time series analysis in line graph form (plotting the dependent variable being examined against the independent variable of time) it is possible to reduce these various distortions by using a number of techniques:

- *moving averages* to show the long term trend
- calculating *seasonal variations* to adjust and smooth out the trend line
- the use of *linear regression straight line graphs* to smooth out irregularities

It must be stressed that the use of these techniques by no means makes the forecasting of a future trend any more *certain;* it merely makes the trend more clear and comprehensible. As we will argue at the end of this Chapter, forecasting is not a science, it is the extraction of the most reliable data for making a best guess.

moving averages

The use of moving averages is the technique of repeatedly calculating a series of different arithmetic mean values for a dependent variable along a time series to produce a trend graph.

A moving average will move forward in time (the independent variable) step by step along the trend line, calculating a new average from the given data at each step, removing in the averaging process data which is literally "out of line" with the trend. Some data will be above the line, some below it; in the averaging process these fluctuations will offset each other to produce a smooth line. The following example shows the sales figures of a company, Arco plc, over 15 years.

Year	Annual Sales £M		5 Year Moving Average £M
1984	10		
1985	4		
1986	8	64 ÷ 5 =	12.8
1987	18		17.6
1988	24		20.8
1989	34		21.6
1990	20		23.2
1991	12		26.4
1992	26		26.8
1993	40		26.4
1994	36		30.4
1995	18		34.0
1996	32		34.0
1997	44		
1998	40		

This chart has been produced as follows:

- the sales figures were plotted on a line graph (see next page)
- a *five yearly* fluctuating cycle was noted
- the sales figures for the first *five years* were added and divided by five to find the first of the moving averages: (i.e. $10 + 4 + 8 + 18 + 24 = 64$; $64 \div 5 = 12.8$)
- the *next* arithmetic mean is calculated over the five years 1985 to 1989, i.e.the average *moves* forward a year: $(4 + 8 + 18 + 24 + 34 = 88$; $88 \div 5 = 17.6)$
- the process is repeated for the following years until the data is exhausted
- the moving average line is plotted on the same axes as the annual sales (see next page)

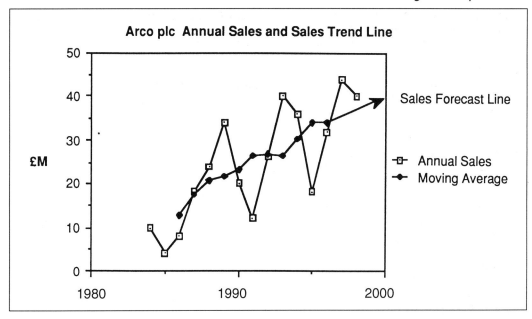

From Moving Average to Sales Forecast Line

It is clear from this line graph that the moving average smooths out the fluctuations, providing an upward moving sales trend line. This line could then be reasonably continued into the future, given that other conditions remained stable, to produce a *forecast of sales* for subsequent years. It is clearly a great deal more reliable than the erratic trend of the annual sales line. On the graph the forecast sales are indicated by the arrowed line.

seasonal adjustments

Seasonally adjusted figures are used when reporting data on a quarterly or monthly basis when the actual figures are distorted by seasonal factors.

When the Government announces its unemployment figures, they are *seasonally adjusted* to allow for factors such as the influx of school and college leavers registering as unemployed on a hopefully temporary basis. In the reporting of business data, such as sales figures, on a line graph, seasonal adjustments can take place to smooth out an otherwise irregular line.

The calculation of seasonal adjustments again involves the process of calculating arithmetic mean averages. The aim of the exercise is to examine the results (e.g. sales figures) for a number of years to produce an *average* seasonal fluctuation figure which can then be used to adjust *future* results as and when they are reported. In the following example the sales manager of W G M Jones Ltd., a company which manufactures train sets, has calculated average seasonal quarterly variations for sales on the basis of five years' figures:

1 January to 31 March	*minus* £2.5M
1 April to 30 June	*minus* £8.0M
1 July to 30 September	*plus* £5.0M
1 October to 31 December	*plus* £12.5M

The positive (*plus*) variation indicates that the company has exceeded the quarterly average sales figure by that amount, and a negative (*minus*) figure indicates that sales are below the quarterly average. Therefore in order to calculate the seasonal adjustment it is necessary to:

- add a minus seasonal variation figure to the actual reported result
- deduct a positive seasonal variation figure from the actual reported result

These calculations are only common sense: the winter quarter contains the Christmas period when sales are higher (by £12.5M in the case of W G M Jones Ltd.) and therefore this seasonal variation of £12.5M must be deducted from the actual reported figure to smooth out the fluctuation.

The actual and seasonally adjusted sales figures for W G M Jones Ltd therefore appear as follows:

Quarters	Sales	Seasonal adjustment	Adjusted figure
£M	£M	£M	
Jan - Mar	40	+ 2.5	42.5
Apl - Jun	30	+ 8.0	38.0
Jul - Sep	50	- 5.0	45.0
Oct - Dec	70	- 12.5	57.5

These could then be plotted in a line graph:

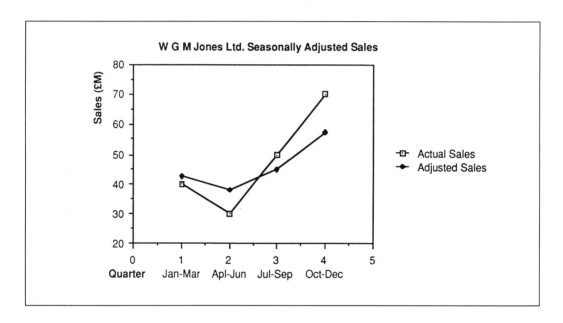

Use of Seasonally Adjusted Figures in Forecasting

Seasonally adjusted figures, as we have seen, are very useful in smoothing out seasonal fluctuations in data relating to past accounting periods. They are also useful in forecasting beacause the seasonal variation figures worked out can be applied to estimates of future results to produce a smoother and more reliable forecast line.

straight line graphs: linear regression

In addition to the moving average, which smooths out cyclical fluctuations, and the use of seasonal adjustments, it is useful when presenting accounting data to be able to produce a simple straight line which smooths out *all* fluctuations. This achieved by the use of *linear regression.*

Linear regression is the production of a straight line plotted by points whose position is calculated by arithmetic mean averaging of the dependent variable over a time series

If we take the sales figures for Arco plc (seen earlier in the Chapter) it is possible to construct a straight line graph by linear regression technique to illustrate the upward trend. This is achieved by plotting *three* points whose position is calculated by arithmetic mean averaging. This process is known as *three point linear regression*. The calculations are as follows:

Arco plc Sales 1984 - 1998

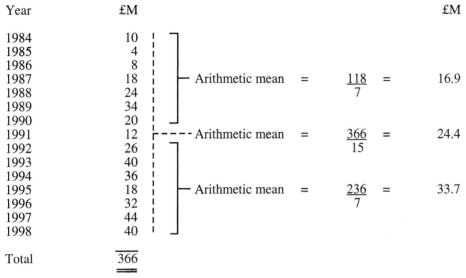

Year	£M					£M
1984	10					
1985	4					
1986	8					
1987	18	Arithmetic mean	=	$\frac{118}{7}$	=	16.9
1988	24					
1989	34					
1990	20					
1991	12	Arithmetic mean	=	$\frac{366}{15}$	=	24.4
1992	26					
1993	40					
1994	36					
1995	18	Arithmetic mean	=	$\frac{236}{7}$	=	33.7
1996	32					
1997	44					
1998	40					
Total	366					

The three points are derived as follows:

- the lower point is the arithmetic mean of the sales figures from 1984 to 1990 = £16.9M
- the middle point is the arithmetic mean of the whole series of sales figures = £24.4M
- the upper point is the arithmetic mean of the sales figures from 1992 to 1998 = £33.7M

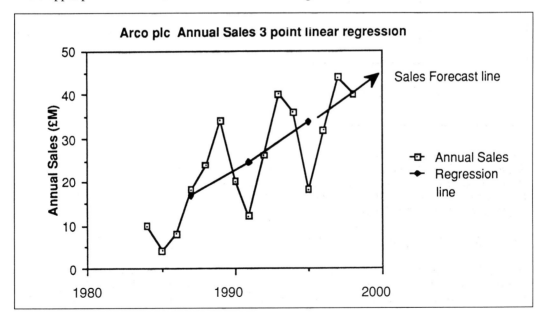

Arco plc Annual Sales 3 point linear regression

Use of Linear Regression Lines in Forecasting

The straight line produced by the three point linear regression clearly shows the upward trend of sales, and could be continued, as in the graph above, to provide a forecast of further sales.

the art of forecasting

As we have seen in this Chapter, statistical techniques are useful for analysing past trends to give a guide as to what will happen in the future. Forecasting is therefore not a science, but more of an art: it can at best be a well informed estimate and at worst a guess. Forecasting is an art which has many uses. Forecasting may be found in:

* internal management reports and budgets used for planning and decision making
* business plans, giving interested parties information about the future prospects of the business
* the annual Report and Accounts and Employee Reports of limited companies, giving shareholders and employees information about the likely future performance of their company.

CHAPTER SUMMARY

❑ Statistics can provide the basic techniques for forecasting.

❑ By examining past trends it is possible to forecast future trends.

❑ There are four basic types of trend: long term, cyclical fluctuation, seasonal variation and irregular fluctuation.

❑ Basic forecasting techniques include moving averages, seasonal adjustments and linear regression.

❑ Forecasting cannot be an exact science, it must be used with care, and only after a thorough analysis of past and present trends.

✍ STUDENT ACTIVITIES

24.1 **Work out** the arithmetic mean, median and mode of the following sequences of numbers:
(a) 1,2,3,3,4,5,6,7,8,9,10.
(b) 1,7,9,12,13,15,15,16,19.
(c) 201,230,289,701,823,832,832,849.

24.2 The following figures represent the daily numbers of staff attending at the works squash club over the last 15 days: 2,5,10,7,4,9,12,10,6,12,14,11,7,13,18

You are to
(a) Work out a moving average on these figures, using as a base for the average the number of figures which *you* think appropriate. Plot the original figures and the moving average figures on a line graph. What general trend do you predict on the basis of these figures?
(b) Work out a three point linear regression line from the same data and plot it on the graph. Is this more accurate than the moving average? If not, why not?

24.3 You are told that the seasonal fluctuation for the sale of toys by Cuddles Inc. of San Francisco is:
Jan - Mar, plus $10.5M; Apl - Jun, minus $4.3M; Jul - Sep, minus $9.7M; Oct - Dec plus $25.2M
The actual quarterly sales figures for the last two years (quoted consecutively by quarter) are:
Year 1: $135M, $105M, $95M, $160M
Year 2: $145M, $113M, $103M, $175M
You are to
(a) draw up a line graph for the two years showing the actual sales and the seasonally adjusted sales
(b) comment on the general sales trend and suggest what the level of future sales might be.

Absorption costing, 155-8
Accounting concepts, 48-9, 52-3
Accounting policies, 111-2
Accounting ratios, 226-33
Accruals, 53
Allocation of overheads, 143-5
Apportionment of overheads, 143-5
Appropriation accounts
    partnership, 74-6
    company, 84
Articles of Association, 82
Assets, 47
Auditors
    external, 3, 111
    internal, 3
Auditors' report, 111
Averages
    mean, 247
    median, 247
    mode, 247
    moving, 248-9
Average cost (AVCO), 131-6

Bad debts, 55
Balance sheet, 46-9
Balancing off, 15, 19
Bar charts, 240-1
Bonus systems, 136-9
Book-keeping, 7
Break-even, 152-5
Budgetary control, 188-91
Budgetary planning, 188-9
Budgets, 185-92
    fixed and flexible, 191-2
    master, 187, 199-200
    zero-based, 192

Capital accounts
    sole trader, 47
    partnership, 76
Cash Book, 28, 29
Cash Book summary, 64
Cash budgets, 195-200
    limitations of, 198
    'what if?' questions, 198
Cash flow forecasts, 195-200
Cash Flow statements, 91-100,110
Company (see limited company)
Computer based accounts, 31, 33-7
Computer graphics, 246
Consolidated accounts, 111
Control accounts, 64
Cost accounting, 118-9
Cost centres, 142
Cost elements, 119-20
Cost units, 142
Creditors' payment time, 212, 228

Current account (partnership), 76
Current ratio, 209, 228

Debentures, 83
Debtor collection, 212, 228
Debtors (control of), 212
Depreciation, 54
Direct labour hour (overhead absorption), 146
Directors' report, 110
Dividend, 83
Dividend yield, 229
Dividend cover, 229
Double entry, 10, 46

Final accounts
    from trial balance, 23
    sole trader, 42-8
    partnership, 73-7
    limited company, 80-7
Financial accounting, 118-9
Financial Reporting Standards (FRS), 91,110
First in, first out (FIFO), 131-5
Fixed budgets, 191-2
Fixed costs, 122-3, 152
Flexible budgets, 191-2
Forecast final accounts, 199-200
Forecasting, 248-54

Gearing, 228
Goodwill, 47
Group accounts, 111

Holding company, 111

Incomplete records, 62
Indexing, 241-2
Inflation accounting, 113

Job costing, 163-6
Journals, 30

Labour costs, 136-9
Labour variances, 179-80
Last in, first out (LIFO), 131-5
Ledger accounts, 10
Ledgers, 7, 28-9
Liabilities, 47
Limited companies
    dividends, 83
    documents, 81-2
    final accounts, 80-87
    limited liability, 80
    published accounts, 105-14
    reserves, 86
    shares and debentures, 82-3
Limiting factors, 186, 198
Line graphs, 239

Linear regression, 250
Liquid capital, 209
Liquid ratio, 209, 228

Machine hour (overhead absorption), 147
Management accounting, 118-9
Manufacturing accounts, 118-23
Manufacturing process, 119
Marginal costing, 155-8
Master budget, 187, 199-200
Materials: see stock valuation
Materials variances, 178-9
Memorandum of Association, 82

Overhead absorption, 145-7
Overheads, 121, 142-8
Overtrading, 219-20

Partnership accounts, 73-7
Petty cash book, 30
Pie chart, 242-3
Piecework rate, 136-9
Prepayments, 53
Pricing policy, 158
Process costing, 166-8
Proportional analysis, 242-3
Published accounts of limited
    companies, 105-14
Profit
    gross, 43
    net, 44
Profitability ratios, 227
Provision for bad debts, 55

Returns, 15
Reserves (company accounts), 84-5

Seasonal averages, 251
Semi-variable costs, 122-3
Service departments, 144-5
Shares (company), 82-3
Single entry systems, 30, 62
Sole trader, 42

Standard costing, 175-81
Statement of affairs, 63
Statements of Standard Accounting
    Practice (SSAP), 110
Statistical presentation of accounts, 238-44
Stock control, 210-1
Stock turnover, 228, 211
Stock valuation, 130-6
Subsidiary budgets, 185-8
Subsidiary companies, 111

Time rate, 136-9
Time series analysis, 239
Trial balance, 19, 21, 48

Units of output (overhead absorption), 146

Variable costs, 122-3, 152
Variance analysis, 177-81

Working capital, 208-13, 215-21
    changes in, 216-8
    control of working capital items, 210-3
    current ratio, 211
    cycle, 218-9
    flow of, 215-6
    liquid capital, 209
    overtrading, 219-20
Work-in-progress (process costing), 166-8

Zero-based budgets, 192